SCHOOL RESTRUCTURING

SCHOOL RESTRUCTURING
INTERNATIONAL PERSPECTIVES

Thomas A O'Donoghue
and
Clive A J Dimmock

Routledge
Taylor & Francis Group

LONDON AND NEW YORK

First published 1998 by Kogan Page Limited

This edition Published 2013 by Routledge
2 Park Square, Milton Park, Abingdon, Oxon OX14 4RN
711 Third Avenue, New York, NY 10017

Routledge is an imprint of the Taylor & Francis Group, an informa business

British Library Cataloguing in Publication Data

A CIP record for this book is available from the British Library.

ISBN 0 7494 2493 1

Typeset by JS Typesetting, Wellingborough, Northants.

Contents

Acknowledgements   *vii*

1. Introduction   1

PART ONE: The background to school restructuring

2. The context   7

PART TWO: Restructuring in four parts of the world

3. Restructuring in England and Wales   25
4. Restructuring in the United States   41
5. Restructuring in Hong Kong   52
6. Restructuring in Australia   67

PART THREE: The impact of restructuring on schools

7. Principals' and teachers' reactions to school restructuring
    (*written with John Hattie*)   84
8. Restructuring and teachers' understandings of their
    curriculum work: a case study   94
9. School development planning: teachers' perspectives   107
10. School-site professionals and parents   120

PART FOUR: The concept of dilemmas

11. School principals' dilemmas in restructuring   137
12. Teachers' dilemmas in relation to their curriculum work   150

PART FIVE: Conclusion

13. Key stakeholders and contemporary educational restructuring: emerging issues   163

References   *178*

Index   *193*

Acknowledgements

Our thanks and appreciation are extended for permission to rework sections of our published papers to the editors of the *Australian Journal of Education, The International Journal of Educational Reform, Curriculum,* and the *Journal of Curriculum and Supervision.* The papers in question are: C Dimmock and J Hattie (1994) 'Principals' and teachers' reactions to school restructuring'; T A O'Donoghue (1994) 'The impact of restructuring on teachers' understandings of their curriculum work' (reprinted with permission of the Association for Supervision and Curriculum Development. Copyright 1994 by ASCD); T A O'Donoghue and C A J Dimmock (1996) 'School development planning and the classroom teacher: A Western Australian case study' (reprinted with permission from Carfax Publishing Company); T A O'Donoghue and S O'Brien (1995) 'Teachers' perceptions of parental involvement in school decision making: A Western Australian case study'; and T A O'Donoghue and T Aspland (1994) 'Teachers' curriculum dilemmas in a climate of restructuring: A Western Australian case study'.

We are also deeply indebted to our colleagues John Hattie and Tania Aspland for their encouragement over the years.

Finally, we wish to dedicate this book to Dr Denis McLaughlin and the late Professor Brian Holmes, whose support was generously forthcoming at crucial junctures in our respective careers. For that support we will be forever grateful.

Chapter 1

Introduction

Educational restructuring is taking place in much of the world, with a deregulated, decentralized system replacing central planning, control and supervision (Cistone, 1989). This change is associated with school-based management, school-based budgeting, and the community management of schools (Lawton, 1992, p.139). There is no shortage of prescriptive theories as to why there should be developments along these lines (Purkey and Smith, 1985; Caldwell and Spinks, 1988; Timar, 1989; Derouet, 1991), although it is important to note that the process can take different forms in different contexts, having been enacted at the national level in the United Kingdom and New Zealand and at the district level in Canada (Hess, 1991).

Restructuring in some countries has also involved significant curriculum changes. In the United Kingdom, for example, while the administrative changes reflect the deregulatory, market-oriented solutions economists might dictate, even to the point of allowing schools to opt out of their local education authorities (LEAs) and to collect funds from the central government, concurrently a core National Curriculum has been introduced which provides the central government with control over the subject-matter content of education (Lawton, 1992).

Educational restructuring has also been taking place in Australia. Here, two related policy initiatives are shaping change in schools (Dimmock, 1995a). The first, resulting in 'macro reforms', involves a shift from centralized governance to decentralised, school-based management. The focus is on change at the whole-school level, primarily affecting governance, management and administration rather than classroom activities of teaching and learning (Chadbourne and Clarke, 1994). The second policy initiative, resulting in 'micro-reforms', concerns school restructuring in order to reform teaching and learning. The concern is to introduce a more flexible, responsive and student-oriented education by targeting changes in work organization, pedagogical practices and learning processes.

While centring on the phenomenon of restructuring in general, this book has a number of specific foci. In particular, it focuses on restructuring in relation to curriculum, teaching and learning. It also highlights the impact of restructuring on key stakeholders at the school-site level, particularly principals and teachers. Throughout much of the world strong emphasis is placed on the role of these personnel in translating restructuring initiatives into practice. However, while advice to them has been plentiful, relatively little of it has been based on contemporary studies. Accordingly, there is a large research agenda to be addressed through conducting a range of both quantitative and qualitative studies on various aspects of restructuring at the school level. Furthermore, such large-scale studies, which by nature would be concerned with generalizations, need to be balanced by case studies along the lines of those reported in the main body of this book. These case studies are of three main types: international policy-oriented studies; case studies based on a qualitative research approach; and statistically based case studies.

A case study is a detailed examination of a single subject, group or phenomenon which provides insight into a particular research concern (Yin, 1984). According to Stenhouse (1978), case study methods involve the collection and recording of data about a case, and the preparation of a report on the case. International policy-oriented case studies can portray the broad background against which the phenomenon of restructuring can be located in time and place. Qualitative case studies allow one to spread the net for evidence widely so that a variety of perspectives can be provided as opposed to selecting a random sample or choosing a sample that would be representative of a total population of participants. Also, they allow one to get as close as possible to the participants in order to unearth those thoughts, interests and beliefs which are of most interest to them, rather than to provide specific findings to *a priori* hypotheses. A fuller appreciation of the situation can be gained by complementing these with statistically based case studies.

The justification for presenting a selection of international policy-based case studies like those reported in this book is straightforward. Comparisons and contrasts with one's own national situation help one to come to a fuller understanding of that situation. The statistically based and qualitative case studies in this book are from Western Australia (WA). These are instructive to an international audience for a number of reasons. First, as Sultana (1991) puts it in relation to case studies in general, they can expose stakeholders involved in similar circumstances in various other parts of the world to material which could help them in clarifying and sharpening their own perceptions. Second, restructuring in WA is interesting because it is a site where various approaches to restructuring, particularly those from North America and Britain, have been mediated and reformulated in various ways. Finally, the nature of restructuring initiatives in WA is such that they lend themselves to an analysis where comparisons and contrasts can readily be made with developments in other societies, particularly in Europe and North America.

Hargreaves (1993) has alerted us as follows to the importance of case studies of this type:

> 'many... policies fail and nowhere is this more evident than in education, where innovations frequently fail quite disastrously. I would argue that one common reason for this is that, in grafting new ideas on to schools, we do it with so little knowledge about the nature of the everyday world of teachers, pupils and schools that our attempted grafts (and various forms of major and minor surgery) merely arouse the "antibodies" of the host which undermine our attempts to play doctor to an educational patient.' (pp. 149–150)

He goes on to argue that case studies can help provide us with the necessary understanding, 'for only when we understand the precise nature of the host body can we design our innovatory grafts with any confidence that they will prove to be acceptable'.

In adopting this position one is mindful of the argument that there has been something of a crisis in scholarly inquiry and knowledge in recent years. As Hopkins (1993) has reminded us, research in the professions (including education) has been preoccupied with the invention and discovery of surefire, prescriptive models which would lead to easily generalizable solutions in each area. Eisner (1983, 1984) has been instrumental in providing compelling arguments which enable educational scholars and practitioners to question such preoccupation. He makes the case that, due to the uniqueness of the practical situations that make up the educational domain, only a portion of professional practice can be usefully treated in the manner of a prescriptive science. The gap between general prescriptive frameworks and successful practice is dependent more on the reflective intuition, the craft and the art of the professional practitioner than on any particular prescriptive theory, method or model.

It is against this background that the usefulness of qualitative and statistically based case studies has to be seen. To put it simply, they are good things to start you thinking. At the same time, however, this is not to argue that there is no sense in which they have generalizability. Stake (1978), for example, argues that case studies may be in harmony with the reader's experience and thus a natural basis for generalization. As Kennedy (1979), in the same vein, puts it, generalizability is ultimately related to what the reader is trying to learn from the case studies. Lancy (1993) provides yet a different angle when he states that such an approach 'is comparable to the law where the applicability of a particular precedent case must be argued in each subsequent case. The reader must decide whether the findings apply or not' (p.165).

The case studies can also be seen as having generalizability in the sense outlined by Uhrmacher (1993, pp.89–90). Building on Eisner's ideas (1985), he argues for the production of cases which describe school life, interpret that life by exploring the meanings and consequences of educational events, and assess the educational significance of events described and interpreted. This 'thematics' approach, Uhrmacher (1993) states, is related to generalizing in social science research. He goes on to argue that, rather than make formal generalizations, one can provide the reader with an understanding of the major themes that run through the cases under study. In turn, these themes provide the reader with theories or guides for anticipating what may be found in other situations; 'these theories provide guidance, not prediction' (Uhrmacher, 1993, p.90).

The three types of case studies – international policy-oriented studies, case studies based on a qualitative research approach, and statistically based case studies – are found throughout this book, which is organized in four parts. Part One consists of a chapter which details the general contextual background. Part Two has four chapters, each examining restructuring in four parts of the world: Chapter 3 examines the situation in England and Wales, Chapter 4 the situation in the USA, Chapter 5 the situation in Hong Kong, and Chapter 6 the situation in Australia.

The chapters in Part Three arise out of the observation that relatively little has been written about the experiences and reactions of those who have adopted and implemented school-based management. Chapter 7 reports a case study which takes up this matter by addressing the following questions: Are principals expected to be managers more than educational leaders, directors of human resources, or promoters of excellence in education? Do principals and teachers consider these role changes will replace their existing duties, or are they perceived to be additional responsibilities? What are the advantages of increased competitiveness, more specialized administrative staff, and greater power to school-based groups? Chapter 8 reports a case study that sought to determine what a group of primary school teachers thought about the impact of restructuring on their work. Chapter 9 reports a case study which set out to develop an understanding of a group of high school teachers' perceptions of the school development planning process at one school. Chapter 10 also focuses on teachers. This time the case study is one of teachers' perceptions of the role which is being mapped out for parents in school decision making in current educational restructuring.

The focus narrows in Part Four to the concept of dilemmas as providing an appropriate frame for examining certain aspects of the impact of restructuring on school-site professionals' understandings of their work. Chapter 11 presents a description, based on interview data, of current dilemmas experienced by school leaders in restructuring. Chapter 12 portrays the dilemmas which have emerged in a group of teachers' conceptualizations of their curriculum work as a consequence of restructuring.

The book finishes with a discussion of emerging issues with regard to the key stakeholders involved in contemporary educational restructuring. In this regard, the focus is on implications for principals, teachers and parents. The chapter concludes with a discussion on emerging policy issues.

PART ONE

The background to school restructuring

Chapter 2

The context

The overall context to this work is contemporary restructuring in education. While there is no simple definition of what 'restructuring' means, a burgeoning educational literature is beginning to clarify its origins, purposes and forms. At the heart of the concept of 'restructuring' lies the recognition of the need for fundamental reform. In this regard, Elmore (1990, p.11) claims there is general agreement that the concept has three main dimensions:

1. changes in the way teaching and learning occur in schools;
2. changes in the occupational situation of educators, including conditions of entry and qualifications of teachers and administrators, and school structure, conditions of teachers' work in schools, and decision-making processes;
3. changes in the distribution of power between schools and their clients, or in the governance and incentive structures under which schools function.

He goes on to argue that while reform proposals typically address a combination of these dimensions, changes on one dimension are not necessarily consistent with changes on others. Furthermore, choosing one dimension over the others as a point of departure for school restructuring can have very different implications for both the process of reform and the results one can expect. He concludes that if school restructuring is to work, 'reformers will have to confront the tensions between these dimensions' (p.11).

Agreement over the comprehensiveness and complexity of the restructuring process is confirmed by a number of scholars. Murphy (1991a) refers to the 'complexity involved in transforming schooling', and to efforts to restructure which 'can begin in a variety of places and employ a number of different strategies depending upon the specific objectives sought' (p.17). Regarding comprehensiveness, he refers to restructuring in America as centring on four strategies: school-based management; parental choice and participation in school decision making; teacher empowerment; and teaching for understanding. He argues that most efforts at restructuring have, to date, emphasized one or two of these, such as teacher empowerment, which became the focus of the restructuring movement at its outset in the USA and, more recently, school-based management and choice. Teaching for understanding and redefining the teaching-learning process have received relatively less attention in most countries.

The comprehensiveness of the restructuring movement is also emphasized by Caldwell (1993), who describes the scope and pace of change in education in the 1990s as 'nothing short of breathtaking' (p.165). The key term, according to Caldwell, is 'restructuring' and it is 'being applied to curriculum, pedagogy, administrative structures, governance, teacher training and retraining, and to the teaching profession itself' (p.165). He argues that in the United States the so-called 'second wave' of reform is sweeping the nation, with almost every aspect of schools and their support systems under examination. In England and Wales, a National Curriculum has been introduced for the first time with nationwide tests at the primary and secondary levels. Most schools now have total control of their budgets, with the ability to opt out of control by their local authorities on the majority vote of parents. School-site selection of principals and teachers has been established for some time. A strong accountability process, based on evaluation of school performance by school review teams, is a mainstay of the system. Furthermore, school governing bodies, with strong parental representation, have had their powers substantially increased.

Dramatic reforms have also taken place in New Zealand with the empowerment of boards of trustees at the school level, *inter alia*, to hire and fire principals. Remaining to provide a framework is a small central authority which has a powerful review and audit function (Caldwell, 1993, p.165). Noteworthy, too, is the pioneering system of self-management in Edmonton, Canada, which has been refining aspects of decentralized schools since the mid-1970s (Brown, 1990). For much of this period the Edmonton system has focused on school-based budgeting, but the system continues to evolve, with one intention for the future being to empower the student body.

EXPLANATIONS FOR RESTRUCTURING

There are at least five major explanations for the emergence of restructuring in education. First, political explanations are based on 'dissatisfaction theory' (Iannaccone and Lutz, 1978). There was dissatisfied public opinion with standards and achievements in education in the 1980s. Politicians found it politically advantageous, therefore, to advocate better schools, which were more responsive to the needs and expectations of the public. This ideology was compatible with the renewed political strength of business interests in the 1980s.

Second, Caldwell and Spinks (1988) interpreted the politico-economic case for restructuring education as based on four values – equality, efficiency, liberty and choice. These writers contended that centralized budgeting, with relatively uniform resource allocation to schools, impairs the achievement of equality and efficiency and, by implication, choice. Their solution was to advocate school-site management, with lump sum budgets allocated to schools, a high degree of community involvement in school decision making, and the fostering of diversity within and among schools to ensure choice (Caldwell and Spinks, 1988).

Third, Perrow (1970) used organization theory to suggest that the appropriate pattern of centralization and decentralization for an organization was determined by the nature of techniques and technology required to accomplish the work, and the nature of the organization's clients. Thus, the more schools are seen as organizations catering for diverse student needs, requiring more specialized teaching and learning, and a wider range of cognitive and affective skills, the more decentralization is likely to be the appropriate structure. The work of Peters and Waterman (1982), which showed that excellent companies combined centralization of core values with decentralization of operational functions, is frequently invoked as a justification for such an approach.

Fourth, the case for restructuring has been justified on the basis of school effectiveness studies. Among the more acclaimed school effectiveness researchers are Purkey and Smith (1985), who used meta-analysis to identify 13 characteristics for school effectiveness. They concluded that in effective schools:

> 'the staff of each school is given a considerable amount of responsibility and authority in determining the exact means by which they address the problem of increasing academic performance. This includes giving staff more authority over curricular and instructional decisions and allocation of building resources.' (p.358)

A fifth explanation for restructuring focuses on the case for teacher professionalism and empowerment. Caldwell and Spinks (1988) noted that in the United States, for example, reports by the Carnegie Forum on Education and the Economy (1986) and the Holmes Group (1986) both advocated the goal of making schools better places for teachers in which to work and to learn – places where they could exert more professional autonomy and leadership.

JUSTIFYING RESTRUCTURING ON THE GROUNDS OF IMPROVING TEACHING AND LEARNING

Many question the need for the restructuring of school systems. Whether they be parents, principals, teachers or academics, there are many who, complacent or not, appear to be reasonably satisfied with the status quo. Why, then, the need for change? Leaving aside the political and economic justifications for restructuring, it is possible to mount a convincing case on educational grounds and, in particular, on the need to reform the approach of schools to teaching and learning (Holly, 1990; Murphy, 1991a).

First, schools are themselves part of turbulent policy environments. Policy goals and statements commonly allude to the main aim of improving student learning outcomes. Many governments have established structures and procedures to render schools accountable for their students' academic performance. Schools are expected to define their purposes in school development plans and to render accountability in terms of student outcomes. Furthermore, system-wide monitoring of standards and student attainments in basic subject and skill areas (such as literacy and numeracy) enable ministries, schools and parents to measure and compare the performances of individual schools against system-wide norms. These demands on schools shift the focus away from a traditional concern with resource inputs to an outcomes orientation. Changing policy expectations thus render the maintenance of the status quo irrelevant, since schools need to search for greater effectiveness in securing improved student learning outcomes.

A second reason for focusing on change in teaching and learning arises out of the changing relationship between schooling and the broad, long-term adjustments in society and the economy. For example, there is the argument that the type of workforce needed for the future will require school and college programmes to reflect the competencies and skills required in competitive global economies. Schlechty (1990) refers to the shift of American society in the late twentieth century from an industrial base to an information base, and describes his vision of schools to meet this change for the twenty-first century. In an information-based society knowledge work, namely work that entails expending mental effort, is the primary mode of work, since information constitutes the main means for its accomplishment. Elmore (1990), adopting such a perspective, has called for major reform of the American school system, arguing that:

> 'In order to sustain our present standard of living and regain our competitive position in the world economy... we will need a better educated workforce, which will in turn mean that schools will have to dramatically improve the way they educate all children.' (pp.1–2)

A new wave of educational thinking in the 1990s reinforces this reconceptualization of teaching and learning. American scholars in particular recognize a shift from behavioural psychology, which has been the source of thinking underpinning the traditional industrial model of schooling, to social cognitive or constructivist psychology as the inspiration for a new model of learning and teaching in the post-industrial information society (Cohen, 1988; Murphy, 1991a).

Third, there is every indication that present trends in social problems such as alcoholism, drugs, crime, vandalism and family breakdown will continue to rise in the foreseeable future. An increasing number of school students are likely to be directly or indirectly affected by these trends. If schools are simply to keep pace with, let alone seriously address, these growing problems and their implications for teaching and learning, they will need to shift from their established cultures and practices.

Fourth, there is growing concern that too many students leave school with little or no success in learning after ten or more years of schooling (Goodlad, 1984; Sizer, 1984). Murphy (1991a), referring to the United States, claims that '25 per cent of all students physically remove themselves from engagement in learning by dropping out of school' (p.52). Of those students who stay, many fail to achieve the school graduation certificate. While it has been customary to blame students for failure to learn, the spotlight is increasingly shifting to the school and its responsibilities to ensure that learning takes place (Chubb, 1988). Many disaffected students report negative attitudes towards school, finding them unfriendly and uncaring places, unreflective of their values, interests and cultures (Cuban, 1989).

A fifth reason arises out of the relative rigidity of schools with respect to changing their approaches to teaching and learning. Some observers claim current schools bear many similarities to their counterparts in the last century. Elmore (1990), for example, describes classroom activity for the average student as 'dull, perfunctory and disconnected from what goes on in other classrooms or in the larger community' (p.8). Faced with the impossible odds of educating batches of 30 mixed-ability children, many teachers lower their expectations of student learning or focus on smaller groups of more able students who provide them with some job satisfaction. In many cases also, the curriculum is still delivered in regimented ways, for fixed periods of time, unrelated to individual students' learning needs, and students still move in step to the next age grade, irrespective of their performance.

Finally, a growing awareness of social justice issues, particularly pertinent for minority groups and the educationally disadvantaged, is adding an extra dimension to the need for schooling to be reshaped. Increasingly, the goal is to improve the learning of all students and to recognize the entitlements of all to a quality learning experience relevant to abilities, needs and interests (Levin, 1987; Slavin, 1988). Pressures for regular and mainstream schools and classes to accommodate students with learning disabilities and behavioural problems serve only to exacerbate the problem, as do policies espousing equity and protection of the rights of minority and underprivileged groups. Schools are increasingly expected, therefore, to cater for the learning needs of all students at a time when the student body is growing more multicultural and diverse.

THE CHANGING ROLES OF TEACHERS, PRINCIPALS AND PARENTS

The changing role of teachers

Since the 1960s the role of the teacher across a wide range of OECD countries has changed because of the changing nature of teachers' work. In particular, teachers have had to deal with a changing clientele because of the massive expansion of education systems arising out of the extensive growth and change in industrialized societies. During the 1960s and 1970s this change resulted in the introduction of a wide range of curricular and pedagogical innovations. As Skilbeck (1990) puts it:

'Learning processes came to the fore to meet the needs of the greatly increased student numbers drawn from all sectors of the community. Curricula were reviewed and revitalized and whole new subjects or fresh approaches to existing subjects were introduced to meet emerging social needs, in working life, in the leisure society and in interpersonal relations and the values domain.' (p.12)

Connell (1980, p.333) has identified the following characteristics of the reforms which teachers tried to put into practice:

1. the encouragement of students to discover facts and think for themselves, to define problems and issues and work for solutions;
2. the introduction of a variety and diversity of approaches, combining individual assignments, group projects and other pedagogical procedures designed to engage students' interests;
3. the fostering of active student expression and creativity.

Skilbeck (1990, p.12) goes on to state that in the 1980s these themes were given more of a social needs emphasis as a result of a growing consciousness of economic challenges and large-scale social problems. While this emphasis continues into the 1990s, with the themes still informing much classroom practice, it is accompanied by an emphasis on pursuing clearly prescribed objectives as outlined in student outcome statements.

In Australia, changes in teachers' work have reflected general trends in other OECD countries. Three broad areas of change have been identified, namely, changes in the student population, changes in teachers' social roles, and changes in teachers' professional roles (Schools Council, 1990, p.21). With regard to changes in the student population, this can be attributed, to some extent, to the fact that Australia, like many other countries, has had an expansion in its education system. This has resulted in increased retention rates, particularly at the upper secondary school level. One consequence is a new cohort of students who many teachers characterize as lacking in interest and motivation:

> 'These teachers' perceptions provide an indication of the mixed feelings excited by the new cohort of students – the concern and uncertainty about how they should be catered for, and the demands on time and energy which are not necessarily new, but which have become more pronounced at this level in dealing with less obviously motivated and able students. The effort being put into attempts to modify teaching practice and course structures can be readily evidenced across the country.' (Schools Council, 1990, p.23)

The situation for teachers has been complicated further by the increased rate at which students with physical and intellectual disabilities are being integrated into the regular classroom.

When considering the effect of changes in the student population on the nature of teachers' work it is also important to keep in mind that Australia has experienced changes in its immigrant population. The consequence for schools has been a significant increase in pupils whose primary language is that of one of the countries of continental Europe or Asia. While specialist teachers have been employed to teach these pupils English, classroom teachers have had to adapt their practices to meet the demands of the multicultural classroom. In this regard, not only have they been faced with the problem of having to try to teach a class composed of pupils with varying commands of the English language, but they have also had to deal with the fact that different cultural groups often have different learning styles.

They have also had to become culturally sensitive in a whole host of ways because of the new cultural assumptions which differing groups of students and parents have brought with them.

> 'On the matter of changed social roles, the following observation has been made: in the past, schools have been organized on assumptions about the family and its work patterns. The gap between those assumptions and social realities is widening, particularly as a result of the increasing participation of mothers in formal, paid work... also, concerns, expectations and standards about the care of children have heightened. Schools as well as families are sharing the implications of this.' (Schools Council, 1990, p.23)

Schools have responded to this situation in a variety of ways, including the provision of counselling and programmes on drug abuse, sex education and delinquency. Not only have schools employed specialists in these areas but they have also encouraged teachers to take up such issues in the teaching of their more traditional subject areas. Teachers have also had to inform their approach to work with a consideration of issues such as racism, sexism, multiculturalism, gender equity, and the environment.

On the matter of changed professional roles, it has been noted (Schools Council, 1990, p.24) that there have been many identifiable changes in teaching practice in the past two decades. One of these changes is the move (particularly in primary schools) to promote situations where, combined with more formally structured lessons, students 'negotiate' what they do. This, of course, requires teachers who have the skills to work in teams and create flexibly organized environments. The curriculum at both the primary and secondary levels has also been broadened. This has led to a change in teachers' work since schools have not employed specialists to teach many of the new subjects but have harnessed the interest and enthusiasm of already practising teachers.

Teachers are also having to come to terms with the technological revolution. In particular, they are having to deal with demands that computers should be playing an increasing role in the classroom. Many are meeting the challenge through introducing pupils to word processing and demonstrating its usefulness within process writing. A much smaller number are beginning to realize its potential for improving teaching and learning through the use of computer-assisted learning and as an information retrieval system through the use of the Network. However, it is clear that there is an enormous amount of work to be done to convince teachers of, and prepare them for realizing, the potential of information technology to enhance education.

Finally, the last two decades have seen an extension of the teacher's role in school management and a much greater involvement of parents on school boards and school councils. Both of these developments are very demanding of teachers' time and energy and, as the next two areas to be considered demonstrate, they have had significant implications for principals and teachers.

The changing role of principals

The advent of restructuring, and in particular school-based management as a central aspect of it, has had significant reverberations on the role of principals in government schools. At no previous time in the history of publicly provided formal education has so much attention been paid to the principalship. Restructuring policies aimed at transferring more functions and responsibilities to schools, at improving their performance, and at holding them to account for that performance have focused attention on the importance of leadership at school level, and in particular, the leadership provided by principals. Principals are seen as the fulcrum on which the quality of restructured schools depends.

While the principal's role has evolved continuously since its inception, restructuring policies have accelerated the form and pace of that evolutionary process. A convenient way of conceptualizing these more recent changes is to recognize the principal's role in the following ways: as both broadening and deepening; as more demanding both inside and outside the school; as incorporating elements of administration, management and leadership; and as subject to a number of interlocking and complex themes. Each of these is now elaborated.

Various scholars (Kimbrough and Burkett, 1990; Rossow, 1990) have captured the all-encompassing nature of the principalship in a contemporary setting. The broadening of the principal's role includes the following areas of responsibility:

♦ educational or instructional leadership – supporting, supervising and monitoring the curriculum, teaching and learning;
♦ management of non-specifically educational aspects of the school (including personnel and human relations management), and resource management (particularly budgetary and financial management);
♦ management of the school community and the external environment;
♦ management and leadership of change.

For principals to operate successfully within each of these management domains or fields, there is an increasing expectation that they possess specialized knowledge and a range of esoteric skills. This can be construed as a deepening of the role and can be illustrated in a number of ways. With respect to the principal's dealings with a host of different individuals and groups in the context of today's litigious society, a knowledge of the law is considered essential. In the context of instructional leadership and the quest for improved student learning, the principal is expected to have expertise in what is considered best practice of the curriculum, teaching and learning. In managing the school staff in a heightened context of performance management, the principal's personnel and human resource management skills are expected to include techniques of selection, deployment, motivation, appraisal and development. In managing closer relations between the school, the community and external environment, the principal is called upon to be a good communicator and a diplomat, and to possess public relations skills. In addition to all of these, the principal is expected to possess competency in budgeting and resource allocation, and to lead and manage organizational change in ways which gain the participation and commitment of both professional and lay members of the school community.

A further frame by which to conceptualize the principal's role is to distinguish between three levels of operation – administration, management and leadership (Dimmock, 1996). Administration may be regarded as referring to the lower level routine tasks, such as attending to correspondence; management, on the other hand, concerns a higher level of function aimed at maintaining expected levels of performance, efficiency and effectiveness among the organization's resources, particularly its human and financial resources. Leadership is considered as the highest level of operation, being concerned with motivating staff to achieve goals they might otherwise fail to set and to perform at levels they might not otherwise reach. In the context of restructuring, the decentralization and devolution of responsibility to school level has caused a very significant increase in both administration and management, particularly for the principal. At the same time other aspects of restructuring policy, such as improved quality of teaching and learning, 'better value-for-money' schooling, and increased attention paid to performance, evaluation and accountability, have placed a premium on leadership, particularly the principal's leadership. While distinctions may be drawn between the three concepts in terms of level of importance, most commentators on the principalship regard management and leadership as equally necessary undertakings for principals' engagement in the contemporary restructuring context.

A further way of conceptualizing and understanding changes in the principal's role is to select key themes characterizing its recent development. These themes derive from the form which school-based management has assumed: the need for the change process to be managed; the influences on the principalship exerted by the changing organizational context; and principals' perceptions and understandings of the new demands and expectations placed on them. The more important of such themes are discussed below.

The change from control by central office to school-based management has necessarily reconfigured the principal's position from being a middle manager in a long hierarchy to being a senior manager in charge of a more self-managing organization. This means that the principal is a key change agent, responsible for managing the change process and bringing about a successful transition to school-based management. In many of the school systems undergoing restructuring, the principal, on behalf of the system, is expected to 'sell' the idea of school-based management to all stakeholders in the school community, often without the benefit of much support from the central office. Simultaneously, the principal is expected to manage and oversee the change process in detail as it manifests itself in transformed structures, processes and practices. The challenge to principals in managing the transformation to school-based management is thus compounded by virtue of the fact that, at the same time as they work towards adoption of the concept, they are concerned with implementation.

A further theme which has exerted an influence on the principalship has been the changing nature of the work context. The switch to school-based management has resulted in a number of significant changes in the workplace which principals are expected to oversee and manage. As a consequence, principals have accumulated new responsibilities and functions. These include the introduction and implementation of school development planning, staff appraisal and performance management, new student-centred curricula, school-based budgeting, and the management of new governance structures, in particular more empowered school councils and boards.

Many of these additional responsibilities have promulgated further changes in the principal's role by necessitating different styles, techniques and approaches to work. Principals are now expected to manage a more diverse set of stakeholder groups than ever before, and these groups are more empowered than they have ever been. Parents, business and local community leaders may constitute an influential group of lay members on school boards or councils. Moreover, principals are having to manage groups of professional teachers who are themselves expected to play more participative roles in school decision making. Many restructuring initiatives are explicit about the principal's obligation to create a climate and culture conducive to shared decision making, collaboration between teachers, and between professionals and lay members of the school community. Yet few situations are to be found where tradition favours such collaboration and, at the same time, principals with leadership styles which accommodate these expectations may be in a minority. Consequently, for many principals the expectation that they share power, authority, decision making and leadership calls for a monumental change in their leadership styles.

There are other respects in which the changing work context of school-based management is creating substantial change in the principal's role. One concerns the emphasis placed on running the school along business lines and according to business principles. Greater delegation of financial responsibility to schools and their subsequent auditing places the onus on principals to oversee the efficient and effective use of school budgets. More than ever before in government schools, principals are having to match income with expenditure. They are having to seek school revenues from multiple sources, and trying to minimize costs and use resources more thriftily in an effort to redirect funds from less to more pressing causes. Another concern relates to changes in the work context, an increasing number of which are being enshrined in legislation. These include health and safety at work and social justice issues, including gender equity, sexual harassment, and protection of the rights of minority groups. Included in this group of changes are attempts to transform industrial relations away from collective bargaining and award systems towards enterprise bargaining and individual and group workplace agreements.

One important change in the principal's work context centres on the increased emphasis placed on performance and outcomes. Not only are principals more accountable for levels of performance and achievement among their staff and students, they are also responsible for putting in place and managing systems designed for their measurement. Examples include appraisal and performance management for assessing teachers; student outcomes-based curricula for gauging student performance; and evaluation and accountability mechanisms, including performance indicators, for judging whole-school performance. The mechanisms, concepts and terminology largely derive from the business sector. Yet those driving the initiatives justify them on the grounds that they will improve the quality of schooling and education.

Another major influence on principals' changing roles are their own perceptions and understandings of the new demands and expectations placed on them. How principals perceive and make sense of restructuring is an important factor in how they interpret their roles. Their interpretation, in turn, shapes their role-taking and their role-playing patterns of behaviour. Recent research suggests that one way in which many principals see their changing roles in a context of restructuring is in terms of dilemmas. A dilemma is defined as an unresolvable situation. It contains elements which defy management in terms of securing a successful conclusion from all points of view. In meeting one set of expectations, it is more difficult to meet others. Dilemmas cannot, therefore, be resolved. They can only be handled and coped with. Choices, compromises, sacrifices, trade-offs and opportunity costs are usually some of the ways in which dilemmas are conceived by principals.

Changes to the principal's role discussed in this section, including the simultaneous broadening, deepening and externalizing aspects, raise the spectre of conscientious principals becoming over-extended professionals. Many responsibilities are being added, but few are being taken away. A ramification has been the stress experienced by principals and the mounting challenge to their self-efficacy as a result of the growing list of expectations placed on them (Dimmock and Hattie, 1996). Increased emphasis on, and provision of, principals' professional development as a means of combating these difficulties has met, at best, with only partial success.

The changing role of parents

Throughout much of the world public education traditionally has been the preserve of bureaucracies which have left little room for non-professional participation in shaping education policy and practice. Parental involvement, where it has existed, has usually been limited to activities such as fundraising, providing school equipment and sitting on various auxiliary bodies such as parents and friends' associations (Stacey, 1991). Reforms which have increased parental involvement in England and Wales originate from democratic principles which were emphasized in the 1970s (Rust and Blakemore, 1990). Beattie (1985) attributes the success of these reforms to the political legacy of parental activism in the 1960s, for which the catalyst was the controversial introduction of comprehensive schooling. The Plowden Report (Department of Education and Science, 1967) stressed the importance of parental support to the child in school. The parent-teacher (PTA) movement also grew rapidly with the keynote being cooperation between home and school. Groups of concerned parents came together in 1962 as the Confederation for the

Advancement of State Education and by 1969 many LEAs were beginning to appoint parent governors. In 1975 a Labour government committed to a more participatory style of local democracy set up the Taylor Committee. Among the themes of the resultant 'Taylor Report' (Taylor Committee, 1977) were that schools needed a body of locally concerned people to ensure their responsiveness to those they served and that parents should be equal partners in such LEA school governing bodies. Communication with parents was also of concern to the Committee and recommendations were made as to what a good school should do to inform and involve parents and enlist their support.

Throughout the 1960s and 1970s a major force behind the development of increased parental involvement in the United States stemmed from concerns about social justice and equity. Much of this new involvement derived from federal social justice initiatives aimed at promoting equity and equality among the poor, black, handicapped, and other minorities. Berger (1991) notes the social justice character of the federally funded programmes such as *Headstart*, *Homestart* and *Follow Through*. It was through programmes such as these that parental involvement in public schooling focused on the potential of education to create a more just society. Their purpose was to provide compensatory resourcing in disadvantaged areas. The federal support given to schools in such areas was conditional on the involvement of parents and the community in the process.

In Australia, it is arguable that the rationale for increasing parental involvement in schooling in the late 1960s and the 1970s also rested on democratic principles through which the right of all education participants might receive greater recognition (Andrews, 1978; Connors and McMorrow, 1990). In seeking to explain the emergence of these democratic principles, Blakers (1982, p.37) observes that opposition to centralized education in Australia arose from a realization among educators that it 'produced rigidity of thinking, adherence to established practices, resistance to change and discouraged community involvement'. The federally commissioned report, *Schools in Australia* (Karmel, 1973), promoted parental involvement in schools and school management (Watt, 1989) and laid the foundation for the establishment of the Australian Schools Commission in 1973. This Commission heralded a new era of federal intervention in education which encouraged community participation and recognized the plurality and diversity of the Australian population. It argued for educational democracy on the grounds that no single model was best for Australia. Beare (1993) argues that in transforming these arguments into practical democratic reform the Commission aimed to empower parents by involving them in making decisions aimed at promoting equity, equality, social justice and choice. A major outcome was federally funded initiatives such as the *Disadvantaged Schools Program, Innovations Program* and the *Participation and Equity Program* (Beare, 1993).

In many countries during the 1980s the forces behind the push for greater parental involvement in education began to change. Lauglo (1990) observes that this was particularly the case in the United Kingdom. He suggests that in order to attract electoral support the Thatcher government's promotion of education democracy was primarily a political instrument, in that it served to shift power away from Labour-dominated LEAs, which had been vocal Conservative opponents over the previous three decades. It is also argued that parental involvement has been used as a means of saving money, by transferring administrative management to school councils, thus removing the need to employ so many central ministry staff (Edwards and Whitty, 1992; Morgan *et al.*, 1993).

In the United States the release of the report *A Nation at Risk* (National Commission on Excellence in Education, 1983) led to the introduction of reform programmes by most states. Subsequently, the language of 'reform' was replaced by the language of 'restructuring'. However Hanson (1991), observing the impact of politics on education in the United States, makes the point that while the Reagan administration was responsible for instigating this nationwide trend, the motivation was to justify a desire not to provide any extra funding, and indeed little extra financial support was allocated.

The issue of the importance of parental choice is also one which came to the forefront as the decade progressed. Commenting on the source of this concern, Bryk *et al.* (1990) identify a return to past traditions in education delivery, arguing that political and public support for parental choice may be traced to the decentralized historical nature of education. Similarly, Boyd (1988) observes that parental involvement in the US was traditionally an integral part of a heavily decentralized education system. Schools were run by elected parent bodies which decided upon curricula, teacher recruitment and most other educational activities related to the school. Accordingly, recent reforms providing for increased parental involvement may be seen as part of a popular parental desire to return to tradition, through which parents might once again exercise greater control and independence (Hanson, 1991).

In a similar vein, Rust and Blakemore (1990) view the forces behind the growth of parental involvement in Norway as having been heavily influenced by local community politics in the 1960s and 1970s. Lauglo (1990) concurs with this view, noting that public acquiescence in educational uniformity immediately after the Second World War was replaced by popular desire for private schooling and government funding of private schools. Regarding Norway, therefore, the concern about choice may be seen as a more 'bottom up' stimulus to parental involvement than is evident in countries such as England and Wales. The forces behind the high level of parental choice now existing in Israel are different yet again. According to Shapira and Hayman (1991), these emerged in the late 1960s and were characterized by parental activism, stimulated by the desire of parents in a pluralist society to provide their children with an education in accordance with their moral and social outlooks.

This brief survey of the various forces behind the promotion of parental involvement in schooling since the 1970s indicates that the pattern internationally is fairly complex. Now, in the 1990s, we appear to have entered a phase where many of these forces have come together with those currently operating under the guise of restructuring. In particular, economic rationalist and corporate managerialist policies have been manifested in education through the introduction and implementation of strategies designed to promote restructuring and secure reform, the effects of which are designed to impact on all stakeholders. 'Economic rationalism', according to Bartlett (1992, p.288), proposes an overarching stress on efficiency and economy, effectiveness and performance, and outputs in the public sector, all of which combine to achieve the goals of the state. The same author defines 'corporate managerialism' as involving the appropriation of private sector models of administration and their application to the public sector with the restructuring of bureaucratic organization to achieve greater outputs for given inputs. This requires a leaner, tighter, more precisely defined management structure, and more precisely articulated policy goals, as well as 'the devolution of action (though not power or authority) to the service agencies at the workface' (Bartlett, 1992, p.228).

A major theme of governments in legitimizing educational policies formulated from such positions is the democratic rights of parents to participate in the education of their children. Tracing the series of education acts in England and Wales, Wolfendale (1992) notes their commitment to the principle of educational democracy. Each of these acts strengthened and formalized parental involvement. More recently, former Prime Minister John Major introduced the concept of a 'Parents' Charter', which was designed to formalize recent democratic reforms in education participation. Citing the rights of parents to choose schools and to participate in school decision making, Major laid claim to be upholding the democratic principles which had traditionally underpinned British society.

In New Zealand, arguments highlighting the democratic rights of parents have also spurred educational reform. The reforms initiated by the 1988 Picot Report into education transformed democratic principles into reality. Parents were given formal decision-making powers within a programme of devolution and school-based management. Responsibility for schooling was transferred from the central education ministry to individual school boards, with each board having an inbuilt parent majority. Parents also received the option of establishing new schools which reflected their educational stance.

Burkhardt and March (1991) argue that recent Australian reforms which have increased parental involvement in school decision making reflect the adoption of corporate management philosophies in education. Similarly, Watt (1989) argues that notions of efficiency, productivity and accountability drive the reforms. According to Gamage (1993, p.141), the proponents support one or both of the following: 'fundamental and pervasive alterations in the way educational reforms were organized and institutionalised and the way in which state schools were governed and held accountable to the public'. Two broad strategies emerged, namely, school site-based governance and school choice. Consideration of these strategies feature widely throughout the remaining chapters of this book.

CONCLUSION

This chapter has centred on the phenomenon of restructuring which has been taking place in many school systems throughout the world over the last ten years. First, a brief exposition on restructuring *per se*, and the nature and form it has taken within an international context, has been presented. A general account of the changing nature of, and expectations regarding, the role of principals, teachers and parents, particularly in regard to curriculum, teaching and learning, then followed. This provides the broad context within which the case studies in the chapters which follow can be located.

PART TWO

Restructuring in four parts of the world

Chapter 3

Restructuring in England and Wales

Educational reforms in the UK since the mid-1980s, as elsewhere in the English-speaking world (notably Australia, New Zealand, Canada and the USA), have combined both a measure of decentralization of management decision making to schools and stronger centralization of control over curricula and the monitoring of educational standards (Boyd, 1992; Levacic, 1995). In mapping these changes in detail, this chapter is in three parts: the first provides a brief account of events leading up to major reforms; the second describes the reforms themselves, the major parts of which are incorporated in the 1988 Education Reform Act (ERA); and the third discusses their significance.

Background to reform

Reforms to the education system in England and Wales had been steadily and incrementally made since the 1944 Education Act. What makes the 1988 and subsequent reforms so important is the wholesale and concerted effort they represent to change in fundamental ways the values underpinning the system as well as the practices pervading it. A key question to ask is, why the impetus for wholesale change culminating in the reforms of the late 1980s and early 1990s?

Several longstanding concerns of governments may be identified as providing conditions conducive to reform. One ongoing issue was government dissatis-faction with standards of achievement in schools. Another issue was the poor performance of the UK economy in terms of international competitiveness and growth and its perceived link to an education system which was seen as well below the standard expected. In short, education was seen as failing to turn out a more productive labour force. Other economic factors were inflationary pressures, the need to control public spending as a proportion of the GDP and a desire to get value for money (Thomas, 1993, p.30). Allied to these economic factors was a reluctance on the part of taxpayers to pay more for education through higher tax rates, which acted as a disincentive to work, yet the desire on their part for better and more educational opportunities. Faced with these imperatives, central government had to find radically different, 'creative' solutions, such as greater efficiency in the public sector and shifting more of the cost of education on to the private sector.

Conservative governments through the 1980s were also able to rely on support for their position from growing public disenchantment with the performance of the public sector, fostered by 'public choice' and 'free market economists' (Levacic, 1995, p.2). There was, in addition, a populist movement for greater participation in the decisions which affect the daily lives of people in relation to the local services they consumed. Some commentators recognize what could be called a 'chronic disequilibrium' in the demographic-economic structure of the UK society (Thomas, 1993). During the 1970s and 1980s, declining school enrolments and fewer new entrants to the labour force were accompanied by rapid growth in the numbers of dependent aged. In this context of a smaller productive workforce supporting a larger dependent population, educational reform can be seen as a response to economic and demographic factors.

Political factors are also central to an explanation of the reforms. The Conservatives, under Margaret Thatcher's leadership, had been elected to power in 1979 with a manifesto committed to a strong educational reform agenda. Thomas (1993) views the gap between the election to office of the Conservatives in 1979 and the ERA as a 'lagged response' to perceived economic problems (p. 44). For much of the 1980s, education remained 'untouched' by the Tories' market-oriented policies; when it came to a third term of office at the 1987 election, educational reform provided just the radical platform the party needed in order to win electoral victory, given the growing public dissatisfaction with education. In addition, the period 1985 to 1987 had been marked by considerable teacher political unrest which enjoyed little public support.

Other reforms incorporated in the ERA, however, such as parental choice of school and supporting access to the private system, are viewed by Thomas as reflecting the ideological commitment of the government to private ownership and markets, a commitment which had steadily increased since the election in 1979. Political ideology, he argues (1993, pp.45–47), also provides an explanation for a number of other reform initiatives. One of these concerns the government's commitment to efficiency which, through its belief in competition and markets, it was also able to argue led to improvement in standards.

In explaining the centralization of curriculum control, a trend which runs counter to the prevailing pattern of decentralization in other reforms in the package, Thomas (1993, p.47) argues that there was a strong desire on the part of the Department of Education and Science (DES), faced with the erosion of some of its power in light of other decentralizing reform measures, to secure more control over the curriculum. It was able to argue consistency with the rest of the reform package by pressing the need for local management, but within national guidelines.

The following section provides an outline of the main policy changes incorporated in school reform in the ERA and subsequent legislation.

THE EDUCATION REFORM ACTS

The Education Reform Act of 1988 provides a convenient starting point for mapping school reform in England and Wales. For the entire post-Second World War period the legislative foundation of the school system had been the 1944 Education Act. Although changes in the system during the decades that followed had been reflected in the passing of many regulations and amendments to the 1944 Act, by the 1980s the need for a new act was indisputable. In addition, a decade of rule by a rightwing Conservative government determined to make sweeping changes to education only served to reinforce the need for a new act as the 1980s drew to a close.

The resultant 1988 ERA and subsequent Education (Schools) Act (1992) provide the legislative architecture for the complete transformation of virtually every part of the school system of England and Wales. The main elements of the dramatic reforms contained in the ERA, are as follows:

♦ The National Curriculum, which for the first time, lays down in considerable detail the content of the curriculum and the assessment of pupils at the ages of 7, 11, 14 and 16.
♦ Local management of schools (LMS), a programme of school-based management which limits the powers of LEAs and devolves funding and resource management to governing bodies and school staff.
♦ Open enrolment, which removes boundary limits on pupil enrolment and enables parents to choose the school they wish their children to attend, subject only to its physical capacity. Since school budgets are linked closely to pupil numbers, schools are encouraged to compete for pupils in order to sustain or increase their income.
♦ Provision is made for schools to 'opt out' of control by LEAs and become 'grant maintained' (GM), thereby receiving their revenue and capital budgets from a funding agency whose members are appointed by the secretary of state.
♦ The incorporation of further education colleges as autonomous bodies, independent of LEAs (Bush and West-Burnham, 1994, pp.1–2).

The main feature of the 1992 Act was:

♦ The introduction of a nationally controlled 'inspection' regime, which ensures that all schools are inspected at least once every four years according to criteria established by the Office for Standards in Education (OFSTED).

In line with the theme of this book, the sections below focus on all of the above reforms, with the exception of that part of the ERA concerned with colleges of further education.

The National Curriculum

One of the foremost features of the ERA is the introduction of a National Curriculum and a national assessment system for children aged from 5–16 years. Subjects are categorized into a 'core' group, consisting of mathematics, English, and science, and a second group of foundation subjects; history, geography, technology, music, art, and physical education. In addition, a modern foreign language is included as a foundation subject for all students in secondary schools. For all subjects there are attainment targets which identify the knowledge, skills and understanding that pupils are expected to have, and these must be specified in relation to four key stages relating to ages 5–7, 7–11, 11–14 and 14–16. Accompanying the attainment targets are programmes of study defining the content, skills and processes which must be taught at each key stage. Finally, the assessment arrangements are prescribed whereby the extent to which students have achieved the attainment targets at each key stage can be ascertained.

Implementation of the National Curriculum was to take place over many years, but from 1989 onwards all schools had to take account of the requirements in their curriculum planning. First to be affected were teachers in infant and junior schools, for whom programmes of study in maths, English and science were quickly published. These schools were also the first, in 1991, to experience the national testing system of Standard Attainment Tasks (SATs), starting with 7-year olds.

Even as the first testing began, modifications were being made. In response to the overwhelming experience among teachers that excessive amounts of time were being devoted to testing, the secretary of state abandoned plans to test 7-year olds across all subjects and instead confined testing to core subjects. However, as Thomas (1993, p.32) recognizes, a new problem was created whereby teachers are more likely to concentrate their time on teaching core subjects.

A further curriculum change in the late 1980s concerned the extension of a more explicit vocational element in the curriculum for all 14–16 year olds. The Technical and Vocational Education Initiative (TVEI) was launched in

1982 under the auspices of the Manpower Services Commission (the Department of Education and Science had no constitutional powers to mandate the school curriculum at that point). Its purpose was to provide a technical and vocational route to national qualifications for those who were not suited to a wholly academic curriculum. Its relative success, together with the government's avowed intent to strengthen its control over the curriculum as a means of ensuring a better match between education provision and the needs of the economy, led the government in the late 1980s to extend the vocational element to all students in the age range 14–16. Consequently, a further issue arose as to how to integrate this element within the National Curriculum (Thomas, 1993).

Local management of schools

In many ways, LMS is the hub of the reforms. It is an integrated package, and involved, from April 1990, delegating to schools responsibility for staffing, premises and services. The governing body of the school, with a lay majority, has the final budgetary control. The delegated budget is funded by a formula largely determined by the number of pupils attending, and the tenure of staff is directly related to the ability of the school to meets its expenditure from its budget. If there is an expected budget deficit, staff can be dismissed and there is no obligation for the LEA to guarantee them employment in other LEA schools. Alternative employment depends on the governing bodies of other schools deciding to hire them.

Thomas (1993, p.33) comments that 'this change in the tenure of staff can be expected to lead to greater competition between schools over the enrolment of pupils', a change reinforced by a further provision of the ERA preventing LEAs limiting admissions to popular schools. The degree of inter-school competition for pupils was made keener by the requirement to give parents more information on which to base their school choice. This was made possible through a growing emphasis on performance indicators. The publication of league tables of schools' performance subsequent to the ERA is one type of performance information available to the public. In addition, in exercising their delegated powers, governors and headteachers must take account of their responsibility to provide the National Curriculum. In order to do this, they must develop a management plan showing how the allocation of resources meets the National Curriculum requirements.

Open enrolment

The ERA increased the ability of parents to choose their child's school by making it impossible for a child to be refused admission to a state school if there is a place available. Each school has a specified standard number of pupils, which can only be changed with the approval of the secretary of state, and it reaches full capacity when it achieves that number. It may voluntarily admit more than its standard number, or can be forced to do so if parents make successful representation to an appeals panel.

As Levacic (1995, pp.6–7) states, 'more open enrolment has stopped the practice whereby LEAs protected schools with falling rolls by holding down the admissions of pupils to more popular schools'. In reality, the choice parents can exercise varies greatly depending on local conditions, notably the availability of alternative schools and the existence of spare places. The main admissions criteria for state schools remain proximity to residence, stated order of preference and sibling connection.

Opting out – GM schools

The introduction of GM schools allows the governors of all primary and secondary schools with more than 300 registered pupils to apply to the secretary of state for maintenance by grant from the central government and to cease to be maintained by the LEA. Thomas (1993) declares:

> 'This change and the associated creation of 24 city technology colleges, also independent of LEAs, was designed to increase the range and diversity of schools from which parents and children can choose. In effect, while the organization for the "local management of schools" was intended to make schools more responsive to parents, the organization for "grant-màintained schools", in threatening the viability of LEAs, put pressure upon them to be more responsive, both to schools-as-clients and to parents-as-clients.' (p.34)

A central philosophy behind government reform is clear: competition is a means for improving the reponsiveness and performance of the public education system.

New school inspection arrangements – OFSTED

The Education (Schools) Act (1992) fundamentally changed the ways in which schools are inspected. Formerly, schools were inspected irregularly by a team of Her Majesty's Inspectors (HMIs), an independent group of experienced professionals, who fulfilled the role of a field force monitoring and inspecting standards on behalf of the DES. The chief inspector regulated which schools should be inspected, and trained, selected and monitored inspectors in addition to providing guidelines for inspections. The 1992 Act replaced the HMI system with OFSTED, whose task it was to oversee the inspection of every school at least once every four years.

OFSTED is independent of the Department for Education and Employment (DfEE) (the DES became the DFE in 1992 and the DfEE in 1995), and is headed by Her Majesty's Chief Inspector for Schools. HMIs were reduced in number and relocated to OFSTED. The system of school inspection is now fundamentally changed; for example OFSTED identifies the schools to be inspected, and inspections are now privatized and carried out by teams of inspectors who tender to OFSTED for the contract to inspect schools for a fee. Some of the inspectors are self-employed, others are local authority advisers and inspectors. Both professional and lay members make up the composition of inspection teams, which are led by a registered and trained inspector.

The schools themselves are responsible for generating a lot of the information required for inspection, with the criteria for evaluation being made very explicit. Parents must be consulted as part of the school inspection process and the findings must be discussed with school governors and with the senior management team of the school. A full report goes to OFSTED, is published, and a copy must be made available by the school to anyone who requests it. A summary of the report must be sent to parents, press and local employers.

Governors are required to prepare an action plan in response to the report within 40 working days and parents must be kept informed of progress in implementing the plan. Schools adjudged to be failing are declared at risk, and given one year to improve, after which, if they fail to so do, they are taken over by an *ad hoc* body called an education association which puts in new management. Such a school subsequently becomes a grant-maintained school. Under the OFSTED arrangements school inspection criteria not only cover educational standards, including the quality of learning and school ethos, but also the efficiency of the school and an overall verdict on the value for money the school offers. In this way the quality of management practised by senior and middle managers, as well as governors, is assessed.

THE SIGNIFICANCE OF THE REFORMS

According to Thomas (1993, pp.45–7) the main themes of school reform were underpinned by three concepts which were central to the development of the Conservative Party's ideology after 1979: markets, competition, and accountability. These, in turn, were meshed with other interlocking themes, such as efficiency and effectiveness, changing ownership, and altering the distribution of power, control and influence among the major stakeholders in education. Together these themes form an intricate, complex and reinforcing network of factors determining the direction of policy reform.

In the context of the consumer-led, market-oriented educational culture established by the reforms, there are clear winners and losers in the power, influence and control stakes. Among the 'winners' are parents, employers, headteachers and the DES (DFE after 1992 and DfEE after 1995), while among the 'losers' are the LEAs and teachers. In contrast to the USA, where teacher empowerment was seen as part of school reform, the UK government believed the teachers already exercised too much power, reflected in the phenomenon of 'provider capture'. The government therefore deliberately set out not only to curtail the power enjoyed by the teachers, but also that exercised by the LEAs. Some LEAs, particularly those which were Labour controlled, had obstructed Conservative policy for many years. In addition, LEAs were seen by central government as yet another tier of government, one easily dispensed with in the pursuit of efficiency.

LEAs had owned and administered state schools since 1902. Until the ERA, the LEAs could exercise a considerable influence over the allocation of pupils to schools. By so doing, they were seen by the 'new right' as protecting mediocre schools and thereby preventing standards from being raised. The opportunity provided by the ERA for the schools to opt out of LEA control and become GM institutions thus represented a transfer of ownership. Together with the newly created city technical colleges, established with private sector money (thus breaking the monopoly of state funding), local communities now had diversity of types of schools from which to choose. By late 1994 there were approximately 1100 GM schools in England and Wales, most of them secondary schools, and they represented one-quarter of all secondary schools. Many of the 1100 have been attracted to GM status by the relatively generous levels of funding and by a wish to avoid the effects of local government restructuring. While the number of GM schools might be considered to reflect the success of the policy, it must be remembered that the government's original intention was that nearly all schools would choose GM status. By 1993 the number of GM schools and their combined budgets were sufficiently large to warrant the setting up of a quango, the Funding Agency for Schools (FAS), established by the 1993 Education Act to orchestrate the administration of GM schools. It must be said, however, that many parents and teachers are opposed to opting out and to the existence of GM schools, viewing them as selective and counter to the principle of comprehensive education (Levacic, 1995, p.6).

A key element of the reform package has been the empowerment of parents as clients and consumers of education. Providing them with a greater choice of schools is but one strand of the strategy. A second and related strand has been to ensure that parents are furnished with more information on which to base their choice of school. In 1980 schools were required to publish their examination results. From 1992 the government began the publication of national examination results with the intention of adding other information from performance indicators in due course (Levacic, 1995, p.13). Schools are already required to publish detailed prospectuses, give their governors' annual reports to parents, hold an annual meeting with parents and publish inspection reports. They will in future be expected to meet the ERA requirement to publish their National Curriculum test results. The publication of examination scores and resultant league tables has caused considerable controversy. Those opposed to the idea point out the dangers of a public consuming such information without being made aware of the need to contextualize the data, by allowing for different quality inputs in the form of socio-economic status and value-added measures.

A third strand of the strategy aimed at empowering parents has been to provide them with a greater 'voice' in the running of schools. Attempts to increase parent participation in the governing of schools began in 1980, when the Education Act of that year ensured the representation of elected parents, teachers and community interests on governing bodies, following the recommendation of the Taylor Report in 1977. The 1986 Education Act increased the number of parent-governors, depending on the size of the school, and the ERA greatly expanded the powers of governing bodies by giving them increased responsibility for managing delegated school budgets and staffing. However, in practice most governing bodies are still heavily reliant on the headteacher and the tendency persists for them passively to approve budget plans prepared by the headteacher and senior management rather than play more proactive roles.

The LMS measures were designed both to empower schools and disempower LEAs. LMS was complete by April 1993 for the country as a whole, excluding London, where it was complete by April 1995. The main purpose of the LMS initiative was to create a quasi-market in education. It achieved this by a two-pronged policy of age-weighted pupil funding as the basis for deciding school budgets, and parental preference exercised through choice of school. Indeed, the two were directly linked, since school revenues were based on the number of pupils enrolling, which in fact reflected parental choice. The funding formula based on age-weighting has caused some disquiet between primary and secondary schools, the system being seen to unduly favour secondary schools, particularly the larger schools with sizeable sixth forms.

A further source of controversy has been what Levacic (1995, p.9) calls 'the average-in-actual-out' salary funding principle, on which the DfEE has refused to budge. Schools are funded according to the average cost of staff across the LEA and not according to the actual salaries of the staff they employ. Two schools with a similar number of teachers may therefore have very different staff costs: one might have older staff with many at the top of their pay scales, while the other might have younger staff at the bottom end of their pay scales. Although a four-year transitional period was agreed for introducing the system it did little to quell disquiet over the fact that some schools were seen as clear winners and others as clear losers. The DfEE has insisted that the rationale is inviolable; that schools must operate according to market principles, where the costs and benefits of a decision impact on the decision-making unit itself. Headteachers and school managers are thus induced to consider the cost of a teacher measured against that teacher's performance. The traditional basis on which teachers are paid (according to experience and seniority) is thus changed to a system based more on individual performance and the local situation.

Headteachers' and deputies' pay is now decided by governing bodies, which must take relevant national pay scales into account, but can also make additional payments according to performance.

Some of the above features are unique to UK school restructuring. For example, the direct link between the school's ability to attract pupils and teachers' job security is found nowhere else in the English-speaking world (Levacic, 1995, p.10). If the school at which the teacher is currently employed has insufficient pupils to justify the employment of a teacher, the teacher will have to seek employment elsewhere or face unemployment. The problem is particularly acute for teachers working in schools located in areas of declining population, such as many inner city areas. Here, declining pupil enrolments may be more reflective of demographic trends than poor quality education provided by the school.

The effect has been no less traumatic for LEAs and their staff. Faced with severe competition from the private sector to provide support services to schools, many LEA officers have taken early retirement or pursued careers elsewhere. The conundrum for many LEAs and those who work in them has been the extent to which they should be seen to 'privatize' and take risks in order to compete with private sector providers, while bearing in mind that they are handling local taxpayers' money. The reforms have adversely affected the LEAs more than any other body.

In contrast to the curtailment of the LEAs' powers, the headteacher's position has gained in stature as a result of the reforms, even allowing for the fact that headteachers enjoyed considerable power and influence before the reforms. As Levacic (1995, p.189) comments, 'this is not due simply to the addition of financial management as a further responsibility but to the greater complexity of managing semi-autonomous schools in a quasi-market environment'. The headteacher has had to manage the external environment more proactively, developing the school's public image, undertaking marketing and seeking additional resources wherever possible. At the same time increased pressure on the headteacher has arisen from inside the school with greater responsibility and accountability for the deployment of resources. Not only has the scope of the headteacher's responsibility changed, but the fundamental values context within which the responsibilities are discharged has also undergone transformation. LMS has had the effect of highlighting the 'business side' of school management. Headteachers are thus charged with responsibilities for managing the financial, human and physical resources of the school, while also attending to the quality of the curriculum, teaching and learning provided. Faced with the scope of these challenges it is not surprising that many perceive their extended professional roles in terms of dilemmas (Dimmock, 1996).

In larger secondary schools headteachers have the staff resources to delegate more functions. A deputy, for example, often undertakes curriculum responsibility, while another shares responsibility for resources (including financial management) with a school secretary or finance officer. This arrangement leaves the headteacher as a chief executive overseeing and orchestrating the internal and external affairs of the school. A premium may then be placed on whether the headteacher can keep in close touch with activities on so many fronts.

In smaller primary schools, on the other hand, there is not the scope for delegation, and the principal usually undertakes the budget management role and leaves curriculum management to other staff. Increased workloads arising from the reforms have forced headteachers to delegate and share decision-making responsibility with staff. This increased amount of delegation, combined with a tendency for some schools (now that they have control over staffing patterns and budgets) to appoint more support staff at the expense of senior managers at the deputy level, is tending to create flatter hierarchical structures.

While LMS is generally regarded as having been a success, the experiences described above indicate that reform has not been without its problems. This is hardly surprising given the wholesale and fundamental scale of change.

One further source of difficulty for the government has been the funding of GM schools. From 1994 GM schools had a funding formula applied to them which was different from LEA schools, but it was not a national formula for all GM schools. This was because the central government felt that allowance should be made for local variations according to different levels of education spending across different LEAs. Hence the amount per pupil received by a GM school must correspond to the amount received by LEA schools in its area. However, government policies to restrain local authority spending in recent years have caused hardship to many LEA schools and, ironically, have hurt the GM schools in the process.

In effect, differences between LEA and GM schools are mostly minor. GM schools have total control over all of their resources, while LEA schools have control over 90–98 per cent of theirs. GM schools enjoy total control over their admissions policy, while the LEA still administers this on behalf of its schools. A GM school can more easily change its structure by, for example, adding a sixth form. Nonetheless, as Levacic (1995, p.12) argues, both GM and LEA schools are subject to the same LMS policy context and constraints.

It is generally acknowledged that the ERA omitted one vitally important part of a revamped education system, notably the arrangements by which schools were to be evaluated and held to account (Levacic, 1995, p.14). By the mid-1980s the HMI system had come under increasing criticism. It was seen as lacking the resources to complete comprehensive and regular reviews of every school in its orbit. In addition, while its reports were now being made public, the system failed to produce detailed and specific criteria by which all schools would be evaluated and held to account. In part, too, as curriculum, managerial and administrative reforms to schools multiplied through the 1980s and early 1990s, the HMI system found it increasingly difficult to remain relevant. An entirely new system was thus established under the auspices of OFSTED in 1992. With what success has the new system operated?

In his extensive analysis of accountability systems in general, Macpherson (1996, p.67), commenting specifically on OFSTED, recognizes that much rests on the reliability of contracted inspectors, the induction training they are given, and the ability of local communities to come to terms with the criteria and processes. An OECD report (1995, p.56) concluded that the benefits from the OFSTED system have been the more explicit evaluation criteria and the encouragement to schools to undertake improvement of their own evaluation procedures in preparation for inspection. The drawbacks, however, have been the stress and time placed on teachers preparing for inspection, the effect of which has been to detract attention from teaching.

In two further respects, according to Macpherson (1996, p.67), the OFSTED system has triggered debate. It has heightened awareness of the importance of the validity and reliability of data and of the 'value-added' concept. The general consensus seems to be that the OFSTED process has still to take proper cognizance of reporting scores adjusted for socio-economic status (SES), and using adjusted scores to report school improvement strategies. Comparisons between schools, therefore, in terms of student performance, must remain speculative while SES is not factored in. Rather than focus on value adding, OFSTED reports tend to concentrate on providing information to parents to enable them to exercise choice between schools. This emphasis sits well with the thrust in reform policy to empower parents with the right to school choice and the so-called 'Parents' Charter'.

According to Macpherson (1996, p.69), while both parents and teachers have reservations about the OFSTED system, they remain generally positive. Both groups realize that genuine improvement depends on the quality of follow up in the action plan. Both wish to see improvement in the quality of interaction between inspectors and parents and teachers. Those headteachers of schools which have already been inspected under the new system are even more positive. They believe the system makes a significant contribution to school improvement, especially where the follow-up action plan is a collective effort by the school governors and external advisers.

More critical reviews, however, are also evident. One is that OFSTED inspections focus too much on summative and not enough on formative evaluation. Another is that they favour the well-endowed schools, and therefore disadvantage the less well endowed, by demanding that substantial resource inputs be invested in the preparatory stage of inspection, involving schools in marshalling their own data. Macpherson's general conclusion is that as long as the inspection process fails to reflect adequately the SES and value-added dimension to school improvement, it will be of limited efficacy.

One aim of the ERA was that schools manage their resource deployment to comply with expectations enshrined in the National Curriculum and to promote the learning achievement of pupils in line with assessment targets. There has, in fact, been a significant growth in formalized school planning, particularly since 1992/3. This appears to be promulgated, at least in part, by OFSTED inspections highlighting efficiency considerations in their criteria and by central government and LEA agencies in developing their strategic and performance monitoring roles. Now, also, it seems as if the process of formalized school planning is about to become mandatory throughout England and Wales; the White Paper of the new Labour government, *Excellence in Schools* (Secretary of State for Education and Employment, 1997) states that there will be a requirement for each LEA to prepare an education development plan (EDP), setting out how it intends to promote school improvement and including the performance targets set by its schools in agreement with the LEA (p.28). It is envisaged that EDPs will be phased in and will be fully operational in each LEA by April 1999.

One of the key central government aims in the restructuring process of the late 1980s and early 1990s has been to centralize control over the curriculum for the 5–16 age group in all state schools. The National Curriculum and its associated testing at ages 7, 11 and 14 was thus instituted to accompany the existing General Certificate of Secondary Education (GCSE) taken at age 16 and the post-16 A-level examinations and vocational qualifications. The concept of a National Curriculum as an entitlement for all children had general appeal, especially in areas of the former curriculum (such as science and modern languages) where provision was mediocre and in some cases non-existent for many pupils. Both science and at least one modern foreign language are now mandated for all pupils up to the age of 16.

Nonetheless the government has been forced, under pressure from over-worked teachers, to modify its original intentions. As previously mentioned, an over-ambitious testing policy occupied so much of the teachers' time that there was insufficient left to cover the syllabus. In addition, certain subjects in the National Curriculum (such as English and history) have attracted fierce criticism for their prescriptive and contentious subject matter. A further source of criticism has been that there is far too much mandated content to cover, given the curriculum time available; the government has responded by reducing the amount of subject content matter in the National Curriculum. It has also reduced the number of subjects tested, as well as the length of the tests, and allowed teachers more flexibility (Levacic, 1995, p.14). In the overall context of assessment, including the post-16 age group, the longevity of the A-level examination is surprising. In comparison with broader-based post-16 courses and examinations in other countries, the A-level appears dated and ready for replacement. However, it has become so entrenched and institutionalized that its demise is hard to predict.

Most commentators conclude that the wholesale reconfiguration of organizational and institutional arrangements resulting from the reform measures of the 1980s and 1990s have been successful. Schools are managing their own budgets, and headteachers, senior school managers and parents are generally accepting the new order. There is also general political consensus between the Labour and Conservative parties in support of LMS. It is remarkable how, for the most part, the fundamental changes in values ushered in by the reforms have been accepted by the major stakeholders. Schools are building up sizeable reserves in bank accounts and looking for innovative ways to generate more resources. The new-found freedom is being used to improve the physical environment in some schools and the teaching and learning environment in others. There has been a growth in support staff, while at the same time the teacher-pupil ratio has dropped. Schools appear to be spending more on retaining core permanent teachers and more on support staff to help them.

While few would choose to revert to the former arrangements, there are still seemingly intractable problems to confront, if not resolve. One of these concerns the funding formulae, which determine the all-important sum of money each school receives. The 'average-in-actual-out' salary principle causes widespread dissatisfaction, as do the substantial disparities between LEA funding levels, between LEA and GM schools, and between primary and secondary schools (Levacic, 1995, p.188). One is also less sanguine about the long-term future of the GM schools.

In summarizing the effects of the school restructuring initiative in England and Wales to date, Levacic (1995) uses a four-dimensional framework of cost efficiency, effectiveness, equity, and responsiveness, choice and diversity. She is in no doubt that the first of these, cost efficiency, has been the most successful. Among the ways in which cost efficiency is manifested are greater economies in the purchasing of resources and improved efficiency through adopting resource mixes that better achieve educational aims. Schools are thinking more carefully and critically about their aims, the type of resources they need, the best resource combination, how to budget to achieve their aims, and the fact that they will have to account publicly for all of this.

There are clear efficiency gains in schools having the ability to 'buy in' services as and when they need them and deciding to whom they contract these services. Interesting examples are coming to light of schools deciding to change their mix of resources. One concerns the increased trend to employ more teachers' aides and classroom assistants in primary schools and a wider range of support staff in secondary schools. In this way, as Levacic (1995, p.191) claims, 'schools can increase the ratio of adults to children while reducing the ratio of teachers to children'. While this is cost efficient, it is less clear whether it is cost effective, as judged by whether it enhances pupil learning. Headteachers' impressions are that it is effective, but confirmation awaits empirical investigation.

The second of the criteria used by Levacic concerns the effectiveness of the reform measures. Here the important relationships are input-output ones. Whether increased cost efficiency, resulting in more resource inputs, leads to improved student learning outcomes is the matter at issue. The evidence on this is circumstantial rather than empirical. Knight (1993), for example, found that LMS increased the total resources at the disposal of schools. It was then a matter of whether the schools invested more of these available resources in curriculum, teaching and learning, and on what in particular, within the technical core activities, the resources were invested. Surveys aimed at gauging the perceptions of headteachers and teachers with regard to improvements in the quality of teaching and learning are confirmatory of positive outcomes. But in the final analysis these are still perceptions and not hard outcome data.

Another link in the complex efficiency-effectiveness relationship is between managerial processes and educational outcomes. Both Dimmock (1993) and Levacic (1995) argue that characteristics of school-based management (LMS in the English and Welsh context) share many of the same features as schools judged to be effective, according to the criterion of academic learning outcomes. These school features include goal setting and planning, strong leadership, collaborative decision making and flexibility of resource use. It is then argued that schools undergoing restructuring along the lines of school-based management will achieve the same successful academic outcomes as those achieved by the so-called effective schools. Such causal connections between processes and outcomes and between managerial-organizational and educational aspects of schools remain highly conjectural. While logic and common sense might indicate such relationships, organizational analysts point to the complexities of simply implanting characteristics of effective schools into less effective schools with expectations of the same successful results.

The third of Levacic's criteria, equity, is equally difficult to ascertain. Problems as to what is meant by equity arise. For example, is the term used to refer to inputs, processes or outputs? According to Levacic, there is an absence of hard evidence to conclude that the effects of the quasi-market have been regressive in penalizing those more disadvantaged groups in society. It may be, however, that parents and children in low socio-economic areas are less able to avoid the ineffective schools. Their ability to exercise choice is curtailed. But, as Levacic remarks, the argument for the market mechanism has never been based on its equitable effects; for this, one has to look towards government intervention. If the market creates failing schools, as indicated by their declining enrolments and parents 'voting with their feet', then it is unlikely that such schools themselves have the capacity to retrieve their position within the realities of the marketplace, without government assistance.

In terms of her fourth criterion, responsiveness, choice and diversity, Levacic argues that there is no strong evidence that schools are actively seeking to respond to parental preferences. Many are not entrepreneurial in seeking pupils from outside their normal catchment areas or fundamentally changing their missions. They are, however, more keen to cement links with their traditional 'feeder' schools and to promote their public image, particularly in respect to examination performance.

The English and Welsh experience of school restructuring over the last decade lays to rest the myth that wholesale systemic change of large complex education systems cannot be undertaken with any degree of success. If 'success' is defined in terms of changing values, roles and behaviours of major stakeholders, then the English and Welsh experience has been successful. The jury is still out, however, on whether the multiple and complex reforms have improved the quality of teaching and learning and whether the resultant school system is more or less equitable.

Chapter 4

Restructuring in the United States

INTRODUCTION

Unlike the situation in England and Wales, where reform has been centrally dictated, the approach to educational reform in the United States has been more piecemeal and decentralized. This is not surprising, of course, since the United States is not like England and Wales which has two levels of government (national and local), with education being a function of national government, administered locally. Rather, it has three levels of government – national, state and local – with responsibility for public education being vested in the states, and responsibility for delivery of educational services being placed with local government in all states except Hawaii. On this, Swanson (1995) states:

> 'While providing general oversight, all states in the US. except Hawaii which operates as a single unit, have created approximately 15,000 local school districts to organize and operate schools. Some school districts are departments of municipal government as in England, but most are independent with their own taxing powers. New York is the largest school district with nearly 1,000,000 children... but it is hardly typical. At the other extreme are districts with only a handful of children for whom the districts pay tuition to other districts to provide for their education rather than operate their own schools. More typical is a school district serving 3,000 to 5,000 children in one or two secondary schools and several elementary schools.' (p.6)

To make this observation, however, is not to ignore the significant role which the federal government has played in education in the United States, particularly over the last 40 years. Indeed, it was prompted to unprecedented levels of financial and legislative support for schools, particularly for mathematics, science, and technical education, with the launching of the Soviet satellite, Sputnik, in 1957 (Ignas and Corsini, 1981, p.6).

Reforms continued throughout the next two decades. In the 1960s, schools were called upon to make their programmes relevant to social needs while a significant demand in the 1970s was that they focus on moral development. However, the responses took place against a background where the educational system continued to be financed primarily through local property taxes. The inadequacy of this funding base and the increased expenditures 'led to severe financial problems in many major cities where strikes, early school closings, and severe cutbacks in programs became common during the late 1970s' (Ignas and Corsini, 1981, p.6). Because of the absence of a strong central hand directing education nationally, the situation was more acute in some educational districts than in others. Swanson (1995) captures this situation very well, as follows:

> 'Within a state some districts may spend as much as three times the amount spent in other districts... The variation in the expenditure level is mirrored by variation in the extent of educational services provided by school districts... In addition to financial and programmatic disparities, there are also disparities among districts in the ethnic and socio-economic composition of their school populations.' (p.8)

This observation by Swanson provides a significant informing background to his contention that the United States approached its educational reforms of the past 15 years with a system of public schooling characterized by gross inequities: 'the top 20 per cent of graduates of US high schools are world class in their preparation and are getting better. The next 40 per cent are mostly capable of completing college. The bottom 40 per cent are poorly served, however, and the focus of most concern' (Swanson, 1995, p.8). The particular reforms which have been taking place in response to this situation have been in three relatively discrete waves, each of which will now be considered.

THE FIRST WAVE OF EDUCATIONAL REFORM

Throughout the 1950s, 1960s and 1970s, a substantial body of literature appeared in the United States providing extensive evidence indicating a high incidence of scholastic failure and a steady decline of academic standards in schools. Much of it was summarized by Armbruster in *Our Children's Crippled Future* (1977), to underline the continuing evidence of academic decline over a period of almost 40 years, despite massive increases in educational expenditure and improvements. However, the main stimulus for reform was economic in nature. The dominance of the United States in the increasingly global economy was being challenged by competition, particularly from Japan and Germany, and American business and industry were seen as not responding effectively. Much of this was attributed to inadequacies in the system of public schooling. Yet public schooling was also seen as having the potential to rescue the situation. Reports by the Carnegie Foundation for the Advancement of Teaching (Boyce, 1983) and the National Commission on Excellence in Education (1983), followed, emphasizing initiatives such as increasing standardized test scores, raising academic standards, lengthening the school year, and introducing new salary arrangements for teachers.

From the long lists of detailed recommendations in the reports, the following have been identified by Murphy (1984, p.17) as standing out regarding the improvement of curriculum, teaching and learning:

♦ Whatever the student's education or work objectives, knowledge of the basics is the foundation of success in the after-school years and therefore forms the core of the modern curriculum.
♦ Textbooks and other tools of learning and teaching should be upgraded and updated to assure more rigorous content. University scientists, scholars and members of professional societies, in collaboration with master teachers, should help in this area.
♦ Students should be assigned more homework.
♦ Instruction in effective study and work skills, which are essential if school and independent time are to be used efficiently, should be introduced in the early grades and continued throughout the student's schooling.
♦ The time available for learning should be expanded through better classroom management and organization of the school day. If necessary, additional time should be found to meet the special needs of slow learners, the gifted, and others who need more instructional diversity than can be accommodated during a conventional day or school year.
♦ Persons preparing to teach should be required to meet high educational standards, to demonstrate an aptitude for teaching, and to demonstrate competence in an academic discipline.

The assumption in these proposals was that school professionals had become lax and that the educational system could be revived by tightening educational standards and holding schools more accountable for their outcomes. Consequently, a significant amount of state-level education reform legislation was enacted during the 1980s, as part of the first wave of educational reform. It was not long, however, before serious questioning took place regarding the degree to which the legislation and associated innovations were leading to improved student learning. Goodman (1995, p.3) cites the example of the Individually Guided Education (IGE) project, which was adopted in approximately 3000 elementary schools to improve their abilities to meet the diverse academic needs of students. It called for many changes in the traditional patterns of administration, curriculum and instruction. However, when it was evaluated it was found that it reinforced the ongoing practices, curriculum content and attitudes in the schools; 'schools that created illusory programs simply used the label of IGE to justify the continuation of current routines and arrangements' (Goodman, 1995, p.3).

Various studies of the reforms initiated around the country concluded that they tended to mandate 'more of the same' at the school-site level, 'meaning more required courses in academic areas, heightened teacher certification requirements, a lengthened school day or year, or more defined teacher evaluation practices' (Conley and Goldman, 1995, p.513). These reforms required little change in fundamental practices or organizational structures, and teachers were able to continue their current practices or adapt them incrementally. Also, assumptions about teaching and learning were not challenged or modified.

Soon the call went out for more fundamental and systemic change to meet the goals of enhanced American economic competitiveness. Critics of the state policies that aimed at change through mandates and regulations argued that it was schools as institutions, not students, teachers and curricula, that should be the focus of change. As Timar (1989) has put it:

> 'Tightening curriculum standards, changing teacher certification requirements, or extending the school year, for example, will have negligible effects if schools lack the organizational will and competence to implement them. Furthermore, piecemeal reform policies do not necessarily change the fundamental relationship between teaching and learning. Fundamentally, the critics insist, high quality education is the product of robust organizational cultures, not disparate programs. Instead of improving them, state reform strategies relying on regulations and mandates for new programmes tended to overwhelm schools with additional baggage or mire them in a regulatory swamp.' (p.56)

Effective schools research provided the critics of the 'first wave of reform' with powerful ammunition. Now what was being advocated was teacher collegiality, shared decision making, common goals and clear priorities in order to forge 'the disparate experiences and expectations of teachers, administrators, students and parents into coherent organizational cultures' (Timar, 1989, p.57).

THE SECOND WAVE OF EDUCATIONAL REFORM

The initial response to the criticisms of the first wave of reform was one which recognized that some differences exist between schools and their pupils, and that what was required was a restructuring of public education rather than simply reforming and revitalizing it. Informing this notion was the experience of how a shifting international market for private sector goods and services was producing apparently successful restructuring in a number of multinational corporations (Mitchell and Beach, 1993, pp.249–250). Similar restructuring of service provision and service delivery was being urged on the schools by corporate executives and political leaders. This led to a wide range of suggestions, including school choice and educational vouchers, magnet and other alternative schools, outcome-based learning, and minimum competence assessment, all underpinned by the argument that they would lead to improved student performance.

By the mid-1980s, the reform movement sweeping the country was one which was concerned with redirecting efforts from repairing schooling to restructuring the entire educational enterprise (Murphy *et al.*, 1991, p.135). This movement was legitimated by a number of highly influential reform documents, including those of the Carnegie Forum (1986), the Holmes Group (1986) and the National Governors' Association (1986). Initial efforts focused on empowering teachers, but later efforts centred on school-based management and parental choice (David, 1989; Elmore, 1988).

The central informing concept of 'restructuring', however, was proving to be problematic because of its lack of clear definition. On this, Mitchell and Beach (1993) have commented:

> 'One reason for confusion in the meaning of the term restructuring is that it serves two distinct functions. In its most prominent usage, restructuring is a political concept. It is a symbolic label used to focus reform energies. When used politically, terms have to be interpreted broadly and remain sufficiently vague to be endorsed by a coalition of supporters whose underlying disagreements would keep them from supporting more clearly defined programs of action. In contrast with this political role, restructuring also serves as an important professional concept. Among professionals, the term is used to identify particular approaches to improved school performance. Confusion on the political and professional uses of the concept distorts communication.' (p.250)

Their solution is to focus discussion around six overarching themes, three of which have to do with organizational targets for restructuring while the other three emphasize key operational elements to be reorganized. The organizational targets for restructuring are the school site, the teachers and the school governance system, and the operational mechanisms are parental or student choice, pedagogical strategies and the mix of services to be provided. Hill and Bonan (1991, p.6) also contributed to this task of defining the phenomenon of restructuring, arguing that it may refer to specific changes within a school (eg block scheduling or arranging for one set of teachers to stay with a group of students as long as they are in the school) or to systemic changes (eg eliminating major central office units or privatizing formerly centralized functions, such as the delivery of staff development courses). Similarly,

Hallinger *et al.* (1992), referred to restructuring as consisting of endeavours to decentralize the organization, management and governance of schooling; empower those closest to students in the classroom (ie teachers, parents and principals); create new roles and responsibilities for all the players in the system; and transform the learning-teaching process that unfolds in classrooms (p.330).

Notwithstanding these efforts to bring greater clarity into the debate, however, most attention focused on the notion of 'school-based management' (SBM). According to Linquist and Mauriel (1989), the three fundamental elements of SBM are decentralization, collaborative decision making and advocacy of the school district. The model, which is borrowed from the corporate sector, constitutes a governance plan in which authority and responsibility for the functioning of individual schools are shared between central office and the school-site officials, all of whom are to work as professional, collaborating colleagues. Michaels (1988) defines it as follows:

> '[School-based management] is distinguished... by an exciting and markedly different agenda, including: the individual school as the unit of decision making; development of a collegial, participatory environment among both students and staff; flexible use of time; increased personalization of the school environment with a concurrent atmosphere of trust, high expectations, and sense of fairness; a curriculum that focuses on students' understanding what they learn – knowing "why" as well as "how"; and an emphasis on higher-order thinking skills for all students.' (p.3)

Soon, significant examples of restructuring in accordance with this ideal were being reported from around the country. The state of Michigan eliminated the local property tax as the primary source of financial support of schools and placed almost total responsibility for financing schools with the state. The Chicago school system placed policy-making authority in the hands of lay-controlled boards attached to individual schools. In the state of Kentucky all elements of the education system were modified, including its governance and finance, while a number of states were experimenting with limited voucher schemes. As Swanson (1995, p.14) puts it, site-based management was the order of the day.

Nevertheless, by the end of 1990 there was a growing sense that, despite progress, the restructuring movement was not living up to expectations and the national interest continued to be threatened. Part of the problem rested with the lack of agreement about exactly how schools should be restructured. On this, a study by Hallinger *et al.* (1993) is particularly instructive. In particular, they found a lack of connections made by teachers and principals between new governance structures and the teaching-learning process. In other words, neither the teachers nor the principals seemed to view restructuring 'as a reform designed to assist students' (p.34). Also, neither party 'appeared to have a vision of how schooling might change to accommodate the changing needs of students and society' (p.35). Another issue highlighted in the study focused on the finding that while the teachers explicitly favoured a more active role in technical decision making, they were not convinced that such participation would be authentic. At the same time, administrators questioned whether the teachers wanted to participate and also queried how long their interest would last once the reality of increased meeting time, commitments and conflict set in. Finally, a more fundamental discrepancy was apparent between the views of both parties and those of the policy community driving restructuring. This was particularly salient with respect to the issue of connecting reforms in education governance with changes in classroom practice. Given these findings and those of others, it is not surprising that by the early 1990s calls for more revolutionary reforms began to be heard with increasing frequency.

THE THIRD WAVE OF EDUCATIONAL REFORM

Under the Bush (Republican) administration, a new Secretary of Education, Lamar Alexander, was appointed. Very soon, Alexander suggested a move towards more fundamental and radical educational reforms on the part of the federal government, remarking: 'One of the lessons of education reform in the 1980s is that we've been too slow and too timid. What we need is a populist uprising' (Gigot, 1991, p.6). President Bush quickly followed with the unveiling of the 'America 2000' education plan, an initiative which was continued by the Clinton (Democrat) administration. The plan arose out of a desire to bring focus to the educational reform movement. To this end the state governors, both Republican and Democrat, joined with President Bush and developed six national goals for education to be realized by the year 2000 The National Education Goals Panel was established to monitor progress and to coordinate efforts of state and national organizations. This was a bipartisan effort, with Panel membership being politically balanced, allowing two members of the national administration, eight governors (only three of whom may be from the President's own party) and four members of Congress appointed by the majority and minority leaders of the House and Senate (Swanson, 1995, p.14).

The National Education Goals Panel is committed to five principles to guide standards-based reform (The National Education Goals Panel, 1993):

1. The development of nationwide standards must be highly inclusive, blending expert classroom knowledge with that of researchers, policy makers, and the general public.
2. The standards must not be considered a uniform national curriculum.
3. The standards must be deliberately set at high levels.

47

4. The standards must be viewed as dynamic, subject to periodic review and change.
5. The importance of nationwide standards must be clearly and effectively communicated to the American people.

These principles were developed by the National Council on Education Standards and Testing, which was established in 1991, with the cooperation of the Goals Panel. The Panel also endorsed the Council's recommendations for national standards and related systems of student assessment. Then, in 1994, the Goals 2000 'Educate America Act', was enacted and established a National Education Standards and Improvement Council to develop criteria and a process for reviewing and approving nationwide standards.

Swanson (1995) argues that three broad themes characterize this nationwide approach to reform: 'education reform must be systemic; the nation's commitment to education reform must be longterm; and, to achieve the Goals, state, local and federal governments must form an education partnership' (p.14). However, other partnerships were also emerging. American industry was asked to contribute $150 million towards the $550 million required for the construction of 535 new schools designed to be 'national models of excellence':

> 'The New American Schools Development Corporation was formed by American business leaders in July of 1991 at the request of President Bush. The purpose of the corporation is to underwrite the design and implementation of a new generation of "break the mould" schools. It has pledged to raise $150 million from private sources between 1991 and 1996 to finance the effort, of which $103 million had been raised by the end of 1993. In response to its call for proposals, 686 design teams responded from which 11 were selected to be supported for further development over a five-year period. The overriding criterion for selection was the likelihood that a design would enable all students to reach the national education goals and attain "world-class" standards.' (Swanson, 1995, p.15)

The private sector is also involved in promoting school reform in other ways, including establishing school–business partnerships and creating foundations and trusts. For example, the Tennessee businessman, Chris Whittle, has committed $60 million to the design phase of his Edison project for a network of charter schools to operate in urban areas across the country, while the Minneapolis school board has hired a private firm to run the school system in place of a traditional superintendent.

More controversial have been proposals, particularly by former President Bush, to increase parental choice by allowing federal money for disadvantaged students to be made available for those attending private and parochial schools. This 'old chestnut' has once again not been cracked, largely because of a fear that an exodus to private schools might result and further jeopardize the already endangered finances and status of urban schools. There is, of course, also the constitutional issue. The Supreme Court has always held that the First

Amendment prohibits any public funds going to church-related activities. However, if the third wave of reform is maintained and the contemporary conservative majority in the Supreme Court continues, it might be that a future interpretation of the First Amendment will permit public money to go to religious organizations, so long as all faiths are treated equally and none are favoured.

What the future may hold, however, is much more likely to be represented by current developments in the state of Oregon. Here, in 1991, the legislature passed House Bill 3565, laying out a new vision of schooling for the state's 1200 public elementary and secondary schools. Its stated intention is to create a restructured educational system to achieve the state's goals of the best educated citizens in the nation by the year 2000 and a workforce equal to any in the world by the year 2010. Conley and Goldman (1995, p.517) argue that the act presents a complex framework for systemic redesign of education, pre-school through post-secondary. They go on:

> 'In essence, the act lays out a framework of expectations for student performance and calls on schools to redesign their programs to enable students to meet performance standards. The law does not prescribe the means or structures educators should employ to achieve the act's goals. Its sponsors envisaged it as a "trigger mechanism" to engage educators in serious redesign of schools.' (p.517)

What is being attempted is the use of top-down legislation to promote bottom-up school restructuring (Conley and Goldman, 1995, p.513).

In other states, most notably Kentucky (and British Columbia in Canada), attempts to promote change through legislation have focused on primary education in the first instance. The assumption underlying such an approach is that changes should be incremental and should be implemented gradually and sequentially year by year from early childhood to secondary education. In Oregon, however, the emphasis in the legislation is on secondary education. Two performance- and skill-based qualifications, the Certificate of Initial Mastery (CIM) and the Certificate of Advanced Mastery (CAM), are core concepts. At approximately 16 years of age, a student can obtain a CIM by demonstrating mastery in 11 performance areas, all of which are to be geared to world-class levels. Assessments must include work samples, tests and portfolios, and culminate in a project or exhibition that demonstrates attainment of required knowledge and skills.

The CIM is organized around six broad occupational categories (Conley and Goldman,1995, p.516). It is designed to facilitate school-to-work transition by causing students to give more thought to their career choices as well as to investigate the world of work firsthand while still in school. There is an emphasis on professional-technical programmes in addition to college preparation. Students are provided 'opportunities for structured work experiences, cooperative work and study programs, on-the-job training and apprenticeship programs in addition to other subjects' in combination with a comprehensive educational component (Conley and Goldman, 1995, p.516). Overall, this approach to school reform is designed to work downwards so that elementary and middle schools are forced to examine how they can adapt their programmes to the requirements of the CIM and the CAM.

Another major feature is that site-based councils have been established in every school since September 1995. Teachers form a majority in these councils, but parents and classified employers must also be represented. The councils are responsible for setting goals, approving school staff development programmes and supporting implementation of the Act.

Enhanced public accountability for education is achieved through the Oregon Report Card, a comprehensive report on performance on a school-by-school basis (Conley and Goldman, 1995, p.516), with the Act defining how assistance is to be provided to students who are not succeeding in public education. Included are requirements that schools identify in the primary years students who are not succeeding and employ alternative instructional approaches with them. Additional support for at-risk students is mandated through alternative learning centres (Conley and Goldman, 1995, p.516).

This approach is probably a very good indicator of the way in which other states will move in the future. It certainly seeks to address former President Bush's call for reforms to ensure that every child will start school ready to learn, high school graduation rate will increase to 90 per cent, competency will be demonstrated in five core subjects in grades 4, 8 and 12, American students will be ranked first in the world in both maths and science, and every American adult will be a literate and responsible citizen (Giroux and McLaren, 1992, p.99). However, it is also an approach that is not without criticism, from a number of quarters. The historians urge caution and the adoption of a historical perspective lest the latest wave of reform be simply recapitulating earlier errors.

> 'Curriculum improvement is approached by each new group of reformers as though the problems they are trying to solve have never been recognized before. As a result, there is a failure to build on curriculum work done in the past. The continuity between past and present has too often been a tale of repeated mistakes' (Tanner and Tanner, 1990, p.30).

Others, like Giroux and McLaren (1992) view current trends as being:

> 'rooted in a notion of pedagogy that presupposes that the solution to the problems of American schooling lies in the related spheres of management and efficiency rather than in the realm of values and politics. Similarly, teachers are increasingly being asked to adopt pedagogical models dominated by the dictates of technique, implementation, "what works" and measurement.' (p.104)

They view what is happening as 'a direct assault on the issue of cultural difference' (p.106) in its language of consensus and uniformity. In this, they are echoing the voices of post-modernists, critical theorists, social reconstructionists and post-structuralists who, despite the differences which separate them, are all calling for a fundamental reconceptualization of the understanding of public schools and of the social purposes they should serve. In particular, they are concerned with issues of inequity. Inherent in their call is a radical reconstruction of the current educational system in order to serve the twin goals of social justice and pluralism (Capper, 1994).

Others, like Snauwaert (1993), promote a very different approach to restructuring, arguing that school governance should be based on principles of participatory democracy. And, finally, there are individual schools which have taken it upon themselves (rather than employing consulting experts) to 'rethink fundamentally what it means to educate children' in the United States (Smith, 1993; Wood, 1992). One is tempted to suggest that it is this 'grass roots' movement that holds out the greatest potential for transforming the nation's schools. Only time will tell whether or not this is the case. We can only wait anxiously and observe with interest.

Chapter 5

Restructuring in Hong Kong

INTRODUCTION

School restructuring policy in Hong Kong is remarkably similar to policy initiatives introduced in other systems, notably England and Wales, Australia and the US. This is not surprising, since the main policy platform on which school management reform is built, the School Management Initiative (SMI), is heavily based on an exported model of school restructuring from Australia. Although reforms to schools and curricula in Hong Kong have been steadily advancing for a number of decades, it can be argued that it was not until the early 1990s that administrative restructuring assumed a wholesale, systematic and coordinated effort.

This wave of restructuring has centred on three major policy initiatives: the SMI (Education and Manpower Branch and Education Department (EMB & ED), 1991), the target-oriented curriculum (TOC) (Education Department, 1994b) and Quality School Education (QSE) (Education Commission (QSE-ECR7), 1996). In common with the restructuring of school systems elsewhere, these initiatives can be conceived as two pronged, one aimed at reforming the administrative, managerial and governmental aspects of schools, the other targeted at changing the curriculum, teaching, learning and assessment. Unfortunately, as elsewhere, the two prongs of this policy agenda tend to be seen as discrete rather than interrelated. In common, too, with reform initiatives elsewhere, policy documents representing both administrative and curriculum reforms reflect subtle shifts in emphasis over time. The SMI, for example, was driven by a school effectiveness agenda, while the QSE is firmly underpinned by the notion of quality education. The administrative and managerial aspects of Hong Kong's restructuring of its school system are enshrined in the SMI and QSE-ECR7, while curriculum reform is represented by the TOC.

Following a description of each initiative below, a brief commentary is provided on selected aspects of policy.

THE SCHOOL MANAGEMENT INITIATIVE (SMI)

After several decades of education policy focused on quantitative and logistical concerns, particularly coping with student numbers, in 1991 the Hong Kong government turned its attention to improving the quality of education, a theme which has dominated policy for most of the final decade of the twentieth century throughout much of the world.

In its policy document, the SMI, the Hong Kong government (EMB&ED, 1991), set out the background prompting, and the proposals for, the reform of the school system. In common with school restructuring in western countries, the motivation came from a desire for a general overhaul of the public sector. This is perhaps not surprising given that Hong Kong was a British territory and that public sector reform had been a strong political thrust of the Conservative Party in that country throughout the 1980s. In addition, a firm of international management consultants was employed to advise on how basic principles of public sector reform could be applied to education. These principles are set out in the SMI policy (EMB & ED, 1991, p.9) and summarized, as follows:

♦ a continual review of the existing base of public expenditure;
♦ a systematic evaluation of results;
♦ a better definition of responsibilities;
♦ a closer match between resource responsibilities and management responsibilities;
♦ appropriate organization and management frameworks;
♦ clearly defined relationships between policy makers and their executive agents; and
♦ more management and less administration.

The consulting exercise resulted in the conclusion that the education service in Hong Kong had the following weaknesses:

♦ inadequate management structures and processes;
♦ poorly defined roles and responsibilities;
♦ the absence or inadequacy of performance measures;
♦ an emphasis on detailed controls rather than frameworks of responsibility and accountability;
♦ an emphasis on cost control at the margins rather than cost effectiveness and value for money.

It was also stated that the legal framework for managing schools was outdated. However, as Wong (1995) has noted, the tightening of administrative and financial controls over the schools had been the department's own doing, caused by the proliferation of its policies over the years. The net outcome was the stretching of its own resources and the stifling of school initiatives.

In the international context of school restructuring, Hong Kong's SMI is the equivalent of the local management of schools (LMS) in England and Wales, 'school-based management' in the United States and the 'self-managing school' concept in Australia. As previously noted, the SMI is to be seen within the context of general reform of the public sector with its greater emphasis on accountability for performance. However, it is also to be seen within a second context, that of school effectiveness, with its characteristic features of devolution and delegation of decision making according to the principles of subsidiarity. Typically, such restructuring involves complex changes in roles, rules and relationships of stakeholders. While delegation of financial responsibility to schools provides them with greater flexibility of resource use, curricular frameworks often turn out to be more centrally controlled than before. School accountability increases not only to the central office, but also to community representatives on school boards and councils. Hong Kong's SMI displays all of these hallmarks.

The SMI aimed to define more clearly the roles of those responsible for administering schools, particularly sponsors, managers and principals; to provide for greater participation by teachers, parents and former students in school decision making and management; to encourage more systematic planning and evaluation of school activities; and, finally, to give schools more flexibility in the use of their resources.

In certain respects, Hong Kong's school system has been configured in a unique way. There is, first, the central bureaucracy, the Education Department (ED). Most primary and secondary schools are classified as 'aided', meaning that while they are publicly funded, they operate under a Letter of Agreement between the Director of Education and the schools' sponsoring body, of which there are many. They also operate under a code of aid setting out the procedures to be followed in return for public funds. The sponsoring body, which must be an incorporated, non-profit making organization, contributes the initial cost of furnishing and equipping the premises, nominates the first supervisor, and has a say in subsequent changes of management committee membership. The school supervisor is a member of the school's management committee and is regarded as a point of contact between the management committee and the department. A small minority of Hong Kong's 1250 schools are not aided, and therefore have no sponsoring body. They are known as government schools and are subject to the direct control of the ED.

The 18 recommendations contained in the SMI can be conveniently grouped under five headings: new roles and relationships for the ED; new roles for school management committees (SMCs), sponsors, supervisors and principals; greater flexibility in school finance; participation in decision making; and a framework for accountability (Wong, 1995).

New roles and relationships for the ED

The first two recommendations concern the relationship between the ED and the aided schools. The ED's relations with the aided sector were to change, from detailed control over all aspects of school management (including student placement, curriculum, funding and equipment) to one of support and advice. In other words, the ED's control was to be relaxed to allow for devolution of authority and responsibility to schools.

New roles for SMCs, sponsors, supervisors and principals

Recommendations 5–8 focus on clearer definitions of the roles for those responsible for the delivery of education in the schools. In ensuring that schools provide a quality service, a revised framework of control was deemed necessary, placing clear responsibility on SMCs and principals for effective school management. Accordingly, every SMC should produce a constitution setting out the aims and objectives of the school and the procedures and practices by which it would be managed. The role and legal contractual position of the sponsor regarding school management should also be clarified, as should the roles and duties of the supervisor in relation to the SMC and principal. In addition, the role and responsibilities of the principal should be set out in a principals' manual.

Greater flexibility in school finance

Recommendations 11–15 relate to financial management, with the main thrust being a proposed block grant to cover all non-salary expenditures and to allow each school the flexibility to decide its own spending pattern within the policy framework set by the ED. Schools were to be given the discretion to use savings from up to 5 per cent of a teacher's salary for any staff or non-staff spending and, in the long term, salary and non-salary grants could be merged. They were also to be encouraged to seek non-government sources of funding, such as donations, for 'above standard' items.

Participation in decision making

Only recommendation 10 applied to changes in school decision making. The whole framework of school-level management should promote participation in decision making by all concerned parties, including all teaching staff, the principal, the SMC and, to appropriate degrees, parents and students. SMI specifically singled out many teachers as isolated from decision making; few teachers, for example, sat on SMCs. Few schools had parent-teacher associations or parents who sat on SMCs. Closer contact between schools and parents was urged, to foster more effective learning.

A framework for accountability

Three recommendations relate to instituting an accountability framework. Recommendation 9 laments the fact that there is no requirement on schools to have any formal procedures for evaluating the performance of staff, an omission which hinders the assessment of staff strengths and weaknesses, and hampers the provision of relevant staff development and the operation of an equitable promotion system. Accordingly, a staff reporting or appraisal system was recommended and schools were urged to consult their SMCs and to look at the ED's own appraisal form as a possible start.

Whereas recommendation 9 deals with individual accountability, recommendations 17 and 18 are levelled at whole school accountability. Recommendation 17 suggests that each school produce an annual school plan setting out its goals and activities for the coming year, against which it can be held accountable. Such a plan would allow the school to assign priorities, allocate its budget, and provide the community with information about school direction. Recommendation 18 proposes that each school prepare an annual school profile covering its activities in the previous year and detailing its performance by developing indicators in a number of key areas, such as student achievement in core areas, non-academic activities, and a staff and student profile, giving details of turnover, qualifications and competence, and parental occupation and housing type, respectively.

In keeping with its predecessors in the west, the philosophy of exchange underpins Hong Kong's SMI restructuring policy, whereby each school is given greater flexibility and responsibility for managing its own affairs in return for rendering greater accountability for its performance to the central bureaucracy as well as to newly empowered SMCs. These committees were to be composed of representatives from the school community.

A key aspect of the SMI document is the third chapter, which is devoted to Australian and American ideas on school effectiveness (slight reference is also made to Singaporean and British ideas). The American research findings of Wilson and Corcoran (1988) are well cited and a comprehensive account is given of the school collaborative decision-making model advocated by Caldwell and Spinks (1988) in Australia, which is strongly advocated as a model for Hong Kong schools to follow. The strong recommendation to support Hong Kong's school restructuring with a school effectiveness model is unequivocal.

Unlike many of its western predecessor school reform programmes, SMI was introduced as a voluntary scheme. The first cohort of 21 schools joined in 1991, and by 1993/94 more than 100 schools were participating, out of a total of approximately 1250 schools. The government's adoption of an implementation strategy relying on voluntary opting in by schools revealed its preference to increase membership by persuasion rather than by legislative coercion. Even by 1996/97, still only a minority of schools (under one-quarter) had chosen formal membership, an outcome regarded as somewhat disappointing. It is worth recognizing, however, that although many schools had chosen not to become formal members of the SMI scheme, they were, in fact, implementing policies which were in sympathy with the SMI strategy.

Two surveys have been conducted on SMI progress. The second (Education Department, 1994a) found that all member schools had constituted their school management committees, with extensive involvement of principals, and to a lesser extent teachers, but with minimal involvement of parents and alumni. Most of them were successfully managing their decentralized block grants. There was evidence of more systematic planning, with all schools having an annual plan, including statements of mission and goals. Such planning, however, may be illusory, since involvement appeared to be confined to the senior levels of staff, even monopolized by the principal. The implementation of staff appraisal schemes also appeared to be causing difficulties, particularly among teachers whose understanding and acceptance of the idea was problematic.

A number of other findings are also noteworthy. First, respondents indicated an increased workload, with especially heavy demands falling on middle managers. Second, there was evidence that the reform had not penetrated to any great extent the work of teachers at the classroom level. Third, some evidence suggested that school personnel felt a lack of support from system level. Finally, some complained of time constraints (Cheng, 1992). These latter findings confirm the reactions and responses to restructuring experienced by participants in other education systems (Dimmock, 1995a).

QUALITY SCHOOL EDUCATION (QSE-ECR7)

Five years after the introduction of the SMI policy, the Education Commission (EC) published its seventh report in the form of a consultative document called *Quality School Education* (Education Commission, 1996). This report not only continues the trend set in motion by the SMI but adds a significantly different complexion. It is not unusual for governments to publish second and subsequent documents when undertaking restructuring initiatives – experience of restructuring efforts in the west suggests that a succession of policy initiatives and documents over time seems to be the norm. Restructuring is more of an evolutionary process than a one-off transformation.

There is a significant shift in emphasis between SMI and QSE-ECR7. Whereas SMI primarily aims to introduce a system of school-based management, founded on the body of school effectiveness research, the strong thrust of QSE-ECR7 is to develop quality schools possessing quality cultures, and to introduce a framework by which to monitor and assure quality. Again, the marked change in nomenclature from 'effective schools' to 'quality schools' is in line with shifts in the west, and with developments in relevant and related academic literature.

Problems in the school system are recognized by the EC to centre on the lack of a quality culture. They cite as evidence the fact that many schools do not have development plans linked to goal achievement; most schools do not have clear targets for both academic and non-academic students; and many do not have appraisal systems to assess the performance of principals and teachers. In addition, there is poor support for schools in promoting a quality culture. Moreover, principal preparation and teacher training programmes are regarded as inadequate in preparing a cadre of professionals who can cope with the changes required, and the Education Department does not promote quality development in schools. School community members also believe that there is insufficient incentive for schools to take the initiative or accept responsibility for achieving quality education. Schools feel hamstrung by the inflexibity in funding and believe that funding levels are not related to performance. There is also little recognition of the 'value-added' efforts made by schools to develop their students' potential.

As a consequence of their deliberations, the EC's strategy was embodied in 35 recommendations with additional suggestions regarding implementation. The recommendations can be grouped as follows: a framework for developing and monitoring quality school education; preparing for quality school education; assessment of performance; incentives to encourage quality school education; school-based management; and funding flexibility. A brief outline of each is provided below.

The framework for developing and monitoring quality school education

The EC recommends the setting up of a quality development commission to advise the director of education on quality school education. In addition, a new whole-school approach to school inspections is advocated. The present inspection divisions should be reorganized into a quality assurance inspectorate to coordinate resources for periodic comprehensive assessment of the performance of each school. At school level, school development plans, annual budgets and staff appraisal schemes should be institutionalized. Teachers should contribute to the improvement of quality education through active participation in the SMC and the School Executive Committee (SEC), a second tier executive arm of school management, chaired by the principal and responsible to the SMC. In an effort to make school management more robust, greater attention should be paid to the following: meeting the needs of students according to their abilities and aptitudes; the identification of meaningful input, process and output indicators by which to judge school quality in line with a value-added approach; and the participation of schools of similar background in quality circles, an idea borrowed from Japanese corporate management, to share experiences and work towards continuous improvement.

Preparing for quality school education

To equip key players to build quality schools, the government and teacher education institutions should provide appropriate courses, especially in financial and human resources management.

Assessment of performance

In order to assess school performance, the EC thinks it desirable to develop performance indicators and to introduce the concept of value-added achievement. This, it says, will provide an equitable base for school self-evaluation and external quality assurance. Schools should also develop as soon as possible a proper appraisal system for assessing the performance of teachers and principals.

Incentives to encourage quality school education

In order to build a quality culture, the EC states that it is necessary for the government to provide incentives for schools to strive for continuous improvement. Consequently, a 'quality development grant' should, it says, be introduced to fund worthwhile innovative projects on a competitive basis. Cash awards could also be available to a small number of schools which demonstrate the most impressive value-added performance. This should raise the morale of teachers. It would be up to the principal to decide, after having consulted with the SMC, teachers and parents, how the money should be used.

School-based management

The SMI established a framework for greater accountability for school-based management with the participation of teachers, parents and students. This system is helpful in the achievement of school goals and formulating long-term plans to meet student needs. Accordingly, all schools should practise school-based management in the spirit of the SMI by the year 2000 so that they can develop quality education to meet the needs of their students.

Funding flexibility

A block grant comprising the school, class and administration grants should be provided to all aided schools to give them greater flexibility to allocate funds according to their needs. Consideration should be given to government schools to have the greater flexibility that aided schools enjoy.

While the two initiatives of SMI and QSE-ECR7 embody Hong Kong's attempts to reform school governance, management and administration, the so-called target-oriented curriculum (TOC) constitutes their parallel in curriculum reform.

THE TARGET-ORIENTED CURRICULUM (TOC)

Restructuring of Hong Kong's school curriculum, like its management counterpart – the SMI and QSE – is following trends established elsewhere. The introduction of the target-oriented curriculum (Education Department, 1994b) has been described as a shift of curriculum ideology from academic rationalism to social and economic efficiency (Lee and Dimmock, in press). Writing about the National Curriculum in Britain, on which the TOC is partly based, Kelly (1990) described the three underpinning ideologies governing curriculum reform as 'instrumentalism', 'commercialism' and 'elitism'. Instrumentalism refers to the emphasis on economic considerations in curriculum planning; commercialism to the view of education and curriculum planning as a national investment rather than a social service; and elitism supports a meritocratic version of educational equality, namely, survival of the brightest students as indicated by academic performance.

In line with major curriculum developments in Britain, Australia, and North America, the TOC is an attempt radically to shift the way in which curricula are planned, taught and learned. The former curriculum, which can be described as academic rationalist, emphasized strong boundaries between subjects, a focus on subject-specific goals, general cognitive development, and a syllabus-dominated, "what the teacher is expected to teach" approach. By contrast the present curriculum, which can be described as economic-instrumentalist, is characterized by weak boundaries between subjects, with a focus on broad generic skills such as problem solving, critical thinking and reasoning, inquiry, communication and conceptualization (Morris, 1995), and is regulated by what students are expected to learn and achieve in the form of learning outcomes. This shift from a teacher- to a student-focused curriculum is also intended to achieve an important reorientation away from whole-class teaching and assessment towards more rigorous assessment and measurement of individual student performance against set targets.

In short, the heart of the TOC policy centres on notions of what policy makers regard as 'improved practices' of teaching and learning based around more learner-centred approaches, the division of the curriculum into progressive learning targets and objectives for four key stages of learning, and the development of content, teaching methods and assessment strategies geared to the learning targets. Emphasis is placed on setting learning targets and on close assessment of individual children in terms of target achievement. In accordance with the introduction of the TOC, a framework of learning targets and related support materials is being developed for the three core subjects of Chinese, English and mathematics. A pilot scheme began in 20 primary schools in 1993. Despite some teething problems, it was decided that the TOC should be introduced to primary 1 classes in 70 primary schools in 1995. Eventually, it will be introduced to the lower secondary school curriculum.

In summary, international observers of Hong Kong's attempts to reconfigure its policy framework aimed at the reconstruction of its school system would not be able to differentiate it from similar reform initiatives in the west. Nothing distinguishes the package of initiatives as distinctively reflecting a set of Hong Kong conditions. Even the changes in terminology and in the directions and intentions of policy during the 1990s, from school effectiveness to quality schools and schooling, and from traditional teacher-syllabus-centred curricula to student learning outcomes' curricula, replicate trends identifiable throughout much of the western world.

A COMMENTARY ON HONG KONG'S SCHOOL REFORM INITIATIVES

The SMI portraits of effective schools and their characteristics, as portrayed by research studies conducted in western countries, are held up as models for schools in Hong Kong to follow. While the danger of assuming that western models are applicable to Asian societies is all too readily apparent, there is a second, equally important misleading assumption being made. This concerns the impression that once a checklist of effective school characteristics is identified, schools need only adopt the same characteristics to become effective. The truth is that while we may be clear about the characteristics of effective schools, we are much less certain about how to make schools effective. In short, existing schools need to undergo reform and change in order to secure improvement and effectiveness. Moreover, each school has its own distinct culture and dynamics, a consideration which brings the focus back to management processes and culture.

Most commentators would agree that even among the one-quarter of schools which have adopted school-based management and the SMI policy, there has been no fundamental change in their culture. Indeed, this partly explains why at the end of 1996 QSE-ECR7 was published. The document's emphasis on quality schooling recognizes the necessity of building a school culture at the heart of every school which values and focuses on quality education. However, such emphasis is not apparent in the SMI policy, which largely reflects administrative and structural changes. School reform policy in Hong Kong is thus characterized by at least two problems which bode ill for the achievement of quality schools. The first is an inherent weakness in the substance of the policy itself, namely, an over-concentration on structural administrative, governmental and managerial concerns at the expense of the cultural-symbolic and pedagogical; and in not identifying how the former can be connected to the latter. The second problem relates to major flaws in policy implementation.

SMI, QSE-ECR7 and TOC all focus exclusively on policy objectives and implementation strategies rather than on the operational details of implementation. Yet the processes involved in managing a reform or innovation at the point of service delivery invariably determine its fate and its effect. Educational management and policy is traditionally fragile when it comes to operational implementation of policy reform in schools. It is at this point that culture seems to be a critical influence in determining the degree of receptivity to change. In the remaining sections of this chapter some of the issues concerned with operationalizing the implementation of Hong Kong's school reforms at school level are addressed.

Planned reforms to teaching and learning

Although the SMI and QSE-ECR7 documents are primarily concerned with management issues, there is a tacit understanding that the ultimate objective is improvement in the quality of teaching, learning and curricula. Presumably, therefore, the reform of school management structures and processes is seen as instrumental to such improvements. Indeed, QSE-ECR7 (EC, 1996) states the fundamental aim, as follows:

> 'School education should develop the potential of every individual child, so that our students become independent-minded and socially-aware adults, equipped with the knowledge, skills and attitudes which help them to lead a full life as individuals and play a positive role in the life of the comunity.' (p.1)

In particular, two recommendations of QSE-ECR7 address issues of direct concern to teaching and learning. The first refers to the need for a pluralistic school system 'to cater for the needs of students according to their abilities and aptitudes', and the second to the aim of developing fully 'students of different abilities in the spirit of equal opportunities' (p.39).

These recommendations imply major reforms in the ways in which students and teachers are to be grouped for learning and in the teaching methods to be used. However, on a practical level, taking into account present conditions in classrooms, it is difficult to imagine how one teacher with a class of 40 students can possibly meet the expectation of catering to different abilities in a spirit of equal opportunity. The implication is that teachers must change their teaching methods and approaches towards more student-centred strategies.

This implication is borne out by the TOC policy. For example, the TOC *Programme of Study for English Language* (Curriculum Development Council, 1995) advocates 'learner-centred methods and strategies for teaching' (p.43) and that 'learning should be experiential rather than instructional since students learn best through activities that demand involvement' (p.41). It goes on to advocate how teachers can 'cater for individual differences' by being 'sensitive to each student's needs, evaluating each student's development of cognitive ability, judge what materials will challenge each student, arouse the student's interest, respond to and help the student who needs extra help, and appraise each student's capacity to learn and improve' (p.44). Teachers are to develop learner independence and they are reminded that they should not spoon-feed; rather, they should 'plan and organize learning, provide direction, guidance and resources, model certain behaviours, help students execute activities, be a companion in the exploration of knowledge, and assess and record students' activities in order to give feedback and provide for further development' (p.46). These are the essential restructuring principles advocated for the new curriculum and for classroom practice in Hong Kong's schools. How well adapted are current teaching-learning conditions in Hong Kong's schools to meet these expectations?

Current classroom conditions in Hong Kong's schools are not favourable for achieving more student-centred and individualized schooling as advocated or implied in the TOC and QSE-ECR7 policy documents. Most Hong Kong classrooms are cramped and crowded and it is commonplace to find 40 students in a class; desks are formally arranged in rows. Classrooms are typically small, so that both students and teachers have to work in very confined spaces. Opportunities for mobility and flexible classroom layouts are therefore out of the question. Most classrooms are not well equipped by western standards, having no more than the bare essentials of a blackboard, desks and chairs. These conditions dictate that teachers have little alternative but to adopt a narrow range of teaching methods, most based around didactic methods. Opportunities for catering to the variability of student needs and abilities as well as introducing more flexible student-centred learning approaches would appear to be severely curtailed by physical and financial resource constraints.

Decentralization and school-based management

It is convenient to discuss many of the administrative and managerial school reform measures under this heading. These measures include decentralization, collaborative principals' leadership style, school development planning, parental involvement, staff appraisal, and professional development and training.

Decentralization

Decentralization and transfer of the responsibility for school management from the Education Department to the school lies at the heart of the SMI policy in Hong Kong. In tandem with this responsibility goes an obligation for schools to be more accountable for the ways in which they execute these newly acquired functions. However, while schools are expected to assume greater responsibility and accountability, they do not feel they are being given the commensurate powers and authority necessary for the proper discharge of these obligations. From their viewpoint, this detracts from the appeal of joining SMI. Many schools feel there is insufficient appeal, attractiveness and advantage for them to opt in to SMI.

A further unintended outcome of SMI may be the strengthening of principals' power and authority at the expense of others involved at school level. To put it another way, devolved responsibilities, and to a lesser extent power, are transferred from the system centre, but only as far as the principal's office. This may well have happened in many Hong Kong schools where the principals' power in relation to teachers and parents was already traditionally strong. Decentralization to date may merely have served to underscore this chasm. In such cases it is incumbent on principals to delegate and empower others in the school community, not to monopolize the power and authority for themselves if the spirit of reform is to be achieved.

Principals' leadership style – from autocratic to collaborative decision making

A strongly advocated feature of both the SMI and QSE-ECR7 documents is the required change in principals' leadership style, from an authoritarian to a more collaborative, participative one. For example, the SMI stated that 'because proper management structures and processes are lacking, some principals are insufficiently accountable for their actions and see their post as an opportunity to become little emperors with dictatorial powers in the school' (EMB & ED, 1991, p.14). It goes on to refer to a lack of educational and managerial leadership in schools. Effective leaders, by contrast, 'would provide strong support for school-based management and collaborative decision making within a framework of school objectives, and provide the link between the school and the SMC' (EMB & ED, 1991, Annex 2). This belief is reinforced in QSE-ECR7 – where the recommendation is made to set up a two-tier management structure in schools – a SMC and a SEC. The SEC would be the executive arm of the SMC and be headed by the principal. This could be interpreted as a clear attempt to disseminate some of the present power and authority exercised by principals. In addition, QSE-ECR7 advocates that the teachers' role should be more than just classroom teaching: 'Teachers should participate in school management to help develop the various school activities in a professional way' (EC, 1996, p.30). Teacher participation is envisaged in the SMC and SEC. This represents a further sharing of decision making by principals.

Collaborative leadership styles are currently advocated as key facets of school restructuring policies in the west. The assumption is that such leadership styles bring multiple benefits, including better quality decisions, sharing of workloads, and greater staff commitment to implementing decisions. Even in western societies, however, some of these supposed benefits appear more rhetorical than real, with many western principals testifying to the slowing of decision making once collaboration is practised. There is also the main impediment caused by the difficulties of achieving collaboration. This occurs because, first, school cultures are traditionally more individualist than collaborative; second, the concept itself is capable of many interpretations and may occur at different organizational levels; and, third, difficulties arise because collaboration is inextricably intertwined with power, authority and responsibility. In sum, leaders are often reluctant to collaborate when they fear loss of personal power and control, especially in situations where they are ultimately held accountable.

Parental involvement

SMI refers to the fact that very few schools have parent-teacher associations or parental representation on SMCs. It goes on to claim that close contact between schools and parents could foster more effective learning, and should be encouraged in all schools. The same point is repeated in QSE-ECR7.

A considerable body of research undertaken in western countries confirms the benefits to children's learning arising from close parental involvement in their children's school work and its extension into homework; parental assistance to teachers in class; and provision of a stimulating social and home environment where learning is encouraged. It would be safe to assume that the same findings apply to other societies, including Hong Kong. However, the emphasis in SMI and QSE-ECR7 is on securing greater parental involvement in school decision making through involvement in institutional structures (namely PTAs and parent associations) the main purpose of which is to increase pluralism, generate school funds and make schools more accountable to the parent stakeholder group. It is highly questionable whether the latter measures have an effect on improving the quality of education or levels of student learning.

Staff appraisal

Both the SMI and QSE-ECR7 are unequivocal about the necessity to introduce a staff appraisal system. The importance of appraisal, as set out in the SMI, is its assessment of staff strengths and weaknesses, clarification of staff development needs, and its contribution to ensuring a meritocratic basis for promotion. The same arguments are repeated again in QSE-ECR7, only this time appraisal is seen as part of a quality assurance process. In reality few schools, even those which were part of the SMI scheme from its initial phase, had made much headway by 1997 in introducing an appraisal scheme; and Hong Kong is not alone in this respect. Difficulties of implementation, whether due to the unions or to those philosophically opposed to the idea at school management level, have been encountered in most systems, irrespective of culture and context.

Hong Kong's schools are therefore not exceptional in encountering implementation difficulties. Part of the problem, however, is that there has been no strong push from the ED for schools to move on appraisal. In addition, advisory committee documents (Education Department, 1992, 1993) on appraisal allow considerable school flexibility and discretion by not setting down helpful guidelines and operational suggestions as to how school staffs might best establish the practices and procedures. This situation typifies a key dilemma of reform: the ED is either unwilling or unable to provide to schools detailed guidance and direction on implementation, thereby leaving it to each school to work out its own response; schools, however, rarely seem to possess the technical knowledge, expertise, initiative, will and resources to make the reform happen.

Professional development and training

High priority is accorded in SMI and QSE-ECR7 to the professional development of principals, teachers and other key players. This is rightly seen as a prerequisite for the successful implementation of restructuring policies. Both reports, however, are extremely cursory in detailing the form and delivery such training should take or the standards to be met. In view of the fact that successful implementation is acknowledged by all three documents, including TOC, to rest heavily on professional development, it is disappointing that they give so little attention to the quality and type of professional development deemed necessary.

It is a truism that the restructuring of any system of education depends on the quality and preparedness of its workforce, and Hong Kong's school system is no exception. Major changes to curriculum, teaching and learning, and to governance, management and administration are predicated on professional development. One can rightly claim that a lot more thought is needed about the substance or content, the delivery methods and the quality of professional development required. The question of whether suitable providers of such professional development exist is another matter. Visions of the newly restructured schools and of the improved quality education they deliver should guide decisions on the knowledge, skills and attitudes needed by school leaders, teachers and other stakeholders. As Muller and Watts (1993) caution, organizations 'often adopt first-rate strategies that are implemented by managers with second-rate education and training. When these managers work in out-of-date work environments, the result is that the organizations become third-rate' (p.361). These profound words are just as true for Hong Kong's school reforms as they are for others in this book.

Chapter 6

Restructuring in Australia

INTRODUCTION

State education authorities have, since their inception in the late nineteenth century, controlled public schooling in Australia. This situation developed because of the desire to give equal educational opportunities to all children, no matter how remote their place of residence. Until very recently, the Education Department in each of the nation's six states and two territories was centrally responsible for such matters as curriculum, school buildings and supplies, leaving examinations, teacher salary determinants and payments, staffing appointments, and transfers between schools.

This situation has been of great interest internationally over the years: Gamage (1993) has noted that eminent North American scholars such as Kendall (1938), Butts (1955) and Jackson (1961) criticized the control, conformity and preoccupations with efficiency and examinations which they discovered in Australia. They emphasized the importance of decentralization and breaking down the bureaucracy on the grounds of administrative and economic advantages and effectiveness. Butts (1955) argued:

> 'I wonder… whether you miss something of the vitality, initiative, creativeness and variety that would come if the doors and windows of discussion and decision were kept more open all the way up and down the educational edifice. The two-way flow of educational ideas might lead to more broadly based decisions, and therefore more democratic ones.' (p.16)

He went on:

> 'I have the feeling that the time is ripe for serious long-term planning with respect to the possibilities of genuine decentralization in educational policy making and financial support. Some regions and some communities in every State are now surely large enough and vital enough to be classified as school districts worthy of greater autonomy in the handling of their educational affairs.' (p.16)

However, while New South Wales (NSW) initiated some reforms in 1948, and Queensland and Tasmania followed shortly afterwards, it was not until the early 1970s that the prospect of loosening some of the major bonds of centralization was seriously considered across the country.

Today, the situation is very different. The major source of change has been summarized by Gamage (1992) as follows:

> 'Especially in an era where the federal government (Commonwealth) has a declared policy objective of taking the country into the 21st century with a much more advanced scientific and technological base, by prolonging the period of training of the youngsters in the education system and also by developing the higher education sector as an export industry by spending billions of dollars, change is everywhere in the system.' (p.5)

This situation has not been arrived at overnight, rather, the move over the last 20 years away from a strong centralized focus has been gradual, faltering, spasmodic and characterized by surges. Also, while there does seem to be a national trend towards devolution, Caldwell (1993) is correct in pointing to the very great differences which have emerged among the various states and territories in the context of eight autonomous public education systems in Australia, with varying histories and traditions, varying political parties and priorities, and different stages of development. Nevertheless, Angus (1995) has identified three 'cycles of reform' which provide a useful framework for considering the broad restructuring developments that have taken place since the early 1970s. This chapter considers each of these cycles in turn, with particular reference to developments in Western Australia (WA), this being the state where the case studies reported in the remainder of book were conducted.

THE THREE CYCLES OF REFORM

The first cycle of reform

Beare (1987) has argued that the 'watershed' for the present-day restructuring taking place in Australian education occurred in the 1970s, when federal intervention weakened the centralized dominance of the states. This, in turn, had its origins in the policies of the Labour Government elected in 1972. In May 1973, the Interim Committee for the Australian Schools Commission (1973) published its report. One outcome was the establishment of the Australian Schools Commission, whose functions substantially increased the federal government's financing of aspects of kindergarten through to grade 12 schooling.

According to Shinkfield (1981, p.54), the emphasis in the 1976–78 period was to improve learning of basic skills; explore ways to 'open up' the school; involve students in decision making; integrate 'special' children into ordinary classes; help handicapped children get employment; promote cultural pluralism; meet the special needs of Aboriginal children; compensate for isolation; bring school and community closer together; promote the feasibility of recurrent education; reduce the disadvantage of girls; cater for children with special skills.

The following position of the Interim Committee for the Australian Schools Commission (1973) was also influential:

'The Committee favours less rather than more centralized control over the operation of schools. Responsibility should be devolved as far as possible upon the people involved in the actual task of schooling, in consultation with the parents of the pupils whom they teach and at the senior levels with the students themselves. Its belief in this grass roots approach to the control of schools reflects a conviction that responsibility will be most effectively discharged where the people entrusted with making decisions are also the people responsible for carrying them out, with an obligation to justify them and in a position to profit from their experiences.' (p.10)

Also, the federal government, through the Schools Commission, allocated money to teacher-innovators for any purpose that had the potential to advance the progress of education. Marsh (1980) cites the example of the 'Special Projects Programme' which welcomed and indeed acceded to most requests by individual teachers for a variety of curriculum proposals, 'from mini-buses for excursions to converting old train carriages into workshops' (p.14).

As Angus (1995) points out, funding was disbursed to schools via state and local committees comprised mostly of school and community personnel: 'the committees largely bypassed the state department offices' (p.7). He goes on:

'In most cases, state authorities were ready to accept the funding, but retained control by renegotiating details of school-initiated proposals before allowing them to proceed. As events unfolded, very few proposals directly challenged the central decision-making authority of state departments. Pulling in its horns, the Schools Commission sought to achieve its devolution goals by provoking a head-on contest between the Commonwealth and the states over administrative structures.' (p.7)

After a decade of special-purpose funding by the federal government, most of the programmes were abolished, having largely failed to shift the balance of administrative power and control away from states and towards more grass roots control at school level. In hindsight, it might seem paradoxical that an initiative involving federal funding was aimed at promoting greater devolution.

The federal government also became involved with education in the states through the Curriculum Development Centre (CDC). The CDC was formally instituted by an Act of Parliament in 1975, and was 'charged with the brief of developing school curricula and materials, research, dissemination and publication of material' (Marsh and Stafford, 1988, p.210). Piper (1992) contends that its arrival was of key importance, since 'it institutionalized the Commonwealth's entry into the curriculum area and legitimated the concept of national curriculum development' (p.21). Written into the CDC Act was the principle of cooperative development between the federal government and the states.

Cabinet directed the CDC to 'seek a contribution in kind to projects from the states which matched its own' (Connors, 1980, p.20). One important example of a project governed by this requirement was the 'Language Development Project', which was a major national initiative in English language education. It had a central team located at the CDC and eight local project teams in the states and territories. The CDC also funded school-based curriculum projects. Marsh (1980, p.14) explains that teachers were able to attract small grants to develop particular curriculum ideas, ranging from the use of simulation packages to the development of a primary school curriculum in a particular subject. By the end of the 1970s it was clear that major changes had occurred in the way in which curriculum planning was carried out in Australia. Musgrave (1979) was able to note that there had been:

'a movement from massive prescription by state education departments and university examination boards to much option at the primary level and minimal prescription, largely at year 12, at the secondary level. More scientific methods are now used to develop curricula and related materials.' (p.135)

The emphasis on school-based curriculum planning by national bodies, and the state education department initiatives for in-service training, provided strong incentives for class teachers to plan, develop and implement their own curricula.

The second cycle of reform

The second cycle of reform in the Australian education system, termed by Angus (1995) 'state government initiated reform', began in the mid-1980s. In contrast with the earlier cycle, the federal government played no part in the reforms. Rather, a major change in political values swept through the public sector, including education. A number of policy documents, including *Quality of Education in Australia* (Quality of Education Review Committee (QERC), 1985), were published, all of which were underpinned by a strong politico-administrative ideology that had been sweeping through much of North America and Europe (Pusey, 1991; Wilenski, 1986). Economic rationalism and corporate managerialism were about to shape the restructuring of Australian education.

A major reason for this change in policies derived from economic difficulties in the 1980s, which led to an examination of the contribution made by education to the economy and an assessment of the quality of schooling. The establishment of the QERC to gauge 'value for money' from federal expenditure on education, and to gear education nationally more closely to labour-market needs, signalled an end to growth in federal spending. The dramatic shift in values between the reforms initiated in 1973 and the QERC is described by Smart (1988, p.157). He argues that while the early reforms were primarily concerned with financial and educational inputs, QERC was required to establish that there were identifiable educational outcomes from federal aid. The change from a concern with inputs during the relatively prosperous 1970s to a focus on outcomes during the financially stringent 1980s was starkly evident. This is true as much for WA as it is for the rest of the country.

Soon after the QERC report came the government of WA's White Paper, *Managing Change in the Public Sector* (Western Australia Parliament, 1986), which outlined the problems facing most state governments in the 1980s; balancing community demands for more and improved services with policies of tight budgetary restraint (Dimmock, 1990). The White Paper delineated a number of key principles for reform in the public sector, including responsiveness and adaptability to the needs of the community, flexibility in the use of resources, and accountability and responsibility to government for standards of service and funding. Efficiency and effectiveness became the prime objectives, although some attention was also given to equity.

During this period, in WA, the newly elected Burke Labour Government had initiated an extensive review of education in what was perhaps the most centralized state education system in Australia (Smart and Alderson, 1980). The subsequent *Education in Western Australia* (Beazley, 1984) recommended wide-ranging educational reforms, including the provision of greater community participation in school decision making. As a consequence of these pressures the reformist Minister for Education, Robert Pearce, requested the Western Australian Government Functional Review Committee to review the education portfolio in order to streamline the structure of the Education Department and to improve coordination and resource management (Western Australia, Functional Review Committee, 1986). The result was the report, *Better Schools in Western Australia: A Programme for Improvement* (Western Australian Education Department, 1987) which promoted the rationale that good schools create a good system. This report was the blueprint for restructuring the school system in WA, based on devolving authority and decentralizing responsibilities to a future system of self-determining schools with community participation. Emphasis was placed on decentralizing responsibilities to principals and teachers, devolving power to school councils, and making school personnel more accountable to both their local communities (through school councils) and to government (through performance monitoring and auditing).

Angus (1995, p.8) is unambiguous in his recognition of the motives for the new wave of reforms throughout the country. Governments were under pressure to improve and extend services; at the same time they were expected to tighten public expenditure on education, which was by far the largest item in state budgets. The purpose was to get better value from the education dollar spent rather than to achieve expenditure cuts. This thinking permeated all services in the public sector. It was driven by a four-step paradigm of means and ends: a clear articulation by state governments of the desired ends; the provision of resources to local authorities (schools), conditional upon agreement to achieve the stated ends; the empowerment of local authorities (schools) to determine the means; and further provision of resources by the centre conditional on the local authority demonstrating progress towards the achievement of the agreed ends (Angus, 1995, pp.8–9). This corporate management philosophy was founded on central offices sharpening the focus on systemic priorities while devolving to schools the authority and means by which they could achieve the agreed outcomes.

Major planks of this corporate management policy in education are clearly identifiable: a mandatory development plan in each school; single-line budgets for schools in place of the previous specific funds controlled centrally; formally constituted school decision-making groups (with staff and community representation) to endorse plans and authorize budgets; an external auditing capacity, with both educational and financial functions; central offices more focused on defining policy guidelines and standards than in the past; and decentralized school support services based at the school or local level (Angus, 1995, p.9). Angus concludes as follows regarding the outcome for education in Australia:

> 'Australian education systems constitute a kind of patchwork quilt. Management structures vary on a state-by-state basis. While it is unlikely they will ever assume a uniform pattern, they have moved towards devolved structures of one kind or another since the Commonwealth's initiative in the early 1970s.' (p.9)

By 1994, some of the key characteristics of the 'state of play' regarding the second cycle of devolution in Australia were: all school systems had experienced significant cuts in out-of-school administrative and support staff; the political and management policy makers in all systems favoured further devolutionary steps; the major focus for change was in the areas of equipment, buildings, flexible staffing, local selection of administrators and teachers, the development and strengthening of school councils and the establishment of school charters.

The 'second wave of educational reform' was also felt in the area of the curriculum. In May 1981, under the Fraser Liberal Government, the incorporation of the CDC as a unit of the Commonwealth Department of Education reduced its operations to a minimum. In 1983 the Hawke Labour Government reconstituted the CDC, but as a division of the Commonwealth Schools Commission rather than as an independent authority. Piper (1992, p.22) states that the new programmes initiated by the revived CDC were located in the states and territories, often in state education departments, with each state and territory entering into separate contractual arrangements with the CDC for the production of curriculum resources. Finally, on 1 January 1988, the CDC became a unit within the Schools and Curriculum Division of the Department of Employment, Education and Training (DEET) and its emphasis shifted away from progressive education towards mathematics, science and vocational projects. This, Barcan (1993) contends, was the result of the federal minister of DEET, working through the Australian Education Council, putting pressure on the states and territories 'to fall into line' (p.348).

The third cycle of reform

The third cycle of educational reform noted by Angus is termed 'the tripartite alliance'. This cycle arose out of government, business and unions from the late 1980s onwards agreeing on the need to restructure education, along with other industries, to improve the competitiveness of the Australian economy and workforce. Within education it resulted in 'professional' and 'industrial' issues becoming intertwined. Significant reports were *Teacher Quality: An Issues Paper* (Schools Council, 1989) and *Australia's Teachers: An Agenda for the Next Decade* (Schools Council, 1990). These reports commented on the widespread view that the morale and standing of the teaching profession were declining. This was attributed to the quality of entrants, the unattractiveness of teaching as a career, the work life and practice of teachers, and the inadequacy of the mechanisms for recognizing and rewarding the quality of teaching in terms of career paths and status. However, it was the federal government's quest to improve efficiency and productivity at the workplace which largely defined reform policy in connection with teachers and teaching. This has occurred in particular under the aegis of reward restructuring and enterprise bargaining.

Since the late 1980s the Australian system of industrial relations has been gradually changing from one based on a highly centralized model to one which focuses on the workplace. The traditional approach, emphasizing arbitrated decisions by central tribunals in order to achieve uniform wage increases without any consideration given to productivity, is being replaced by the practice of negotiation at the enterprise level. In pursuit of efficiency and productivity at the workplace, legislative reforms have occurred at both federal and state levels which present opportunities for individual enterprises to negotiate agreements, defining terms and conditions which are considered to be most appropriate for their circumstances.

Traditionally, teachers' terms and conditions have been set out according to an industrial award which is issued by an industrial tribunal and applies to all employees within a particular sector of the education system. An award is also binding on all employees and is legally enforceable. Negotiations dealing with award claims are conducted between the relevant union and the employer. If no agreement can be reached between the parties the case is put before the industrial tribunal for conciliation and arbitration. Under this arrangement, teachers have expected salary increases to be linked to rises in the cost of living and that relativities with other occupations would be observed.

Concomitant with the federal Labour government's commitment to micro-economic change, the concept of award restructuring was introduced as a means of improving productivity by upgrading the skills of the Australian workforce. The basis for award restructuring was articulated by the National Wage Case decision of 1988, when the Industrial Commission adopted the 'structural efficiency principle'. As Blauer and Carmichael (1991, p.24) assert, this principle is, in itself, a demonstration of a new imperative which is now driving education efforts in Australia. In other words, education is predicated to an increasing extent on the need to develop a society which has a highly competent workforce responsive to the demands made by changing patterns of work, and the need for Australia to be economically competitive in the international market. In the case of schools, this involves improving the skills of their major resources, teachers, and providing them with a better work environment.

In January 1989 a national bench-mark rate was established which asserted that teachers' work and qualifications were substantially the same throughout the country and so, therefore, should be salaries. The following year the Federal Industrial Relations Commission ratified the introduction of the Advanced Skills Teacher classification (AST). The award was silent on what exactly constitutes an AST, but it was intended that the classification should be a recognition of exemplary teaching and provide a new classroom-based career structure which would progress from level one to level three. This initiative has been described as 'the jewel in the award restructuring crown' (Chadbourne and Ingvarson, 1991, p.3) because of its potential to make a significant contribution to the reforming of teachers' work. Nevertheless, since its inception it has been fraught with difficulties and there is some doubt as to whether it will be able to fulfil its original promise (Chadbourne and Ingvarson, 1991; Ingvarson, 1994).

Union negotiations with employers focused on trading salary increases for structural reforms that would generate increased productivity. While initially these trade-offs were based around salary increases in return for clarification and acceptance of teachers' duties and responsibilities, after some time the bargaining process began to focus on what constitutes best practice in work organization. Late in 1990 unions and employers in Australian state education systems agreed on the National Project on the Quality of Teaching and Learning (NPQTL), a scheme to promote in schools a restructuring process which, it was believed, would lead to the improvement of teaching quality and student learning.

Early in 1991 the federal government initiated the NPQTL in order to advance the cause of award restructuring. Its main purpose was to provide a forum for cooperative work involving such key stakeholders as government and private employers, education unions, and the federal government. According to Durbridge (1991, p.89) the work programme which it devised included the transferability of entitlements from one state to another, a framework for qualifications, accreditation and possibly registration, the analysis of current and alternative work organization with its related career and reward consequences, the management and support structures in schools with their accountability and appraisal mechanisms, the nature of teacher education, and the induction and professional development needed to sustain the various operations. The continued decentralization of the industrial relations system to the workplace was represented by the introduction of enterprise-based bargaining.

Shaw (1995, p.3) has pointed out that this period witnessed a dramatic change in the focus of industrial relations legislation which culminated in the Industrial Relations Reform Act of 1993. Previously the focus of industrial relations was exclusively on awards, but now the legislation emphasizes agreement as the predominant industrial instrument. The rationale behind the new Act was expressed clearly by the then federal Minister of Industrial Relations, Laurie Brereton:

'Under this system of enterprise bargaining, the parties involved will have a greater responsibility for determining the outcome of their agreements. The changes in industrial relations will open the way for Australian workplaces to meet the challenge of being more productive and internationally competitive.' (Niland, 1994, p.17)

This development represented a further step in the continuing reforms that the federal Labour government had introduced over the past decade. With the encouragement of the Federal Industrial Relations Commission, the principles of enterprise bargaining and enterprise agreements have also been endorsed by the state jurisdictions, where provisions have been made to provide formal frameworks detailing the proper processes and structures required.

The overriding importance of award restructuring has been the injection of 'productivity thinking' into the 'education industry' and the endorsement of the notion of an association between reform, productivity and salary (Angus, 1992). This perspective has been further reinforced by means of legislation supporting the principle of agreements negotiated at the workplace, either in conjunction with or completely replacing the relevant award. What now remains to be seen is if the ideas regarding teachers' work and conditions that are prompted by the new regime of industrial relations can be put into action, and if schools have the ability to deal with the complex process of bargaining.

The government's programme for economic restructuring and micro-economic reform also resulted in a major push towards developing a national curriculum. However, moves in this direction had been underway since the late 1970s, when the conservative 'back-to-basics' movement swung the pendulum back towards greater curriculum control and away from the importance which the Australian Schools Commission had attached to pursuing a more progressive curriculum, with a concern for the development of the individual and for social justice. This is not to overlook attempts at further progressive reforms in some states. In Victoria, for example, a new Labour government recommended the introduction of a new Victorian Certificate in Education (VCE) which would:

> 'include the abolition of a status distinction between types of subjects (particularly those counting for university entrance and those not counting), common learnings in English and Australian Studies for all students (a first reaction against the instrumental curriculum), limits on over-specialization, and an insistence that all studies (subjects) have theoretical and practical aspects. Perhaps more revolutionary, all studies were to consist primarily of work requirements and these were to be linked to authentic assessments which weighed how well tasks were done. Pen and paper tests were to be used only when appropriate.' (Collins, 1995, p.5)

However, conservative forces coalesced to ensure that only an extremely 'watered-down' version of this new curriculum was put in place. Nevertheless, it had wide influence throughout the country.

WA took a different route. Here, in the late 1980s, the lower secondary school curriculum was divided into seven component areas, each accorded equal status: English, languages and communication; mathematics; personal and vocational education; physical education; practical and creative arts; science and technology; social studies. Nearly 300 units were prepared within these areas in order to give students a greater degree of choice and participation in decisions which affect their education. Units were allocated to a stage of progress from 1–6, with varying entry points for students. The plan was that students would have time to complete between 12 and 23 units each semester, or 72 units or more during years 8 to 10, with schools also being able to plan their own additional units if required.

These developments, however, were soon overshadowed by the concerted movement towards introducing a national curriculum. Several authors (Cumming, 1992; Kennedy, 1992; Piper, 1992) date this movement as beginning in 1988, with the publication by John Dawkins, the minister heading a recently revamped DEET, of *Strengthening Australian Schools* (Dawkins, 1988). This identified a 'national effort for schools' in six areas: a common curriculum framework; a common approach to assessment; priorities for improving the training of teachers; increasing participation rates in post-compulsory education; improving equity in education; maximizing investment in education. These aims were clarified in 1989 in the Hobart Declaration which posited ten goals for schooling in Australia. It was signed by the

Australian Education Council (AEC), which comprised the education ministers of the Commonwealth, states and territories. The same year the AEC established the Curriculum Corporation as the central permanent coordinating curriculum body. It identified eight learning areas, established steering committees for each, and published a schedule for the publication of 'National Curriculum Briefs, Statements and Profiles'.

A concurrent development of significance was the development of employment-related key competencies. These were developed from studies into post-compulsory schooling, an area of great concern in Australian education since the 1980s, when low participation rates beyond the age of 15 were identified. A review of post-compulsory education was commissioned by the AEC in 1990, after the national curriculum initiative had begun. Clearly there was going to be an overlap of interest and the resultant report (Australian Education Council, 1991) did develop some curriculum principles, not just relating to 'curriculum design and development, but a wide range of related aspects such as standards of assessments, educational pathways and learning contexts' (Australian Education Council, 1991, p.53). The focus of the report – the development of key competencies – was further developed by the Mayer Committee (1992) which devised 'key competency strands' and 'key areas of competence'. Then, in 1992, the Carmichael report (1992) recommended a national training award scheme based on the key competencies.

The development of key competencies within a national framework complemented much of the direction of the national curriculum initiatives. Kennedy (1992) argued that the two initiatives – the creation of national statements and profiles and the development of key competencies – were necessary to infuse meaning into the national curriculum.

> 'Where knowledge and understanding need to be made explicit, such as in the key competence areas of cultural understanding and scientific and technological understanding, the knowledge base will be provided by the national curriculum statements... The employment related competencies will be underpinned by the knowledge base of the national curriculum statements.' (p.35)

However, the key competencies, national statements and profiles failed to get national endorsement at the AEC meeting in 1993. Instead, as Collins (1995, p.13) notes, the documents produced were considered separately in each state, and each state has made its own decision about implementation. It remains to be seen what the eventual outcome will be of the states' reassertion of their right to go against the policy of the federal government in education when initiatives of the latter are seen as threatening the states' independence.

Recognition of these three waves or cycles of reform, and the multiple factors underpinning them, provide an important background to understanding contemporary educational restructuring in Australia. A loss of confidence in the abilities of central bureaucracies to administer education systems, a changed political and economic landscape, a belief in consumerism and the wider involvement of all stakeholders (including parents, business representatives and teachers) in collaborative decision making, and the quest for more effective schools, were all prominent factors in the restructuring movement. At the same time, the states showed themselves unwilling to sanction greater centralization at the federal level in the curriculum. Specifically regarding WA, in the second half of the 1990s, the 'centre' still retains absolute control over staffing, has considerable power over policy and guidelines (especially for the curriculum), and has devolved much administration to local schools. At the same time, it expects more accountability from schools. In this respect the system is probably more 'centralized' than ever in the history of education management in the state. In becoming 'decentralized' by offering schools more discretionary powers over how to achieve the state-set goals with respect to the state-set curriculum, however, the forces of decentralization and centralization sometimes coexist in the three major decision-making areas of curriculum, human resources and finance.

The WA system is more accurately described as one focused on increasing school-based initiatives with regard to methods of learning. It is likely to be a long evolutionary process before political decentralization of curriculum, staffing and finance becomes a reality. Devolution, in the form of less empowered school decision-making bodies rather than more empowered school councils, is also proceeding slowly. Finally, in the WA education system, as in most others, particular emphasis has been placed on the role of the school principal and, to a lesser extent, on teachers and parents, in the translation of restructuring initiatives into practice.

The remainder of this book is taken up with the consideration of case studies which raise a significant number of issues regarding the manner in which the restructuring initiatives are impacting on these key stakeholders.

The impact of restructuring on schools

PART THREE

The impact of restructuring on schools

INTRODUCTION

Initiatives to restructure school systems throughout the western world have focused so far largely on their organizational, administrative and governmental configurations. Characteristic features of these new arrangements – school-based management, devolution of responsibilities to principals, empowerment of teachers and school councils and the encouragement of parental participation in school governance – are by now familiar (Malen *et al.*, 1990). Shifting patterns of power and control between school and central office are more complex. Typically, the 'centre' provides an explicit policy framework, with system guidelines and targets. While schools are given more discretion over the allocation of resources and the means by which they perform their work, the centre monitors their performance and ensures their accountability not only to the centre but also to newly empowered school councils.

In tandem with restructuring policies, some governments have expressed concern for the quality of schooling, incorporating curriculum reform and quality of teaching and learning. The relationship between the developments in curriculum, teaching and learning on one side, and restructuring of administrative and organizational aspects of schools on the other, remains ambivalent. Are they more accurately conceived as separate reforms or are changes to curriculum, teaching and learning to be seen as part of restructuring? Whatever the response to this question, the links between desired teaching and learning outcomes and the new organizational and administrative configurations expected to deliver them are rarely explicated. The basis on which the connections are made remains more an act of faith than coherent exposition. There is evidence that administrative and managerial restructuring does not necessarily impact on the curriculum (Caldwell, 1990). Indeed, the effects of restructuring in Australia to date appear to have concentrated on administrative structures in central, regional and district offices and on devolving and decentralizing administrative responsibilities to principals and school councils. The effects of restructuring seem not to have penetrated classrooms to affect how teachers teach and students learn. In the United States context, Hallinger *et al.* (1993, p.22) argue that the voice of teachers and administrators on restructuring has hardly been heard, having been 'drowned out by the din created by academics, policy makers and business persons' (p.23).

The same concern led Bell (1991) to argue from the English context that discussions about school management, both by practitioners and by academics, had been more concerned with structures and processes of managing than with 'demonstrating how effective management of those processes can directly facilitate the processes of teaching and learning' (p.138). Further cause for concern is the absence of evidence to show how school management and organization influence the quality of curriculum provision (Dimmock, 1993). Indeed, surprisingly little is known about how, and by whom, the curriculum is managed in schools.

Studies in the 1980s have shown what principals do to manage the curriculum, teaching and learning (Leithwood and Montgomery, 1982; Rowan *et al.*, 1982; Hallinger and Murphy, 1985; Murphy *et al.*, 1985). With the accumulation of knowledge about principals' practices, some researchers had by the end of the 1980s shifted their focus away from principals' behaviour and tasks towards a concern for their thinking and problem-solving processes (Leithwood and Stager, 1989; Leithwood *et al.*, 1994; Hallinger and McCary, 1990). Despite this shift of focus and a body of literature confirming the pivotal role of the principal in creating and sustaining the academic effectiveness of schools, a number of issues remain to be investigated. First, few studies have been undertaken of academically effective schools where principals do not act as educational leaders. Second, few studies have looked at management of the curriculum throughout the school, embracing the contributions of deputy principals, senior teachers and other teachers. To what extent do these compensate for lack of educational leadership by the principal? Third, little is known about the effects of curriculum and management teams on the quality of curriculum, teaching and learning in schools.

The four chapters which are presented in this section point to some directions which research into these areas might take. Chapter 7 reports on the views held by a sample of principals and teachers in Western Australia (WA), at the point of policy inception, of the likely effects of restructuring on changing roles and responsibilities, actual and desired outcomes, changing power and influence relations, personal values, and difficulties in meeting new expectations. Data were collected using the 'School Management in a Decentralizing System Questionnaire'. There was a remarkable degree of consistency between the reactions held by principals and teachers. Both groups predicted that decentralization and devolution would increase their workloads and broaden their roles, and that all roles would increase in importance. Principals would require more human and technical management competencies, while teachers would assume more non-teaching duties. The problem of the extended professional is apparent. Notwithstanding difficulties and drawbacks, principals and teachers believed that restructuring would lead to better, more effective and more efficient schools. In a pattern of changing power and influence relations, both principals and teachers predicted that school decision-making groups, parents, principals and teachers would experience gains, while the Education Department, employers and students would experience no change.

Chapter 8 reports a case study which sought to determine what a group of primary school teachers thought about the impact of restructuring on their work. The analysis indicated that, in general, teachers viewed restructuring largely in terms of its perceived influence on their curriculum work.

Furthermore, teachers evaluated particular developments associated with restructuring using at least three related frames:

1. the extent to which what is happening does not take into consideration the complexity of the teacher's curriculum role;
2. the extent to which what is happening is not empowering teachers to engage in curriculum decision making; and
3. the extent to which what is happening is affecting teachers' classroom work.

The focus in Chapter 9 is on a study aimed at understanding teachers' perceptions of one aspect of restructuring, namely, school development planning. It considers the general background to school development planning in WA and then outlines the methodology of the study. Three major interrelated propositions with regard to the teachers' perceptions of the process are then discussed. First, the teachers in the school perceived that the introduction of school development planning is part of a wider agenda by the government to devolve as much responsibility for administration as possible to the school, and particularly to teachers, with the primary aim being to reduce the cost of the central administration. Second, they perceived that the state Education Department intends to continue its strong control over the direction and operation of the school and, as a consequence, they feel restrained from engaging enthusiastically in school development planning. Third, they perceived that school development planning, in forcing them to adopt a 'whole school' approach to defining problems and to developing strategies to solve them may, in the long term rather than immediately, have some positive outcomes at the classroom level.

The case study in Chapter 10 is concerned with teachers' perceptions of the emergent role for parents in school decision making as part of current educational restructuring. In WA, since 1987, the public education system has experienced considerable restructuring. Among the changes is the fact that parents in public schools now enjoy a 50 per cent representation on school decision-making boards. Three major themes concerning teachers' perceptions of parental involvement in school decision making emerged from the study. First, the teachers in the study perceived that, currently, central policy makers are promoting parental involvement in school decision making without being cognizant of its possible negative impact on teachers. Second, there was a perception among teachers that parents' concerns are beginning to receive greater acknowledgement at the school level than teachers' concerns. Finally, parental involvement in school decision making is having an impact on teachers' perceptions of their curriculum decision-making role.

Chapter 7

Principals' and teachers' reactions to school restructuring

INTRODUCTION

Despite the rationale for, and much acclaimed benefits of, decentralization, it is not difficult to envisage the problems arising in moving from an entrenched centralized system. Community and parental inexperience and feelings of inadequacy in relation to participation in school affairs, and changes in the tasks and roles of principals and teachers would suggest that the achievement of self-governing schools is a challenging, evolutionary process. The simultaneous demands for excellence and quality, for economic restraint and accountability, and for an adaptive and responsive system able to meet the needs of a rapidly changing technological society also contribute to the complexity of the change process.

There have been relatively few research studies of the reactions of teachers and principals to the current trends towards devolution of control to individual schools in government systems. Little has been written about the experiences and reactions of those who have adopted and implemented school-based management responsibilities. It is likely that greater knowledge of the reactions of teachers and principals, who are expected to implement policy at the school level, will provide insight into the difficulties of transforming entrenched attitudes and practices. In turn, this may enhance the success of current efforts at decentralization and devolution.

A variety of concerns present themselves: one is the possible changes to the roles and tasks of principals following the implementation of devolution policy; another relates to the perceptions which principals and teachers hold of possible and desired outcomes of such a policy. A further issue incorporates possible shifts in the pattern of relationships, responsibilities, influences and the balance of power in education, as perceived by principals and teachers. Finally, there are possible difficulties that schools may face in meeting new expectations in a restructured system. Principals, as major participants, have perceptions and attitudes pertaining to the changes, to their perceived roles and to their new responsibilities, as well as to the newly created school decision-making groups.

The study reported in this chapter addressed the following questions:

♦ Are principals expected to be managers rather than educational leaders, directors of human resources or promoters of excellence in education?
♦ Do principals and teachers consider these role changes will replace their existing duties, or are they perceived to be additional responsibilities?
♦ What are the advantages of increased competitiveness, more specialized administrative staff, and greater power to school-based groups?
♦ How is the power base changing?
♦ What are the perceived difficulties of devolution and decentralization?

These issues, generated from the research literature, were used as the basis for developing the School Management in a Decentralizing System Questionnaire (SMDSQ), administered to principals and teachers when the legislative changes introducing devolution in WA were in their initial stage, in 1988 and 1989. In presenting the results of the study it is acknowledged that the effects of major changes are unlikely to be clear in their immediate aftermath and that the implementation of a decentralization policy is likely to be a long, evolutionary process.

METHOD

The study was conducted in primary and secondary government schools in metropolitan and rural WA. The 24 schools participating in the study were evenly divided between primary and secondary. The schools selected represented a purposive sample, deliberately chosen for heterogeneity, thus maximizing the results within the group sampled. Altogether, 153 teachers and 24 principals responded to the questionnaire. The sample was similar in proportion to the population of teachers and principals in WA. Forty per cent were males (compared to 35 per cent in the population), but there was a smaller proportion of male respondents in country districts compared to the whole population (16 per cent vs 34 per cent). The largest group of respondents were aged between 31 and 45 years (42 per cent), had 15 years or more experience in schools (45 per cent), and were located in metropolitan schools (85 per cent). The majority of respondents were trained at colleges of advanced education (65 per cent), while 27 per cent were trained at universities. About 22 per cent had undertaken further tertiary courses. Of these, 53 per cent had completed, or were completing, a Master's course, 68 per cent had at least two tertiary qualifications, and 24% had completed some units in educational administration, mainly at the Master's level.

The SMDSQ was the data collection instrument used in this study. The content of the questionnaire was based on factors identified in the literature as central to school-based management (Brown, 1990; Caldwell and Spinks, 1988; Chapman, 1987; Guthrie, 1986). Construct validity was also taken into account by administering the questionnaire to a group of 45 experienced primary and secondary teachers and principals undertaking a Master's degree in Educational Management. This group was asked to evaluate the items for relevance and modifications were made as a result of its assessment. There were no items appearing on more than one scale, hence there was no need to deal with problems of item overlap. A series of factor analyses was undertaken on the various scales to devise a set of dependable and coherent scores.

Two major types of scale were used. The first asked respondents to indicate their perceptions of the importance of a set of management tasks for principals by selecting one of five scores for each of three periods of time: past, present and five years from now. For example, using the task 'Setting up a school-based decision-making group', respondents had to answer for the past, present and future, using the following categories: very important, moderately important; of little importance, unimportant, or uncertain. The second type of response used a five-point Likert scale, ranging from strongly agree to strongly disagree. The questionnaire took approximately 25 minutes to complete. Respondents were informed that information was confidential and that they would not be identified individually. This was a condition which, it was hoped, would increase the likelihood of obtaining honest responses.

RESULTS

Changes in the principal's tasks

For all five scales there were significant overall differences between the means of the respondents for the past, present and future. For the present, responses indicated that school planning and policy making, managing the external environment, managing non-human resources, managing teacher resources, and staff selection and development were much more important than in the past, and would become even more important in the future. Respondents thought that the principal would assume responsibility for more tasks across all five scales.

The greatest change in responsibility relates to staff selection and development and the least change to managing non-human resources. The major changes pertaining to staff selection and development were increased responsibility for selecting teaching staff, arranging staff development courses and providing references for promotional purposes. There was only one significant interaction. The primary school respondents considered that managing non-human resources would be most important in their future role. Their secondary counterparts were less emphatic.

Changes in the principal's role

This set of items relates to changes in three roles of principals identified by factor analysis. There were differences across time for all three roles: leader role, developmental and innovative role, and managing human resources role. There were few moderators to this overall conclusion. Males considered the role of leader to be less important than did females. Primary school respondents, particularly females, considered the developmental and innovative role more important than did their secondary counterparts. The greatest role change for principals was the expectation that they would become important leaders, the second highest expected change saw them as innovators and developers, and ranked third was their role as managers of human resources. It should be noted that the change in all three roles ranged from 'moderately important' in the past to 'very important' in the future.

Outcomes and reactions to school devolution and decentralization

There were no significant differences on these scales between males and females, across ages, or between primary and secondary school respondents. Teachers, as distinct from those in positions of administrative responsibility (deputy principals and principals) were more positive towards decentralization. Teachers, particularly, saw a need for more specialized staff in devolved school systems. There were no significant interactions. There was a tendency for more females than males to consider that schools should be more responsible for staffing, for younger rather than older staff to consider that schools should be more responsible for appraisal, and for secondary rather than primary respondents to consider that schools should be more competitive.

The second subset included the number of years teaching (more than/less than 15 years), and whether or not respondents had received training in educational management. There was only one significant difference. Those who had more teaching experience were more positive about devolution and decentralization. The typical response pattern agreed that restructuring will lead to better schools, displayed a positive commitment to decentralization and devolution, believed that the principal's role would become more managerial, and saw a need for more specialized staff. There was strong agreement that devolution and decentralization would bring additional responsibilities for teachers and principals, and school staff would experience greater difficulty in complying with ministerial policy. There was disagreement with the following propositions: that schools should be responsible for staff selection, that there should be more competition between schools, and that principals and teachers should be locally selected.

Changes in patterns of power, influence and responsibility

Data were generated on the changes expected in the patterns of power and influence among various groups as a consequence of the restructuring policy. The respondents saw no change in the power and influence of the Education Department, employers and business community, and students. However, they did envisage that increasing power and influence would go to the following, in descending order: school-based decision-making groups, parents, principals, teachers, and district superintendents.

Respondents were also asked if the school or the Education Department should be responsible for various tasks, or if they should be shared between the school and the department. The following table presents the preferred pattern for each of the tasks:

Table 1 *Percentage of respondents relating to responsibilities for various tasks*

	School	ED	Shared
Teacher appraisal	34	3	63
Staffing/transfer	7	32	61
Accountability	27	8	65
Initiating innovation	36	3	60
Financial management	41	5	54
Community development	68	2	30
Curriculum research	2	64	35
Monitoring standards	4	36	60
Principal appraisal/promotion	2	33	66
Staff selection	14	23	63
Standard setting	17	22	60
Professional development of teachers	8	20	72
Pastoral care of students	80	0	20

Respondents thought most tasks are best considered on a shared basis. However, a majority thought schools should be responsible for community development and pastoral care of students, while the department should be responsible more for curriculum research.

DISCUSSION

A number of findings emerge from this study of the reactions to decentralization and devolution of principals and teachers in the sample of primary and secondary schools in WA. Both teachers and principals expect all roles and tasks of principals to grow in importance in the future. Not one role or task was expected to diminish in importance. This supports the views of Handy (1985) and Duignan (1990), who have argued that decentralization would, for the first time, force principals to draw on a multitude of roles and skills, particularly in the personnel field, but also in technical skills such as budgeting and goal setting. The expectation that principals will undertake tasks as diverse as planning and policy making, management of the external environment, staff selection and management of teachers; and roles as varied as leader, innovator and developer of human resources, presents them with major challenges. Many principals feel a sense of isolation, having to interact with inexperienced councils and other groups for the first time (Chapman, 1987). The multiplicity of roles, all of growing importance, and the increasing number of groups with whom the principal is expected to interact are likely to cause role ambiguity and confusion over responsibilities and accountabilities (Chapman, 1987; White, 1989). Moreover, adaptation to new roles and interactions demands new technical and human competencies. This raises the question as to whether it is possible, let alone prudent, for principals to assume such an exacting multiplicity of roles, even though this study found it would be expected of them.

In meeting this challenge principals will need to focus on priorities, delegate and share responsibilities, encourage team management and facilitate collaborative decision making. There is confirmatory evidence that each of these is beneficial and places emphasis on principals' cognitive processes, and their ability as problem solvers and personnel managers (Leithwood *et al.*, 1994). More participatory decision making may improve enthusiasm and morale, particularly of younger staff (Chapman, 1987), while there is the likelihood that self-esteem, morale and efficiency of all staff may be enhanced (White, 1989). Greater empowerment of teachers was claimed by Caldwell and Spinks (1988) and Hunter (1989) to increase their professionalism. There is also evidence that collaborative decision making, consultation and participation have positive effects on principals' effectiveness (Chapman, 1986).

Respondents expected the greatest change in principals' roles and tasks to be in the performance of a staff selection and development function at the school level. This finding needs to be set within the particular context of WA, which traditionally has had a highly centralized education system, with the centre controlling all personnel selection functions. Moreover, the handing over of responsibility for staff selection to the school level has yet to happen. A further finding of note was that females more than males emphasized the importance of the principal's leadership role. This may reflect the growing awareness and expectations of women towards positions of school leadership, given that women have traditionally been, and remain, under-represented at principal level.

In the sample schools both teachers and principals held positive views of, and were committed to, decentralization, with general agreement that decentralization would lead to better schools. Respondents thought schools would become more effective in achieving their aims and more efficient in using their resources. These positive reactions are confirmed by the findings of Beare (1983), Brown (1990) and White (1989) who, in their interviews with principals, found a recognition of benefits such as flexibility in decision making, in allocation of resources, and in greater discretion over curriculum development at the school site, allowing more appropriate curricula for the needs of all students. This support for decentralization is surprising, however, at least in the WA setting, given the level of industrial dispute and general hostility towards policy makers and central office bureaucrats that the major systemwide change has generated, both before and particularly since this study was conducted. It suggests that teachers and principals are able to distinguish the desirability and potential of policy aims from the politics and strategy of policy adoption and implementation.

Principals and teachers sampled were not wholly committed to all aspects of the decentralization policy. Teachers showed slightly higher commitment to the policy than did principals and deputy principals. Both teachers and principals envisaged a diversification of their roles and an increase in their workloads. Teachers, particularly, saw a need for more specialized teaching and support staff. Presumably they were aware of the increased non-teaching roles that they would be expected to fulfil under school-based management, and the possibility of greater opportunities for allocating resources to teaching and classrooms.

There were also some interesting differences in the results. The majority of respondents thought selection of teachers and principals should not take place at school level, but females more than males considered that schools should be more responsible for staffing. It was interesting that this sample of WA teachers did not support one of the central tenets of decentralization and a perceived benefit of the policy elsewhere, namely, the opportunity for each school to select the staff it wants. This negative reaction may be due to the traditional problems of staffing schools in remote country areas in WA, sometimes hundreds of kilometres from the nearest settlement. The Education Department has always allocated teachers to ensure a supply. School-site staff selection appears to be a central feature of future devolution, and the problem of teacher recruitment in the outback may best be tackled by using incentive payments and other devices. Another possible reason for teacher opposition to local appointments is the inexperience of personnel, and the absence of structures and processes, as well as a culture, to support local staff selection.

If schools are to be held accountable for their future performance it seems reasonable for them to select their staff.

Another finding was that younger rather than older teachers considered that the school, and the principal in particular, should assume responsibility for teacher appraisal. It is probable that older teachers are more resistant to change, feel less secure in a climate of teacher evaluation, and are closer in age to the principal. The majority of respondents were not in favour of greater school competition for students, but secondary principals and teachers were more supportive of the idea than their primary counterparts. In general, the notion of competition runs counter to the culture of government schools, although this is not true of the private system. School competition for students is more likely at the secondary stage, but this does not necessarily explain why secondary teachers are more receptive to the notion of competition. It is difficult to suggest a clear explanation as to why secondary rather than primary staff appear more supportive of competition. One possibility is that secondary teachers are expected to sort children into categories in order to prepare them for the adult world of work and employment, where competition is ubiquitous.

Principals and teachers in the sample allocated all of the major participants in education into one of two groups according to whether or not they expected the participants' power and influence to change with devolution. The respondents believed that the Education Department, employers, business community, and students would experience no change in their power and influence. On the other hand, the greatest increase of power and influence would accrue to school decision-making groups, parents, principals, teachers and district superintendents, in that order. It is not surprising that respondents predicted the largest increase in power and influence for school decision-making groups and parents. Government schools in WA have never had formally constituted school councils or governing bodies, although they have had parent and teacher associations for fund-raising purposes. There have been few channels through which parents have been able collectively to contribute to the government of schools. This led Smart (1988) to comment that a century of non-involvement in educational policy has left a legacy of community and parental inexperience and feelings of inadequacy. Research evidence suggests that high levels of parental involvement in schools is a correlate of school effectiveness (Renihan and Renihan, 1984; Mortimore et al., 1988). Improved communication, teacher-parent support and closer home-school links are some of the benefits.

Principals constitute another group expected to increase their power and influence. This is not surprising given that the responsibilities devolved from the centre will presumably refocus on the principal. Decentralization of responsibility is not, however, the same as devolution of power and influence. Moreover, the creation of school decision-making groups, and the greater involvement of parents and teachers in school management, signify that other participants, besides principals, will experience increased power. As long as it is not seen as a 'zero-sum' concept, it is possible to conceive of an increase in power for principals, parents, school council and others. If it is viewed as a fixed amount, however, then increasing the power of one group necessarily means reducing that of another. This led White (1989) to suggest that devolution may lead to a power struggle between principals, teachers, parents and students. There is evidence from Victoria, Australia, that principals are ambivalent as to whether devolution has increased or decreased their power for this reason (Chapman, 1986).

Most of the respondents thought that the Education Department's power and influence would remain unchanged, even in a policy context of devolution. It is perhaps indicative of the extent to which the centre has monopolized power for so long that principals and teachers could not countenance a diminution in power at the centre, despite the existence of a policy which manifestly set out to transfer responsibilities and power from the centre to schools. This suggests that respondents were distinguishing responsibility from power in the transfer process. Employers and the business community were not expected to increase their power and influence. This response may be surprising to educators further afield, in England and Wales, for example, where curriculum reforms and new sources of funding for schools have brought the business community directly into education. WA still awaits this experience.

The majority of respondents preferred most responsibilities to be shared between the Education Department and school in the new decentralized system, but there is a danger of equivocal division of responsibilities if the details of the sharing arrangement are insufficiently clear. There was a preference for the Education Department alone to undertake curriculum research. This is a disappointing response since school-based curriculum initiatives are normally seen as a key part of decentralization (Knight, 1984). The benefits of school staff developing curricula and selecting instructional materials and methods within a central framework to suit the particular needs of students seem to have been a low priority for principals and teachers. It should be remembered, however, that this survey was undertaken at the inception of the decentralization policy in WA, when teachers' sole experience was of a centre-periphery curriculum development model.

CONCLUSION

The generally uniform responses across principal and teacher groups to the changes associated with system restructuring is a key finding of this study. With few exceptions, there was a consistency of viewpoints. Moreover, the generally positive reactions of both principals and teachers to devolution and decentralization were contrary to the negative comments often attributed to principals and teachers in informal interviews and discussions, and by the mass media. Subsequent studies need to trace the changing patterns of reactions, feelings and behaviours evoked in principals and teachers responsible for implementing the policy at the school level as the policy unfolds.

Chapter 8

Restructuring and teachers' understandings of their curriculum work: a case study

INTRODUCTION

This chapter reports on the findings of a case study that sought to determine what primary school teachers in a school district in the Perth Metropolitan Area of Western Australia (WA) thought about the impact of restructuring on their work. An interpretative methodology was deemed appropriate. The results of the study revealed that teachers generally viewed and assessed the restructuring process in terms of the influence that they perceived it to be having on their curriculum work.

THE CASE STUDY

The setting

In keeping with the goal of probing a range of perspectives, four schools were selected on the grounds that between them they represented a wide variety of social and ethnic groups in WA. A purposive sampling approach in selecting teachers within the schools for interview further enhanced the possibility of accessing as wide a variety of perspectives as possible. As a result of this approach, each group interviewed consisted of a teacher with three years' or less experience, a teacher with between three and ten years' experience, and a teacher with ten years or more experience. Five groups were interviewed in each school, resulting in a total sample of 60 teachers – 30 female and 30 male.

Methods of investigation

The semi-structured, in-depth interview was chosen as the most suitable method for gathering data. The researcher spoke with groups of teachers rather than individuals. In this type of interview, people talk about their lives and experiences in free-flowing, open-ended discussions. Each interview lasted, on average, one hour. Before beginning the interviews, the researcher explained the purpose of the research, reassured the teachers regarding confidentiality, and stressed the teachers' right to remove themselves from the interview process at any time.

An *aide mémoire* was developed to guide the interviews. However, neither the wording nor the ordering of the questions was fixed. In keeping with Goetz and Le Compte's (1982, p.41) suggestion that 'the optimum guard against threats to internal reliability... may be the presence of multiple researchers', the principal researcher conducted each set of interviews jointly with a research assistant so that later, during analysis, they could discuss and agree on the meaning of what was observed. The researchers encouraged the teachers to describe experiences in detail and pressed for clarification of their words. When a particular individual was inclined to dominate the discussion, the researchers directed the discussion to include other members of the group. The researchers also asked cross-check questions in order to elicit an honest account of how the teachers saw themselves and their experiences.

The conversations were tape recorded with the teachers' consent and transcribed. The teachers were asked to check the transcribed interviews and request modifications until they accepted the transcriptions as accurate representations. The transcribed material was then analysed following the procedures outlined by Marton (1988), with utterances in the transcripts categorized on the basis of their similarities and then in terms of their variance. The teachers were allowed to check the analyses and make modifications until the analyses were acceptable. This approach accommodated the variety of voices on specific aspects of the issues within the major categories and subcategories generated.

Analysis

The analysis indicated that, in general, teachers viewed restructuring largely in terms of its perceived influence on their curriculum work. Furthermore, teachers evaluated particular developments associated with restructuring using at least three related frames:

1. the extent to which what is happening does not take into consideration the complexity of the teacher's curriculum role;

2. the extent to which what is happening is not empowering teachers to engage in curriculum decision making; and
3. the extent to which what is happening is affecting teachers' classroom work.

Each of these frames is considered in turn.

Teachers' views on the extent to which the restructuring process does not take into consideration the complexity of their curriculum role

The findings of the study concurred with those of Robertson and Soucek (1991): that although the teachers do not look at the past through 'rose-coloured glasses' and although they dislike much about the old, bureaucratic Department of Education, with its rigid rules and inflexible resourcing and staffing policies, they miss the days of certainty in which 'you knew exactly where everything fitted into the scheme of things' and 'you had a sense of direction'. One of the teachers in the study expressed it as follows: 'We had a very good system with good back up'.

Not all teachers, however, opposed change. In fact, the majority favoured it but believed that it was taking place too quickly. In the words of one teacher: 'People used to say schools were too slow to adapt to the changing needs of society. Now we are going like lightning, but the trouble is no one seems to know where we are going'. One of the interview groups explored this matter further. It pointed out that while the literature from the Education Department and from the schools' administration teams continually stresses that what is taking place is a process that should not and need not be rushed, this is not reflected in practice: 'We have to rush around all of the time. The administration teams are rushing us so much that we cannot possibly give our best to the children'. Others put it differently, stating that they are left with the impression that they are 'running around in circles'. Furthermore, the vast majority of the teachers were adamant that the call for change did not originate from within the teaching force and that those promoting restructuring had no appreciation of the complexity of the teacher's role. The teachers viewed restructuring as a process imposed on them: 'As usual, nobody sought the voice of the classroom teacher'. Accordingly, one is inclined to conclude that those responsible for restructuring appeared to pay little attention to that aspect of the 'change' literature demonstrating that teachers who have no input into an innovation will have no sense of ownership of it and, consequently, little commitment to it (Pratt, 1980, p.428).

However, the situation is not just one of an absence of motivation but also of the presence of a certain degree of antagonism. In this respect, teachers were particularly incensed by much of what they saw as the dehumanizing language of restructuring emanating from the Education Department. In particular, they objected to being referred to as 'human resources' and viewed such a notion as not being consistent with the concept of 'caring' that they see as central to the definition of their role.

The importance that teachers in the study attached to the caring aspect of their work was evident in a number of ways. For example, it constituted the major criterion by which they evaluated the Education Department's present stress on competencies and outcome statements. One teacher put it as follows:

'You can't pay a teacher to be a more caring person. The intangibles are what matter, not just immediate competencies. What about 20 years down the track? What type of person will the pupil be? What about the emotional and social side of development?'

Another, focusing on the large number of competencies being outlined by the Education Department, said:

'The danger with outcome statements is that they will turn into a curriculum; that is what is going to be evaluated, this is what you have to teach, this is what is going to be used to make you accountable. To achieve such a massive number you will work the kids harder, and so pastoral care goes out the window. My early reaction when I saw all those sheets is that you can kiss goodbye to pastoral care as you have so much else to do. You won't have time to sit down and establish personal relationships with the kids.'

This comment echoes Feiman-Nemser and Floden's (1986, p.517) point regarding developments in the United States, where many teachers want student learning to be based on individual needs, yet their schools expect them to improve on standardized test scores, cover prescribed curricula at a prescribed pace, and maintain an orderly classroom.

Certainly not all of the teachers in this study were opposed to schools adopting outcome statements to guide the planning of work. As many of them saw the situation, 'outcome statements have the advantage of giving a distinct focus to your work'. Rather, the teachers seemed to be developing the notion that outcome statements are useful so long as they do not, as one teacher said, 'become the engine that drives your curriculum work, with teachers having to teach towards them solely, since they might become the measure of teacher performance'.

Central to what the majority of the teachers in the study said in this respect is the belief that those promoting restructuring appear not to appreciate that the number and diversity of students in any one classroom create a wide variety of individual and group needs. The only group that showed little concern in this regard were four special education teachers. As one explained, their position is understandable because they have 'much smaller classes, are under much less stress, and work at a leisurely pace'.

The teacher population as a whole expressed great annoyance at what they perceived to be a lack of consideration by those promoting restructuring of the fact that many students do not come to school willingly and that teachers cannot count on students being motivated to learn. In particular, they believed there was no appreciation of the 'caring' role that teachers need to adopt in order to deal with this situation by, as one teacher put it, 'meeting children where they are at'. The importance of the caring perspective was particularly evident in the language the teachers used when describing their pupils. They spoke regularly of 'my kids' and 'my class', and about the fact that although they were not pleased about much that they are now requested to do, they will do it because they 'are committed and love the children'. In fact, their references to their pupils' parents as 'my parents' and 'my mums' indicate that they see themselves almost as part of extended families.

The great importance the teachers placed on their caring role became evident in a number of other ways. They alluded regularly to situations in which they were unable to concentrate fully during school-based decision-making meetings because they were 'too worried about the poor kid who is sick or the poor kid who is being beaten up or the poor kid who is being abused'. More than one teacher apologized for arriving late for the research interview because of the need to attend to a sick or worried child during a break. They also spoke of the importance of their dealing, as appropriate, with a pupil's grief and emotional trauma as a result of the break-up of the parents' marriage. As one teacher summarized it, 'you are the sounding board for the kids. They often have no one else to speak to, so you listen and you get emotionally involved'.

Teachers, then, are largely operating within the Australian education culture fostered in the 1970s, with its concern for equity and community. That decade, as Angus (1992, p.389) has written, fostered a sense that, by educating the 'whole child', schools would 'develop individuals to their full potential while socializing them into communities of enquirers who would contribute to a just society'. The Schools Commission and the Curriculum Development Centre (CDC), both established by the federal government, actively promoted the notion of school-based curriculum decision making and supported it through research and funding. The CDC, in its commitment to a social reconstruction philosophy, also advocated the introduction of a core curriculum (Marsh and Stafford, 1988, p.55). These developments, with their concern for the personal growth of the individual and for social justice, arguably won the support of teachers, since the associated social reconstructionist and child-centred philosophies articulated by policy makers were consistent with the 'caring' language teachers use when speaking about their work.

The teachers in the study reported here also clearly articulated a justification for continuing to place great importance on their caring role in the 1990s. They asserted that as Australian society is characterized more and more by situations in which children's personal relationships outside the classroom are unsatisfactory, the need increases for students to have a good relationship with their teacher. One teacher put it as follows: 'The academic stuff is still important for the kids, but it's almost a lesser priority than their feeling good about themselves and all those attitudinal things'. This understanding suggests the teachers are ascribing an *in loco parentis* role to themselves. The important thing, as they saw it, is for the children to have available an adult with whom they can maintain a good relationship. Teachers see themselves as being that adult, as desiring such a role for themselves, and as being best placed to fulfil that role:

> 'You know what's important. You teach those kids every single day. You know how they tick. The administration team and the school psychologists see the kids in a once-off situation. We teach 32 kids, see them interacting with other kids, see a totally different side of them. We need to meet those kids' needs over and above the curriculum, especially when it comes to social issues, values issues, health issues, because we see that every single day.'

In the teachers' view, the breakdown of the family unit is the most serious issue that should concern teachers and, to deal with it, the teacher must be 'psychologist, nurse, mum and dad, social worker, and teacher'. However, they felt that those promoting restructuring in WA do not place a high value on this issue, and that it will be even less valued in the future. That prediction would appear to anticipate lowered morale among the teachers.

The teachers also perceived that 'the real reasons' for restructuring reveal a lack of respect for the complexity of teaching. The most frequently cited of these 'real reasons' was that the Education Department believed that financial savings would occur if schools were given budget responsibilities. However, teachers were not annoyed so much by this cost-saving agenda as by their perception that those promoting devolution were not open about this matter and sought to legitimize their actions by arguing that their proposals would lead to a better education for the pupils in the State.

The teachers' other perceived 'real reason' for restructuring is more cynical in nature, that is, that the politicians in power are promoting change so they can be seen to be politically active, or, as one teacher said, 'seen to be doing something'. Once again, the issue for teachers was that this move has curriculum implications. Their attitude is captured very well in Sutherland's (1985) observation, made in relation to developments in the United Kingdom, that:

> 'fashions succeed each other and teachers – theirs not to reason why – are expected to change content and methods of their work in due conformity, following and climbing on each successive band-wagon as it comes along.' (p.226)

The teachers echoed these sentiments in a number of ways. One alluded to going through a stage when she and her peers were told not to stress the learning of multiplication tables, only to be told the opposite later on, with no consultation on either occasion. Another noted:

> 'It all comes from outside the system. Someone has done a study or a brainstorm. Take handwriting, for example. We are now on the third method we have had to use. Similarly, parents point out that pupils cannot spell and say, "it's the bloody teachers fault". But why is it? We were discouraged from doing it.'

Finally, a small number of teachers argued that 'the motivation is to put the school in the front line'. What they are referring to corresponds with Weiler's (1989) argument with regard to developments in Norway, that because the policy domain is so heavily contested, the Education Department is anxious to 'diffuse the sources of conflict, and to provide additional layers of insulation between them and the rest of the system', while at the same time keeping ultimate control over the content of the curriculum. The teachers in this study expressed the notion in such terms as: 'before, if you had a problem you got in touch with the Education Department; now you are in the firing line', and 'before, the Education Department was there to soften the blow. Now you are on your own while the department dictates the parameters within which you can work'.

Teachers' views on the extent to which they are not being empowered to engage in curriculum decision making

Nearly all of the teachers agreed that their respective school administration teams had gone to great lengths to establish communication networks within the school community. The following is a typical comment: 'There are a lot more committees in the schools. We have committees for everything – textbooks, language, curriculum, maths, budget, science, social studies, music and so on'. However, they also made clear that their experience confirmed that achieving consensus and promoting action are much more complex than simply having many committees. They offered a number of examples to substantiate this proposition: 'There is no mechanism for the textbook committee to liaise with everyone else'; 'You may not be on the same committee next year even if you want to be'; 'New staff come each year, and you go back over the same ground with them, explaining the rules of the committee structures and trying to win their support for them'.

The majority of the teachers favoured the concept of collegial decision making. This view was aptly summarized in the words of one teacher: 'We feel it is right we should have a say in the running of the school and in curriculum decision making'. What is frustrating for them, however, is their perception that, although they are encouraged by the principals of their schools to participate in decision making, the principals can and do occasionally disregard their decisions: 'You get a consensus and it is not overruled immediately, but later down the track a totally opposite decision comes across when something totally different is put in place'.

Some teachers were annoyed by what they viewed as the contrived nature of the decision-making process. They spoke of the process being 'a big cover-up to make it look like we are all having a say'. Three of the teachers in the study stated that they had decided not to participate in any more decision-making meetings because of their 'fabricated nature'. They argued that decisions were predetermined and that they would take no part in such a 'questionable process'. An equally small group argued that the latter perception was correct and pointed to inconsistencies in the process: 'Nobody asks what our ideas are for professional development. We are told what will take place'. Unlike their more radical peers, however, they stated that they were not prepared to make 'an equally principled stand', because involvement in meetings was necessary for their professional advancement and 'to ensure that we are not penalized by being transferred to teach at unfavourable locations'.

Most teachers perceived that the principals regularly disregarded their decisions because devolution of decision making had not been underpinned by legislation delineating with whom authority lies: 'There must be boundaries to what the principal and we can do, but we do not know what the boundaries are'. Their explanation of this situation was that 'because the management bears the final responsibility, it has the final say'. One teacher voiced the understanding as follows: 'We don't know how far we can go in decision making, but if you get down to the legal nitty gritty, I still think you cannot go past the principal'. Another stated, 'Now there is this freedom, but your freedoms are not down in black and white, so the principal has the final say'.

One outcome of this situation, as perceived by the teachers, is that no fundamental changes take place. They described the decisions that have been made as ones concerned with such 'trivial issues as what kind of flowers to have around the school, where they are to go, how the grounds should be laid out, and what kind of choir uniforms we should have'. Of most concern to the teachers, however, is that the curriculum decision-making process in which they are being asked to participate is bounded by 'system imperatives'. As one teacher expressed it, 'We can only make decisions as to what we value within the syllabus. The school encourages adapting the existing curriculum, not developing a new one'. Here one is reminded of Tye's (1992) comment regarding restructuring in the United States:

> 'If people at the school level are to be empowered to make decisions about curricula of their schools, they will also have to be empowered to purchase and develop their own instructional materials and even their own standardized tests. This means that statewide curriculum frameworks, statewide adoption of textbooks and statewide testing must become things of the past.' (p.13)

Teachers in this study clearly recognized that schools are not free to design their own generic curriculum from 'first principles'. Rather, schools must make decisions within the broad frameworks provided by the Education Department, and teachers who wish to develop alternative programmes must justify their intention to the department's regional office, which may grant approval. As teachers understand it, this process detracts greatly from the credibility of the argument that decision making is being devolved to empower teachers.

A number of other factors exacerbate teacher frustration on this matter. One of these is, as a teacher said, the fact that 'so much is being plonked in the curriculum and nothing is being taken out'. An example chosen to demonstrate this conclusion was the desire 'to mainstream more and more disabled students with no drop in the overall teacher-pupil ratio and no increase in financial or human support'. Some argued that they were beginning to think that they were not as good as they used to be, that they were losing confidence in their own ability, 'trying to cope with everything and cope with the class'. One example to illustrate this concern noted:

'You may have a timetable worked out for your class for the year, then other things outside of your control cause you to change it, such as an all-school decision to emphasize a particular subject. You had no say in that, but you must fit it in.'

Ball (1993) has made a similar observation about recent developments in England and Wales. He argues that school development planning has replaced teacher planning with head teacher and/or governor planning. He goes on to say:

'Teacher participation relates not to involvement for its own sake, as a collegial, professional or democratic concern, but for the purposes of the management of motivation. The school development plan signifies and celebrates the exclusion and subjection of the teacher... they are the objects of management relegated to the status of human resources.' (p.117)

However, a small but significant cohort of teachers in the study reported that their feelings of incompetence had forced them to rethink their professional standing, and an emerging outcome is a reaffirmation of their professional competence: 'I go into the classroom and teach in the manner I consider best. That, now, is when I feel empowered'. Another stated: 'I go into the classroom and engage in passive resistance. They never come and check up on you. They don't check to see if you understand or can do what they tell you to do. That's when I am finally empowered'.

Teachers' views on the extent to which the restructuring process is affecting their classroom work

Teachers in the study tended to view as a distraction any activity that did not contribute directly to the tasks of classroom teaching. This finding corresponds with those of Campbell and Neill (1990), who studied British primary school teachers. When asked how they would use more time if it were available, the British teachers said they would dedicate it almost exclusively to within-class contact. Such a response is, of course, to be lauded, given the well-documented relationship between effective teaching and the proportion of time teachers actually spend engaging pupils with learning tasks (Anderson, 1990; Myers, 1990). It is also understandable given the long-established fact that classrooms are complicated and busy settings, serving a variety of purposes and incorporating a variety of processes and events, including managing groups, dealing with individual needs, maintaining records, promoting learning, and formally and informally evaluating student abilities (Jackson, 1968).

In this respect, what was particularly annoying to teachers in this study was the number of decision-making meetings held during class time, which required that the class teachers be replaced by 'relief' teachers. The class teachers believed that these interruptions affected the quality of pupil learning. Further, they believed that the meetings have not resulted in any significant contribution to what they described as their 'real job' of teaching pupils.

Many of the teachers believed that the time and energy devoted to the meetings could be invested more profitably in classroom teaching. As one teacher said, 'We were trained as teachers – we are here for the kids – the more time we put into meetings and so on, the less time there is for the kids'. They also asserted that administrative tasks took up much time. Teachers on school-subject committees had to sort out budgets, find out about equipment and order it, and fill out invoices. For one teacher, these new demands mean that he now does 'things which work rather than experiment with teaching ideas'. Another teacher commented about the situation as follows: 'Because I haven't time… I haven't time to think through this whiz-bang science experiment, so I decide to do magnets, as I've mastered that and can get through it without much preparation'.

This situation is troubling if one accepts Shulman's (1985) contention that quality teaching requires teachers to work at elucidating subject-matter knowledge in new ways, recognize and partition it and clothe it in activities, emotions, metaphors, exercises, examples and demonstrations. Such activities require what is clearly becoming less and less available: significant amounts of teacher time. Teachers in this study regularly closed their statements with the comment, 'We appear to have less and less time to prepare our lessons properly and give our best to the children'.

Another consequence of the new demands on teachers is that they no longer have free time during lunch breaks; time that was once occasionally used to do extra work with pupils. A similar situation in England and Wales has alarmed the teachers' unions, which have judged it 'unhealthy' that teachers must devote so much of their spare time to their jobs (Assistant Masters and Mistresses Association, 1991). Accordingly, what now seems to be happening internationally is a proliferation of the circumstance recognized by Wise (1979) nearly 15 years ago in the United States, namely, a tremendous increase in the administrative work of teachers that constrains them and takes time away from teaching.

Teachers' time, then, is a commodity in short supply. Time was of major concern to the teachers in this study. Not only were they required to perform more non-teaching duties during school hours, but they also found they had to do many things after school that once were done by the deputy principals. The consequence of this circumstance was simple: teachers believed they could not give their best to the children because 'everyone is stressed out'. One teacher put it as follows:

> 'If teachers aren't in a state to teach kids properly and effectively because they are worn out, it's all a waste of time. You start to get tired. You cannot think and be as creative as you would like to be because of all the new pressures and things to be done.'

Another observed:

> 'I'm so far behind in my marking it's awful. That's the biggest thing for me that suffers. I'm marking more on the spot than ever before, not just over the shoulder marking, but "let's stop ten minutes before the end and mark it together as a class". Otherwise I'd have that plus maths, science and project work at night.'

This frustration was accentuated when teachers requested help on matters related to the curriculum. Restructuring meant that educational support was either not available or was available in such a superficial way as to be considered of little value.

The teachers also had a gloomy view of what the future holds because of what they saw as a trend towards ignoring issues of equity. In particular, they were concerned that further devolutionary thrusts would result in compulsory payment of fees by parents and that, consequently, some schools would be truly disadvantaged. One teacher aptly summarized this concern: 'Better schools will employ better teachers. They will be able to afford their higher salary demands, while the lower socio-economic schools will only employ beginning teachers'.

Teachers also feared the possibility that each school will be given a capitation grant based on the number of pupils in the school and that this grant will be insufficient for the purchase of a wide variety of equipment, such as reading materials and computer software, for pupil enrichment. The wealthier areas, unlike the poorer areas, will be able to provide these extras through local fund-raising, but the system will not ensure that resources are shared among different social groups. The teachers spoke passionately and repeatedly about this concern, suggesting that relegating the issue of equality of educational opportunity to a place of secondary importance would betray what the nation represents.

This view was exemplified by one teacher who nodded enthusiastically after listening to a colleague argue that there was a great danger current restructuring could lead to severe disadvantages for children in lower socio-economic groups, even at the primary school level. The supportive teacher then responded, 'Good on you, that's very Australian of you'. Perhaps unwittingly, what is beginning to take place is a form of professional development akin to that proposed by Smith and Zantiotis (1988), that is, a 'transformation' that focuses on the purposes of schooling and the self-social empowerment of individuals and groups. If this development truly is occurring, it is ironic, given that those promoting restructuring are concerned with telling teachers what their outcomes must be and how they must strive to meet national priorities and enhance international competitiveness (Smyth, 1991).

Teachers in this study offered useful suggestions for improvement of schools. They made clear that, while they favour change, the speed of the process has been too rapid and should be slowed down. They welcome programmes aimed at developing their decision-making skills, along with programmes, resources and time to improve their administrative skills. Another important debate raised during the interviews is whether primary school teachers should be subject specialists who move from class to class like their high school colleagues.

CONCLUSION

Some Australian educators contend that restructuring is having a major negative impact on teachers, but very little evidence is available to contest or to substantiate such claims. The research described in this chapter revealed that teachers viewed and assessed the restructuring process largely in terms of its perceived influence on their curriculum work. They saw this influence as being very negative. Furthermore, they could not foresee improvement in the future, and in some respects they anticipated a deteriorating situation. The overall result is low teacher morale.

Findings of this case study also suggest that those responsible for restructuring took little cognizance of that aspect of the 'change' literature demonstrating that teachers who have no input into an innovation will have no sense of ownership of it and, consequently, little commitment to it. Even those who would like to proceed on the assumption that education is a business cannot afford to ignore findings such as those of Peters and Waterman (1982) and Ouchi (1981). These findings show that, although the most successful companies are characterized by a lean head office with power and authority devolved to subsidiaries in the field, further improvements in production and success depend on the existence of human relations among management and the workforce that are based on trust, subtlety and intimacy. In other words, productivity will improve if people feel they have more control over their destiny, are trusted while having the opportunities to contribute to decision making and, as a consequence, feel better about themselves. The case study described in this chapter indicates that this situation has not been reached. Hopefully, this and other insights offer a challenge for deliberation and reflection, and a source of power to promote professional growth and to lead to transformative action.

Chapter 9

School development planning: teachers' perspectives

INTRODUCTION

As part of the restructuring movement, school communities in many parts of the world are increasingly engaging in school development planning. This process includes determining the school's purpose, setting performance indicators, developing a management information system, setting priorities (including resource allocation), compiling the school's strategic plan, evaluating performance and rendering accountability for performance (Hargreaves and Hopkins, 1991). Teachers are instrumental in the creation and successful implementation of this process and its emergent plans. Accordingly, it is appropriate that studies should be undertaken of teachers' perceptions of school development planning in a variety of settings.

Educational policy makers, in introducing school development planning, have made many assumptions about its benefits, few of which are grounded in empirical research (Hargreaves and Hopkins, 1994). These assumptions relate principally to improving the quality of education while at the same time enhancing public accountability. Similarly, while there is literature which prescribes how best to go about the process of school development planning, relatively little published work, apart from that of Hargreaves and Hopkins (1994), exists which describes the actual experiences of stakeholders at the school level in implementing such processes.

In Western Australia (WA) school development planning was not formally adopted as part of government educational policy until 1990. It is not therefore surprising that few studies have been reported to date on its effects within schools. Nevertheless, a body of research literature needs to be generated on the experiences associated with the process. The study reported in this chapter is one contribution towards such literature.

THE BACKGROUND

Educational restructuring and trends towards devolution have been accompanied by the introduction of new concepts and paradigms of school management. Among these is the notion of the 'self-managing school'. The underlying philosophy is grounded in a planning process, the basis of which involves participative goal setting by the stakeholders who form the school community. These stakeholders include parents, community representatives, teachers, students, and the school administration, all of whom work collaboratively in guiding the development of the school. It is assumed that school effectiveness is enhanced by such a process, in contrast to the direct assignment of goals by a central authority (Dimmock, 1995a). Likewise, it is argued that more efficient resource allocation is likely if resources are directed according to each school's priorities, as determined by its collectively set school development plan.

In sum, advocates of school development planning argue that school efficiency and effectiveness are enhanced by each school developing its own plan, taking into account system guidelines and priorities, and having local community involvement in the process, rather than basing its work on plans drawn up by bureaucrats at system level who are removed from local conditions (Dimmock, 1995a). By directing the collective energies of the school on to matters of local relevance, within the broad priorities set at the system level, it is believed that the quality of educational outcomes can be enhanced. In addition, it is argued that by utilizing a collaborative process in school decision making accountability is increased to the local community.

This model of school governance and management is now evolving in many countries and across all Australian states. In June 1989, for example, the Department of School Education in New South Wales launched its official policy in *School Renewal: A Strategy to Revitalise Schools Within the NSW Education System* (Scott, 1989). The strategy was based on the assumption that principals and their staff know best how to respond to the educational needs of their students. Each school, within the framework of overall department goals, should 'develop its own renewal plan as the basis for its ongoing programme of school improvement and professional development' (Scott, 1989).

Many of the foregoing factors and trends characterizing the push towards devolution, school-based management and more general restructuring are also reflected in developments in WA over the past decade. A 'Functional Review' conducted by the Education Department resulted in the publication of the document, *Better Schools in Western Australia: A Programme for Improvement* (Western Australian Education Department, 1987). This report set out the plan for a more devolved, school-based management system. The overall intention was to maximize effectiveness as indicated by the achievement of goals and the economic use of resources. These changes focused on the establishment of school-based decision-making groups (school councils), performance monitoring and school development planning (Dimmock, 1990). It was argued that by decentralizing responsibility to schools and increasing their accountability to local school communities, the 'self-determining' schools could maximize their effectiveness and efficiency.

In 1990 an industrial agreement between the Education Department and the State School Teachers' Union of Western Australia launched the implementation of the devolution process in the state over a period of five years. A detailed plan which focused on the monitoring and reporting of school performance, school-based decision-making groups and school development planning was agreed for the first phase of its implementation. However, while the policy background to this restructuring of the government school system (Bamblett, 1992; Goddard, 1992), the underlying policy assumptions (Dimmock, 1990) and the impact of policy changes on school principals and teachers (Dimmock and Hattie, 1994) have all attracted research, little if any attention has been aimed at clarifying stakeholders' perceptions of the school development planning process. The following case study was developed as one contribution to meeting that need.

THE CASE STUDY

Methodology

This study aimed at understanding teachers' perceptions of the school development planning process at one school. A state government secondary school in the Perth Metropolitan area was selected and given the pseudonym Western Senior High School (SHS). The School provides education for 1000 students from Year 8 to Year 12 level. It has a staff of 70 teachers organized into traditional subject departments, a principal and two deputy principals. A wide variety of relevant records was sought, including school documents, Education Department statements and circulars, and participants' personal records. Semi-structured in-depth interviews were also used (Taylor and Bogdan, 1984, p.76; Minichiello *et al.*, 1990, p.101). In all, 30 teachers were interviewed. Their classroom experience ranged from new graduates on their first school appointment to teachers who had been teaching for over 20 years. They had been at the school for varying periods of time, ranging from six months to 12 years, and they taught in a variety of disciplines. They included some with special responsibilities and roles such as head of department, curriculum coordinator, extension programme coordinator, year level coordinator, and classroom teacher. The school principal and two parents – the chairperson of the school council and vice-president of the school's parents and citizens' committee (P & C) – were also interviewed.

Twelve interviews in total were conducted, each lasting approximately 40 minutes to one hour. The interviews with teachers were conducted mostly in groups of three or four. The parents was interviewed individually at their respective private residences. General principles for conducting interviews as specified by Spradley (1979) and Measor (1985, pp.63–73) were followed and a variety of data obtained.

During the interview, an *aide mémoire* (Burgess, 1985) was used as an interview guide. It consisted of the following three sets of questions:

First set of questions
What do you understand by school development planning?
What are the stages through which the school development planning process has evolved in the school?
How have you been personally involved in this process?
Can you identify the stages through which the school has moved in developing the school plan?
Could you describe the stages through which the process has passed?

Second set of questions
Who were the participants at each stage?
What role have you played in the school development planning process?
What was the significance of this role?
Do you feel you have made a contribution to the development of the plan?
What groups in the school community can you identify as having been involved in the planning process?
What roles did these groups play in developing the plan?

Third set of questions
What are the perceptions of those who have participated in the process?
Would you have liked to have been more or less involved? Elaborate.
Do you feel the process has been valuable or otherwise? Explain.
What, from your perceptions, are the problems with the school development planning process in this school?
What aspects of the process in this school are pleasing to you? Elaborate.
What factors facilitated this process?
What changes, if any, would you make to the planning process if you had the opportunity?
What do you feel are the strengths of the process in which you have been involved?

The wording and ordering of the questions were not fixed to allow for flexibility. The *aide mémoire* was used to jog the memory of the interviewer about the major issues. As themes arose in the interview they were developed in a lengthy 'conversation piece, not an inquisition' (Simons, 1982, p.37). Probes were used so as to encourage the interviewees to describe their experiences in detail and constantly to seek clarification of their words. Cross-check questions were asked to elicit an honest account of how the interviewees saw themselves and their experiences. The interviews were tape recorded and the transcribed data were analysed using both open and axial coding (Strauss and Corbin, 1990).

Analysis

The school development planning process undertaken by Western SHS moved through two stages, very similar to those prescribed by the WA Education Department. This is not a coincidence and can be attributed to the school principal's ability and willingness to follow government intentions with regard to implementation.

The first stage involved the establishment of the school decision-making group, to facilitate participation not only of the school's senior administrators, but also of teachers, parents and, where possible, students. The second stage involved the school development plan. This took place along the lines of the model proposed by the WA Education Department. As each part was worked through, 'school development days' were held to explain to all staff what the purpose and process were and to gain their input. This involved dividing staff into small groups, which later reported back to the whole assembly. The outcomes from staff involvement served to inform the school council in its deliberations. Subcommittees of the school council were then formed and reported to meetings of the full school council.

Concurrently, the deliberations of the school council were displayed on prominent staff room notice boards and blank spaces were left for staff to write comments and suggest alterations. Minutes of school council meetings were also displayed. Regular newsletters were sent to all parents informing them of progress and displaying the draft statement, and they were invited to comment. In addition, teachers had the opportunity to propose ideas regarding the school's mission statement at regular whole staff meetings. These were then collated and forwarded to school council members to inform discussion.

The process described above was repeated as each part of the school development plan was worked through. The first part involved the development of a school purpose statement and performance indicators (PIs), and the second the development of a management information system (MIS) for each of the priority areas set by the school council. Subsequently, the school became involved in setting new priorities for the next planning period, developing strategies to achieve them and allocating available resources.

With the basic school development plan now in place at Western SHS, the process began to operate through its cycles. The determination of an MIS for each priority area is an ongoing process, as each planning cycle generates new priorities and places existing ones on a maintenance basis. At Western SHS, after the completion of one 12-month planning cycle, numeracy joined literacy and post-compulsory curriculum initiatives as priorities. This resulted in the mathematics department staff being made responsible for preparing draft student outcome criteria and recommending appropriate data to collect in regard to numeracy. The process has also been repeated for the new priority area of health education, while science and social studies have been added for the current planning period. The school development planning process will continue each year, some priorities being added and others deleted, for each cycle, as collectively decided by the school community. Over a period of time all the PIs determined in the second step of the school development planning model will be developed with an MIS and appropriate strategies decided upon for their attainment.

Teachers' perception of the school development planning process

Three major interrelated propositions with regard to the teachers' perceptions of the school development planning process emerged from the analysis of the data:

1. The teachers in the school perceived the introduction of school development planning as part of a wider agenda by the government to devolve as much responsibility for administration as possible to schools, and particularly to teachers, with the primary aim being to reduce the cost of the central administration.
2. They perceived that the WA Education Department intends to continue its strong control over the direction and operation of schools and, as a consequence, they feel restrained from engaging enthusiastically in school development planning.
3. The teachers perceived that school development planning, in forcing them to adopt a 'whole school' approach to defining problems and to developing strategies to solve them may, in the long term rather than immediately, have some positive outcomes at the classroom level.

Each of these propositions, with their various qualifications and nuances, will now be considered in turn.

Proposition 1
This proposition can be viewed, in interactionist terms (Blackledge and Hunt, 1991, p.234) as expressing the 'significance' which the teachers attach to school development planning. In other words, it captures the broad perspective within which they locate and view the process. This, in turn, can be summarized as being the nature of the teachers' awareness of the relationship between educational restructuring initiatives and the general political agenda within WA.

It is clear that the teachers are cynical about the motives behind the promotion of such restructuring initiatives as school development planning. In particular, they speak of 'the real reason' being the Education Department's belief that financial savings will occur if schools are given 'one-line' budgets to be allocated on the basis of their individual school development plans. One of their reasons for this is that the Education Department increasingly uses the language of the world of management and efficiency. Other reasons are also forthcoming. Some speak of the department wishing to delegate as much responsibility as possible to each school so that blame can be reapportioned to the schools if things go wrong.

According to others, another motive behind the promotion of school development planning (and again one about which they are cynical) is that politicians are promoting change so that they can be seen to be politically active, thus courting popularity with parents. Again, however, the teachers present no arguments to substantiate this contention. What they do argue is that there is an unwillingness to devolve major curriculum decision making from the system to the school level, and that this detracts greatly from the credibility of the argument that decision making is being devolved to empower teachers.

In general, what the teachers are alluding to is that schools are not free to design their own generic curriculum from 'first principles'. Rather, schools must make decisions within the broad frameworks provided by the Education Department and teachers who wish to develop alternative programmes, or 'fine-tune' programmes to meet particular students' needs within the general framework, must justify their intentions to the department, which may grant approval. At the same time it needs to be stressed that, in highlighting what they perceive to be an inconsistency in the Education Department's position on devolution, the teachers are not arguing that they would welcome greater freedom in the areas of curriculum design and development. In fact, they seem quite content to work within the present curriculum parameters.

Proposition 2

There are at least three major reasons for this second proposition: the nature of the process, the sources of information to which the teachers were introduced while they were engaged in the process, and the personality of the principal. With regard to the process itself, the teachers were particularly sensitive about what they perceived as an attempt to engage them in 'one correct way' of going about school development planning. It would not, however, be fair to interpret this as a rejection of the model to which they were exposed, but as their being uncomfortable with what one teacher referred to as 'the lock step' way in which they were required to operationalize it.

In essence, what the teachers seemed to be saying is that the school development planning they experienced is 'a useful thing to think with'. It constitutes, as one teacher said, 'a helpful starting point for discussing how one should go about the process in one's own particular situation'. However, they felt that there was no encouragement of flexibility, creativity or adaptability to tailor a procedure to the unique context of their school.

Teachers went on to point out that the need for creativity became very clear in the failure to enthuse parents about the process. This they attributed partly to the requirement that, while the school council is responsible for formulating the objectives and priorities of the school in the school development planning process, it is the principal who must be responsible for formulating the strategies (after consultation with the staff) for their achievement. This situation exists as a requirement of the Education Act 1929, Education Amendment Regulations (No 3) 1991. The consequence is a perception among some staff that parents are not seen as full and equal partners in the process. This adds to the teachers' belief that 'the authorities are not sincere about this business of empowerment of all stakeholders through restructuring'.

There is also a general perception among the teachers that the parents share the latter sentiment and that, as a result, they are not enthusiastic about engaging in school development planning. This enables teachers to understand why, as one of them stated, 'both the P & C and the school council at Western SHS have had difficulty in obtaining parent representation which could impact upon the decision-making process'. He went on: 'I'm very disappointed in parent involvement. Here, with 900 students, you can only get 15–20 parents involved'. In a similar vein, the deputy principal observed: 'You virtually have to beg parents to come along and be on the school council'. Another teacher remarked: 'It's the same people on the school council as on the P & C. The parents only come to those things that directly influence their children'. A parent, the chairperson of the school council and vice-president of the P & C, seemed to concur with the views expressed by the staff when he commented:

> 'I was concerned as a parent that things could go in the wrong direction as far as the future education of my children. So I went along [became a parent representative] on the basis of wanting to look after my interests. There wasn't any altruism at all.'

Another parent member of the school council added insight into parent attitudes towards participation when she remarked that 'it is difficult to get parent participation in anything, so anyone who remotely shows interest gets a job'. Concern also exists amongst the teachers regarding the ability of parents to influence the school council in decision making. According to the Education Department, a formally constituted school decision-making group consists of equal numbers of parents and staff representatives. At Western SHS the school council consists of four elected members of the P & C, four elected members of the staff, the school principal (who is an ex-officio member), and two elected members of the student council. Although the school council consists of equal numbers of parents and teachers, the teaching staff, in reality, dominate any voting. The principal remarked:

'It is sort of equal, except for who turns up at the meetings. The teaching staff are very responsible and make sure they attend all the time. The parents are usually missing one or two. So we always have the numbers.'

Consequently, the teachers in the school perceive that parents do not wish to be involved in the planning of school activities as a whole, but are primarily interested in the welfare of their own children's education. An overall consequence seems to be that the teachers, in turn, are not inclined to engage enthusiastically in the school development planning process.

The second major reason for the teachers' perceptions that the WA Education Department intends to continue its strong control over the direction and operation of schools is the nature of documentation provided to them while they were engaged in the process. In particular, when it came to deciding the purpose statements, they were, as one teacher phrased it, 'bombarded with summaries of, and extracts from, the Finn (Australian Education Council, 1991), Carmichael (1992) and Mayer (Mayer Committee, 1992) reports'. This series of federal government-initiated reports, in keeping with the national agenda of harnessing education for the demands of industry and the production of versatile, multiskilled workers, stressed the need to develop generic and specific work-related competencies in all students. Within the school development planning process at Western SHS the principal regularly informed the teachers that these, along with the Education Department's mission statement, 'are the statements which are the parameters within which we operate'. The outcome, as one teacher sees it, is that, 'there is nothing very Western SHS about our goals'.

The consequence for the teachers is that they perceive the school development plan as really having been imposed on the school by national goals, by the Education Department and by divisions within the department. In particular, they are sceptical as to how representative are the school's purpose and PIs of their own school community views. In short, teachers believe they are assigned objectives by the central administration. A number of comments reflect this attitude, including: 'I think the school purpose statement comes pretty naturally out of the general WA philosophy of education. From school to school, you won't find much variation in their mission statements'.

The third major reason for the teachers' perceptions on this issue can be traced to the personality of C, the principal, and the manner in which she goes about school development planning. She is certainly highly regarded by staff at Western SHS and by bureaucrats within the Education Department, particularly because of her very efficient organizational skills. As a staff member, currently on the school council, and a member of the school development planning committee, put it: 'C is very good at setting agendas, making it clear what is to be done and following it through'. Ironically, however, it is that same characteristic which has generated a climate bordering on what Hargreaves (1993, p.109) calls 'contrived collegiality', a situation which occurs when:

'spontaneous forms of teacher collaboration are discouraged or usurped by administrators who capture it, contain it and contrive it through compulsory cooperation, required collaborative planning, stage-managed mission statements, labyrinthine procedures of school development planning, and processes of collaboration to implement non-negotiable programs and curricula whose viability and practicality are not open to discussion'.

This climate is restraining the staff members from engaging enthusiastically in school development planning. In particular, there is a reluctance to take ownership of the process because of the requirement that they must engage in it whether they wish to or not. The matter is not helped by C's perception of her role as implementing efficiently, without question, government policy within her school. Indeed, it is accentuated by her willingness to express the view that she promotes school development planning because, as she regularly puts it, 'we are employed by the government and if that's their policy, and these are things we need to do, then that's fine by me.'

Proposition 3
In general, the teachers spoke of school development planning and other innovations associated with restructuring as distractions which do not directly contribute to the tasks of classroom teaching. This, it would appear, stems from a belief that the time and energy devoted to the planning process and associated meetings could be invested more profitably in classroom teaching. Nevertheless, despite this view, and after taking into account the generally cynical nature of their rationalizing of the reasons underpinning school development planning and their negative attitude towards the manner in which the process has taken place at their school, there is also a feeling that perhaps there might, after all, be something worthwhile in the general concept of school development planning.

At the time of this study the teaching staff at Western SHS had come to perceive the school development planning process as a structured system which had the potential to facilitate decision making. Teachers admitted that engagement in the process creates the necessity to examine performance and take appropriate action. One teacher commented that the process 'forces you to examine strategies to overcome identified problems. Changes have occurred after the process has been followed'.

The committee system through which much of this functions was certainly not without its frustrations. More than one teacher remarked: 'You can't do a thing in this school without a committee'. Nevertheless, many seemed to think that the process had potential to promote worthwhile dialogue. As one teacher stated, 'plans have certainly been taken to the whole staff and spoken about. They have been discussed very broadly throughout the school'. The existence of a formal and structured system of decision making at Western SHS has also acted as a means of focusing school community attention on to identification of problem areas and how to address them. One teacher commented on this as follows: 'Everything which is happening in the school must have some link back to the plan'.

The development of a mind-set that school activity must be continually linked to the school development plan has created a new approach to problem identification and problem solving which previously did not exist to the same extent. This approach has involved a coordinated planning effort by the 'whole school'. In particular, it has necessitated a change in thinking at the subject-department level. An example of the change in such thinking can be seen in the setting of literacy and numeracy as priority areas for the school to pursue through its curriculum. This change has involved an acceptance by all teachers, regardless of their subject area, of responsibility for achieving the school objective. As noted by a head of department:

'Within a lot of departments the teachers thought that, traditionally, literacy is something they do in English, and numeracy is done in mathematics. They thought of their subject area as a separate compartment, and didn't think of education as a broad continuum. But now, literacy and numeracy have really been brought to the fore, and we are thinking about these priorities and applying them to our classroom even though they were not normally our responsibility.'

In a similar vein, the deputy principal stated:

'The setting of definite priorities has made teachers feel better about tasks, for example, the use of consistent formats, such as column graphs in both maths and science. Also, the use of across-school agreements like the "literacy plan" which involves all teachers using the same kind of referencing, the same formula for letter layout, and so on.'

Generally, it would seem that these 'across-department' strategies have been received positively by teaching staff and school administrators alike.

Some of the specific aspects of the school development planning process have also been identified as containing ideas which the teachers feel are worthwhile. More than one teacher spoke of the PIs bringing a 'greater focus and awareness to areas of need, both at the school level and the department or school subject-area level'. Also, in relation to the structure of PIs, it was argued that 'this new focus on student outcomes is a most important change in thinking'.

The development of strategies to attain priorities was also met enthusiastically by some members. The special education teacher perhaps best represents these staff in the exclamation:

'Strategic planning has been a huge plus. The programmes are now different. They're tailored to the students' needs. The basic student outcomes are so generic, you can interpret them as you choose for your group.'

The condition which requires that for resources to be allocated to carry out different strategies for achieving priorities, the staff must demonstrate that the activity is clearly connected to an objective of the school development plan has also been favourably received. In particular, it is seen as being a fairer way of proceeding than previously. One staff member commented that 'in the past the person who shouted the loudest got the dollars. Now the priorities in the school development plan determine the money allocation'.

It certainly seems that the resources under the control of the school are now being allocated in accordance with the school development plan priorities. This is illustrated in the case of the curriculum priority area of post-compulsory education, where a teacher noted:

'Had we not had a focus upon post-compulsory education within the school development plan, we would not have set up a careers centre. The post-compulsory area was determined as a priority, and funds were forthcoming.'

Another staff member expressed his delight that, 'a new vocational programme will be introduced next year because of the focus upon post-compulsory education'.

CONCLUSION

School development planning, like so many other restructuring policies, has been formulated, adopted and implemented by the WA Education Department, using a top-down strategy. Teachers, as elsewhere, have been marginalized in the development of this, as in other aspects of policy, yet they invariably constitute the key agents of implementation. It would be fortuitous, therefore, if the rationale for, and intended benefits from, school development planning, as conceived by the Education Department, were perceived and received by teachers in the same light.

School development planning is seen by the Education Department as a key plank in its policy portfolio. In brief, it constitutes one of the major mechanisms through which the department is enabled, first, to redistribute administrative responsibility and power; second, to create a wider, more dispersed pattern of involvement in school management, governance and accountability; and third, to encourage schools to improve the quality of school management and leadership, teaching and student outcomes.

From the teachers' perspective, school development planning looks some-what different, and this chapter underlines the importance of understanding how teachers value a particular change and its impact upon their work. The teachers clearly expressed the view that what is going on is an attempt by the department to hive off some of its work to the school, thereby saving money.

In short, they see it as an administrative cost-cutting exercise. Some teachers also believe it is an attempt to pass to schools responsibility for functions which the department finds too hard or too politically embarrassing to handle.

In many cases during the analysis of the data it occurred to us that the teachers were unable to substantiate, elaborate or underpin their perceptions with coherent arguments. In other words, the bases of many perceptions held by them seem to be either emotive, non-rational or influenced by pre-existing views on contextual matters. This did not, however, make them any less influential. In particular, they displayed an element of caution and cynicism towards the department's support for school development planning. While engagement in the process constituted a potentially large additional burden of work for them, it was not simply the distracting effect they thought this would have on their teaching duties that was of concern. Central to their perception of the whole process was their belief that the department intended to continue its strong control over the direction and operation of their school. This, in turn, gave rise to a sense of manipulation and a consequent feeling of reluctance to engage enthusiastically in the process.

Further, although the school effectiveness literature endorses close collaboration between teachers, parents and school administrators in decision making, there may be negative consequences which are too important to ignore. Teachers in the study perceived a lack of parental interest in participating in school development planning and questioned the ability of parents to make a useful contribution. In this respect, the notion of 'contrived collegiality' is appropriate to the teachers' perception. However, an equally held perception of school development planning among the teachers was that in forcing them to adopt whole-school approaches to problems and strategies there might, in the long term, be some gains at the classroom level in the quality of teaching and learning.

Ultimately, the justification for studies such as are presented in this chapter is that teachers play a crucial role in the implementation of any school innovation. In formulating, adopting and implementing policies, therefore, it is prudent to take cognizance of teachers' perceptions of the status quo and the changes mooted, in order to refine the substance of the policy and build in allowance for the implementers' point of view. While policy makers continue to ignore teachers' perceptions of policy changes, both in the early stages of development and subsequent stages of implementation and maintenance, it is tempting to conclude that school reforms will continue to meet with only partial success.

Chapter 10

School-site professionals and parents

INTRODUCTION

In 1987, the Western Australian Education Department (1987) established a plan for restructuring schools and devolving administrative authority and responsibilities to the school and to parents. Among the major vehicles it identified for achieving these goals were school-based decision-making groups and school development planning (Dimmock, 1990). The recommendation that parents be involved in school decision-making groups for the management of schools, and in school development planning, marked a great change. This recommendation was elaborated on in three documents published by the WA Education Department: *School Development Plans – Policy and Guidelines* (Education Department, 1989); *School Decision Making Groups* (Education Department, 1990); and *School Financial Planning and Accountability* (Education Department, 1991). The participatory principles contained in these documents were formalized in what the Australian Education Council (1991, p.89) termed a 'landmark industrial agreement' between the Education Department and the State School Teachers' Union of Western Australia. At the same time, the union made it clear that there was a limit to the extent to which it was prepared to cooperate when it succeeded in stalling the Education Department's proposals to introduce parental control over staffing in public schools. The opposition was on the grounds that such control could lead to an erosion of the professional autonomy of teachers. Presently, however, teachers remain concerned that proposals of this nature are still on the Education Department's agenda, and their concern is not without foundation; in May 1994 the minister of education refused to rule out parental control over staffing.

To a great extent, then, contemporary restructuring of the educational system in WA has as its focus increasing the involvement of parents in school decision making. However, whether or not such involvement will be successful depends to a great extent on the attitudes of teachers. Accordingly, WA teachers' perceptions of parental involvement in school decision making is one of the major questions arising out of current restructuring. It is also the central question underpinning the research which led to the following case study.

THE STUDY

The setting

Constraints of time, finance and accessibility dictated that the case was located in the Perth Metropolitan area. Within this area a school district considered to have the potential to yield a wide variety of perspectives was identified. Four primary schools were selected within the district. These included a school in a predominantly middle-class area, a school in an educational priority area, a school from an area of mixed social class and a school with a multicultural student population. A purposive sampling approach was then adopted in the selection of teachers within the schools for interview in order to access as wide a variety of perspectives as possible (Merriam, 1988).

Methods of investigation

The semi-structured in-depth interview was considered to be the most suitable method of data gathering (Taylor and Bogdan, 1984). Interviews were conducted with groups of teachers. This type of interview brings together groups of people to talk about their lives and experiences in free-flowing, open-ended discussions and enables the researcher to interpret their views. Before commencing the interviews, the purpose of the research was explained to the teachers and the importance the researcher placed on maintaining confidentiality was stressed, as was the right of the teachers to remove themselves from the interview process at any time. In conducting the interviews, general principles as outlined by Measor (1985, pp.63–73) were followed. An *aide mémoire* consisting of the following sets of questions was developed around the central research question, but neither the wording nor the ordering of the questions was fixed.

a) The report *Better Schools in Western Australia* recommended major changes in parental involvement in schools. What is your understanding of the changes that were proposed in relation to parental involvement? Is there any particular aspect of *Better Schools* about which you feel strongly?
b) Do you think parents should be involved in schools?
c) What sort of involvement should they have?
d) What about parental involvement in school management? At the moment, do parents have any involvement in school administration? Who gets favoured in resolutions? Are parents involved in deciding school policy and direction? How do you feel about this? Is there ever any conflict? Are you ever involved?

Are parents involved in any way in deciding the structure of the school day, the school term, and the school year? How do you feel about this?

At the moment, do parents have any involvement in curriculum decision making in the school? How do you feel about this? Is there ever any conflict?

Are they ever involved in deciding the aims and objectives of the school?

Are they involved in any way in deciding what subjects you teach?

Are they involved in any way in deciding what content within subjects can be taught?

Are they involved in any way in deciding how you teach? Do they ever come into your classroom?
e) Given all that we have just spoken about, what form do you think parental involvement is going to take in the future? What do you think parental involvement in schools should be in the future?

As themes arose, they were pursued with the teachers. Probes were used to encourage them to describe experiences in detail and to constantly press for clarification of their words. Also, cross-check questions were asked in order to elicit an honest account of how they saw themselves and their experiences. The conversations were tape recorded with the teachers' consent and were then transcribed. The transcribed interviews were 'checked back' with the teachers for modification until they became acceptable accounts of their positions. The material was then analysed following the procedures outlined by Marton (1988, p.155), with utterances in the transcripts being 'brought together into categories on the basis of their similarities and categories being differentiated from one another in terms of their differences'.

Analysis

Analysis of the interview data revealed three major themes concerning teachers' perceptions of parental involvement in school decision making. First, the teachers in the study perceived that, currently, central policy makers are promoting parental involvement in school decision making without being cognizant of its possible negative impact on teachers. Second, there is a perception among teachers that parents' concerns are beginning to receive greater acknowledgement at the school level than teachers' concerns. Finally, parental involvement in school decision making is having an impact on teachers' perceptions of their curriculum decision-making role. Each of these themes will now be considered in turn.

Teachers' perceptions that central policy makers are promoting parental involvement in schools without being aware of its possible negative impact on teachers

The teachers in the study perceived that state-level educators at the present time are attaching greater significance to parents' concerns than to teachers' concerns. They are suspicious that the reform agenda regarding parental involvement in education has been driven by forces which are not of an educational nature, which are beyond their control, and which do not recognize the central role teachers play in education. Consequently, they revealed that they are beginning to feel a sense of powerlessness regarding the course which education events are taking in WA.

One teacher's comments typify the nature of teachers' reactions to the perceived exclusion of their profession from state education: 'It's not a joke any more. A new Education Department head gets the job and makes changes, a new education minister does the same, and teachers suffer. It's not easy'. The same teacher went on to suggest that 'the education hierarchy has little real understanding of the teaching and learning processes in schools' and thus, 'is not aware of the impact of their reforms upon teachers'.

Teachers remarked that often they only hear of changes when they are leaked to the media or when the State School Teachers' Union somehow finds out about them. They were especially resentful of what they saw as a secretive process which resulted in the production of the *Better Schools in Western Australia* report (Education Department, 1987) and of the suddenness of its implementation. One teacher, referring specifically to the impact state-level education politics has upon school-level decision making, suggested that teachers currently feel they are being gradually and deliberately distanced from school decision-making procedures. A related perception of many of the teachers was that both teachers and parents have not been given enough time and opportunity to adapt to their new relationship, and also that there has been too much change over too little time. One teacher referred in particular to the advent of school development plans and the involvement of teachers in associated committees, and claimed that not enough is known about the impact of those changes on teachers, students and schools in general. Kirk (1988) concurs with this viewpoint. He suggests that 'in recent years, as new demands have been placed on them, teachers have felt themselves under pressure to change, even when they did not accept the case for change, or its direction' (p.19). He concluded that it is understandable that in such circumstances teachers should assume an attitude of defensiveness about future innovations which inevitably complicate their task and require more from them.

Teachers also, while adopting a mainly conciliatory tone towards reforms aimed at greater parental involvement, tended to view it in the context of it being just another point in a long series of state-initiated changes and of policy makers favouring parental involvement in decision making over teachers' concerns. In this, they echoed Kennedy's (1992) comments about the spate of educational restructuring throughout Australia in the last decade, his argument that too many reforms are being generated simultaneously and his belief that this may threaten the ideals which are behind those changes. The impact of continuous reforms, as they see it, is that teachers are becoming somewhat cynical and indifferent with regard to assessing the merits of each education reform.

On this matter, it is useful to consider Sizer's (1984) suggestion that a prolonged series of reforms in education systems leads to a deep and abiding cynicism towards new ideas on the part of teachers. Ideas and changes come and go, and the response of teachers is to 'dig in', resulting in their becoming resentful or apathetic. Accordingly, further reform in WA aimed at promoting greater parental involvement at this time runs the risk of alienating teachers who have already endured considerable change in a short space of time.

Another major concern of the teachers interviewed related to the possibility of developments taking place at the state level which would lead to parental control over staffing. One teacher was of the opinion that such a development would 'cripple' teachers; that they would rarely be able to speak out due to fear of parental reaction. Voicing similar sentiments, another teacher was apprehensive regarding the career paths of teachers if parents could hire and fire staff: 'What happens if they get rid of me because they don't like the way I teach, and I want to get another job? I won't have a chance'. He continued: 'Word gets around and the parents will think I'm no good because I was fired from a school'. Teachers were also concerned that parental involvement reforms have been introduced in WA without adequate support being given to teachers to harness such involvement in a professional manner. They made many references to a lack of useful support literature, poor implementation support, and poor information from the Education Department's central office, not just over this issue, but over a wide spectrum. Some were also concerned about the lack of clear guidelines regarding the specific role of parents and the consequences that this could have for the school. Noting the failure of the Education Department to adequately prepare either parents or teachers for the changes that were introduced, one teacher observed that parents and teachers are gradually defining their roles by experiencing a series of conflicts, through which each group is testing limits and creating boundaries.

Regarding considerations thus far, Morgan et al.'s (1993) research on the complexity of establishing decision-making roles within changing school systems is illuminating. They describe attempts by schools to achieve role clarification among teachers and parents, and note that, over time, a precise relationship has not emerged regarding the role of either, the result being continuous misunderstandings, confusion, and some personal ill-feeling. They conclude:

> 'The process of defining clear structures for close and productive parent-teacher interaction, whether through parent councils or other mechanisms, is something which might take considerable time, and quite possibly a number of models may have to be tried out and subsequently either rejected or modified.' (p.8)

In light of this proposition it may well be that, in the present study, the teachers' perceptions that the Education Department's implementation strategies are responsible for problems concerning role boundaries may be only a partial explanation of their lack of enthusiasm for parental involvement in school decision making. Atkin *et al.* (1988) observe that, internationally, there is almost nothing explicit in teacher contracts, education regulations or school-based policies that spell out the nature and extent of their duties toward parents and families. Clearly, parental involvement has generated issues of such complexity that current organizational structures and cultures in schools and in school systems are finding it difficult to cope with them.

Teachers' perceptions that parents' concerns receive greater acknowledgement at the school level than do teachers' concerns

Another of the major perceptions among the teachers in the study regarding parental involvement in schools is that parents' views are of greater concern to the principals than teachers' views. In particular, teachers suspect collusion between the principals and the most influential parents on the school councils. One teacher suggested that teachers favoured by the parents usually received special recognition from the school principal. Another argued that while teacher representation on the board prevented overt partnerships between the principal and the parents, there was an implicit structure of power sharing between the principal, a small group of vocal parents and favoured teachers on the board.

A significant number of teachers stated that, at times, principals try to accommodate parents' views at the expense of most of the teaching staff. They noted that when dealing with staff, principals frequently qualified decisions arrived at with the words: 'I'll put this to the board and see what they come up with'. Accordingly, the perception among some teachers was that their opinions and feelings received less recognition from their principal than did board decisions, and that decisions made in this context are arrived at from a political rather than an educational agenda. This perception may well represent the arrival at a stage in the process of implementing parental involvement which is evident elsewhere in the world. For example, Meadows (1990), considering developments in the United States, and Morgan *et al.* (1993), considering developments in Northern Ireland, reported similar perceptions among teachers.

At the same time, some teachers in the study appeared to appreciate the difficulty of attaining consensus among education participants. One of them spoke of the values competing for the principal's attention and suggested that a principal has to perform a balancing act between the parents and the staff in order to find common ground. However, she also noted in relation to her own principal that 'he thinks that the parents are the important ones here. It causes some friction, but I'm not sure what else is to be done'. Other teachers were even more cynical regarding the principal's deference to the school council. One remarked that the principal, knowing that changes in the future are highly likely, was preserving his good relationship among parents in preparation for future parental control of staffing.

The teachers also expressed some concern regarding the consequences for pupil learning in what they see as the principals' attachment of greater importance to parental concerns over teachers' concerns, particularly regarding the ability of parents to make informed educational decisions. One teacher, drawing on her own observations of the board's operation in her school, remarked that when parents were unsure of issues they tended to side with friends, those who they felt had status, the principal, or those who spoke persuasively. She further noted that parents often just seemed 'out of their depth'. Similar observations have been reported in schools elsewhere. Meadows (1990), for example, reporting on a case study in a Colorado school, observed that community members often followed the opinions of the principal or vocal teachers when involved in school decision making. A consequence of this was that key figures in school decision making tailored their agendas to cultivate parental support, resulting in the rapid emergence of micro-political issues and hostility among both staff and parents. This phenomenon is not recent. As far back as 1976, Elsey and Thomas found that parents generally did not have enough knowledge about the school as an organization to express any opinion on the matter. Consequently, parents were often easily influenced by other figures in the decision-making process.

The teachers interviewed in the present study, while identifying such concerns, also acknowledged that at present there is little firm evidence that parents have actually affected, or are able to affect, the school's teaching and learning to the extent that they fear might occur in the future. Rather, the major problem is that some personal antagonism has been created between the principal and some teachers and parents because of teachers' expressions of resentment that uninformed parents have a forum for airing their views. However, they did refer to certain incidents which had enabled them to form some strong opinions and make them aware of pitfalls. A conflict between teachers and parents in one school was cited by four teachers. The incident involved board pressure on the principal over the innovative and often unusual teaching methods of a particular staff member. Considerable hostility was generated between teacher and parents while the incident was progressing.

In the present study, some of the teachers perceived the reactions of parental decision makers to be irrational, emotive, and outside the intentions of school devolution. Morgan *et al.*'s (1993) research in Northern Ireland noted similar reactions on the part of teachers. They observed that in primary schools in particular 'teachers seem to be on the defensive. They are anxious that parents seem to be making inroads into areas which they see as their province' (p.50). Wolfendale's (1992) research in England also supports this observation, finding that 'teachers are wary of parent intrusion into what they regard as their domain' (p.11).

The teachers in the present study also voiced other reasons as to why it is wrong for the principal to be paying more attention to parents' views than to theirs. They argued that parents' social background in particular affected their ability to make sound and impartial decisions. One teacher remarked that the parents on the board of her school are mainly from well-off backgrounds, are educated and articulate, and seem to think that all children have the same opportunities as their own. She further observed that sometimes these parents seem to be out of touch with the school's social realities, citing examples where some parents wanted to set strict punishments for incorrect uniform, without taking into account the difficult home life that some students experience on a daily basis and the fact that they might not be able to afford the uniform.

This position corresponds with Pettit's (1981) concern as to whether school councils would ever be able to represent and equally involve in decision making 'disadvantaged groups such as migrants, the unskilled, unemployed and low income earners' (p.4). The teachers in the present study feel that they might be able to address this situation to some extent if the principals were to give as much attention to their advice as they perceive them giving to the influential parents on the school councils. However, they are not overly optimistic that such a scenario is likely. In this, they would seem to agree with Watt's (1989) contention that, if devolution is to continue along the path which has been adopted in most states in Australia, it is almost inevitable that social stratification will accompany that devolution.

Parental involvement

Parental involvement in school decision making is also having an impact on teachers' perceptions of their curriculum decision-making role. Most of this involvement at the classroom level involves, as envisaged by school decision-making groups, parents in the role of aides and technicians. While a fairly positive attitude towards such classroom involvement was evident among most of the teachers, this domain was also identified by them as providing the greatest potential for conflict between teachers and parents. In particular, it appears that complications arise due to the lack of definition of the role and position of parents who work in the classrooms with teachers.

Teachers cited many instances of conflict in the arena of parental involvement in the classroom, yet most of them qualified their comments by noting that most incidents were trivial or petty and that they often did not voice their concerns to the parents involved. A grade two teacher remarked that she observed many daily instances of parents moving into what she regarded as teacher areas and of parents assuming the roles of teachers:

> 'It happens all the time, when parents who happen to be in the class with me start to do things that I would prefer they didn't, like disciplining the kids, or threatening the kids that they would tell the teacher. It kind of puts me on the spot, where I'm forced to back up the parent, or where I have to sort of let the parent have my authority because you can't let the students see disagreement between me and the parents.'

Other teachers related similar incidents. Their main concerns generally focused on situations which had the potential to impact negatively on teacher authority.

Commenting on the impact of the system under which she worked, one teacher observed that most of the parents contribute markedly to the classroom environment, doing what is asked of them without complaint, and quite willing to follow the teacher's instructions. She did observe, however, that 'some parents can just be pests – they can interfere in lessons and try to throw their weight around'. The comment was made on other occasions that the success of parental involvement in the classroom depends heavily on the personal relationships that are cultivated between the parent and teacher. For the teachers, this usually involves making sure the parents are at ease in the classroom, ensuring they have worthwhile duties to perform, and recognizing that they have something special to offer.

The personal dimension was dwelt on by one teacher. He drew on observations of parental involvement in his own classroom in forming his opinions:

> 'Parents are a big help in my room – they take reading, maths, they monitor students on the computer, and they make decisions about where a child's at in checking homework, and sometimes they'll keep a child in at recess. That's all fine with me, because I trust their judgement. Sure they've mucked up and made mistakes, but I do as well, even now.'

Another teacher referred to the role of the school and the role of the home in a child's education, and suggested that both were inextricably bound together. On this basis, she suggested that there were contradictions in the attitudes of some teachers that parents should not become involved in classrooms or in anything to do with teaching. She maintained that this viewpoint, if it were to be applied in reverse, would suggest that teachers should have nothing to do with a child's out-of-school life, in terms of setting homework, research projects, school camps and sports. She concluded that it was her belief that more parental involvement in the classroom could only benefit teachers and students by more closely aligning the efforts of home and school.

Overall, most of the teachers had formed positive impressions of parental involvement in the life of the classroom. Where teachers had negative experiences when interacting with parents, they tended to attribute them to the idiosyncrasies of individual parents rather than to parents as a whole. In one case, five of the interviewed teachers referred to one troublesome parent who had progressed through a number of classes in tandem with her child. The teachers believed that the parent was involved in the classroom, and the school generally, in order to bestow favours on her own child and, as one teacher put it, 'push her own barrow'.

Noting the disillusionment that often accompanies such unpleasant experiences, two teachers remarked that they usually remained angry and resentful for a few weeks, but in the long term their more positive relationship with parents began to reassert itself. Another teacher, commenting on a similar issue, stated that 'it was funny because my worst experience at school involved a battle with a parent, but it was also another parent who did the most to encourage me again and get my spirits up'. She went on to argue that her job satisfaction and belief in her teaching ability was actually higher as a result of the incident. The presence of parents had made her ensure that the quality of her lesson preparation was consistently higher than it had been in schools where parents had not been involved, and the delivery of the lesson was given considerably more attention. She also made some effort to ensure that the parents in her classroom were provided for in the lesson plan, leading to a better organized classroom and more effective student learning. She noted that it was rewarding to discuss shared lessons with parents and talk about student behaviour and ways of approaching topics. As a consequence, the teacher believed that her professionalism and skill as a teacher had observably improved, leading to a greater sense of self-worth.

At the broader level, the teachers in the study were very conscious of the fact that the determination of the broad parameters of the curriculum is still the preserve of the Education Department. In particular, they were aware that *Better Schools in Western Australia* (Education Department, 1987) did not devolve curriculum decision-making power to the school level, nor did it envisage the involvement of parents in such decision making. However, this situation was not seen as problematic. One teacher put it very well:

'Sometimes parents wonder at the way things are taught. When they see new curriculum initiatives from the Education Department, they often are pretty interested, but I think they reckon that they don't know enough to come forward and ask, or that they'd seem stupid if they came and talked about it. So I think it'd take some big changes before parents are going to want a part of deciding these things like curriculum.'

Consequently, he concluded, parents have never pressured the school or teachers with regard to the issue.

In probing the matter further, two of the teachers suggested that most parents show little inclination for becoming involved in translating official curriculum guidelines into school programmes because they defer to teacher professionalism and are unsure of their own knowledge of the area. Parents generally, it was felt, seemed to be aware of the training and experience required to gain a sufficient understanding of curriculum issues in order to ensure an informed involvement. As one teacher put it:

> 'In my experience, the parents are usually quite interested in what their children are getting taught, what topics they are learning about. But, past that, they aren't really interested in anything like teaching methods. Parents usually say something like "I'll leave that part of it to you", or "you're the expert on that". They seem to want teachers to make decisions in curriculum because they know its importance, and they don't want to interfere. Their attitude seems to be that as long as we know what we're doing then it's all right.'

At the same time there was a small amount of conflict in each of the schools between parents and teachers over syllabus issues. Such issues were to do with controversial textbooks, including poetry texts given to grades six and seven, the level of specificity and explicitness of health education in the upper primary grades, disputes over grades given to particular students, and the capacity of the school to provide academic extension work for certain students.

Overall, however, it was rare for teachers to be queried about their teaching methods, the sequencing of curriculum content, the way teaching programmes were structured, or the manner of assessment used in the school. Teachers noted that parents were usually aware that teachers were not fully responsible for the curriculum their children received. This supports Atkin *et al.*'s (1988, p.55) contention that, as a general rule, parents appear willing to take a good deal on trust when dealing with curriculum and teaching matters.

CONCLUSION

The general context of this chapter is the increase in parental involvement in school decision making. In particular, it considered the findings of a case study aimed at accessing the perceptions of primary school teachers in a school district in the Perth Metropolitan Area in Western Australia with regard to parental involvement in school decision making. The data analysis revealed three major themes. First, the teachers perceived that, currently, central policy makers are promoting parental involvement in school decision making without being cognizant of its possible negative impact on teachers. Second, there is a perception among teachers that parents' concerns are beginning to receive greater acknowledgement at the school level than teacher's concerns. Finally, parental involvement in school decision making is having an impact on teachers' perceptions of their own curriculum decision-making role.

From a consideration of the first two themes, it appears that parental involvement in school decision making has served as one catalyst for arousing teacher dissatisfaction with various aspects of education policy making and decision making at the state level. In particular, teachers believe that both policy makers and school principals attach as much, if not more, importance to the potential role of parents in school decision making as they do to the role of teachers. What the third theme demonstrates is that teacher dissatisfaction is not directed at parental involvement. Rather, the perception is that the advantages for education that parental involvement might bring are overshadowed by the problems which that involvement highlights, namely, the lack of trust and goodwill between teachers on the one hand and policy makers and school principals on the other.

At the same time, teachers now recognize the permanency of parental involvement in the school. One teacher identified the influence of the teaching staff on her viewpoint, remarking that, in comparison to her previous school, she was surprised at the level of parental involvement at her present one. Evaluating her own feelings with regard to this, she observed: 'I didn't want parents making decisions I thought belonged to teachers, and I didn't want them in my class. I thought that they were just bored or busybodies. After a while I started thinking it was OK. Now I think parents have a lot to offer'.

It is useful here to consider Sultana's (1991) research on the potential for a reconstruction of teacher attitudes as a result of their own experiences and of their observations of others' experiences. He suggested that:

'Despite the general hegemonic nature of schools, when teachers were individually or collectively caught up in dynamic interaction with progressive social movement, then their ideological commitment departs from the conservative and moves closer to liberal and radical grounds.' (p.151)

On this matter, one teacher in the present study noted that previously he had given little attention to the question of parental involvement as long as parents didn't interfere with his teaching, but that once he accepted parents' help in his classroom he realized that it freed him to concentrate on teaching. It may be that what is happening is greater teacher recognition of parents' democratic rights and greater teacher understanding of the role parents play in a child's education.

Watt's (1977) observations (when parental involvement internationally was in its infancy) are helpful in providing a wider perspective on teachers' perceptions in this regard. He suggested that emerging teacher recognition of cooperation is both a product of, and a stage in, fundamental changes in the relationship between parents and schools. Drawing on his research in pre-school environments, he argued that this change has involved the development of different attitudes, relationships and ways of working, and challenges traditional concepts of professionalism and accountability in education.

For many of the teachers in the present study it seems that reconstruction is under way, yet is only at the initial stage of an incremental process. It is possible that the end result of such a process may be a wholesale transformation of the role of both parents and teachers in the school. However, if that is what policy makers and administrators desire, they need to develop a greater awareness of teachers' needs and opinions. As the teachers in the study indicated, it can no longer be taken for granted that they can, or will, absorb changes which create uncertainty and confusion without the result being a lower standard of teaching and, as a result, a lower standard of student learning.

PART FOUR

The concept of dilemmas

INTRODUCTION

Restructuring policies aimed at promoting school-based management, greater parental involvement in decision making, new conceptions of teaching and learning and increased accountability for performance and outcomes all depend for their success on the ability of principals, other school leaders and classroom teachers to respond positively to fast-changing school contexts. Expressed simply, changes integral to restructuring threaten traditional practices, roles and relationships within schools and between schools and their environments (Caldwell and Spinks, 1988; Leithwood, 1992; Murphy, 1993). There are sound reasons for supposing that the challenges presented to school-site professionals by restructuring are perceived as being far from easily managed. Also, both the policies *per se* and the strategies by which they are introduced are generally perceived by them as being problematic. Different elements of the same package of restructuring measures may be interpreted as inconsistent and some of the measures seen as ill conceived. Furthermore, the strategies used by central offices to implement policy at school level are often viewed by them as naive and misconceived, and for many whose earlier careers were forged under more centralized management systems, the changes ushered in under restructuring are unwelcome (Hallinger and Murphy, 1991). They now face decisions as to which roles, relationships and practices to retain, forge or discard. Nor are conditions necessarily appreciably easier for recently appointed school leaders who, with relatively little experience to call on, strive for effectiveness in fast-changing educational contexts.

The concept of dilemmas provides an appropriate frame for examining how certain aspects of this activity are impacting on school-site professionals' understandings of their work. Conceptualizing the work of school-site professionals in terms of dilemmas is both accurate and worthwhile. It is accurate because many confirm that they perceive much of their daily work lives in terms of seemingly unresolvable or difficult-to-handle situations. That is not to say that all events, situations or problems are cast as dilemmas. Some are more clear cut and surmountable. A focus on dilemmas is, however, worthwhile for a number of reasons. First, as Argyris and Schön (1978) note, we learn most about ourselves and others during crises and times of difficulty, when normal patterns of behaviour and response are no longer adequate. Dilemmas may constitute such occasions. Second, restructuring normally has school improvement as one of its aims. Dilemmas may be seen as potential obstructions to school improvement. Improving our understanding of the restructuring dilemmas experienced by school-site professionals and the ways in which such dilemmas are managed is therefore likely to enhance the prospect of school improvement. Third, a better understanding of how school-site professionals make sense of their roles in restructuring might be gained through the concept of dilemmas. This, in turn, could lead to improvement in the preparation and training of school-site professionals.

At the same time, while the totality and complexity of restructuring places a daunting range of tasks and responsibilities on school-site professionals, interest in applying the concept of dilemma through which to gain understanding of their conceptions of how it is impacting on their professional lives has only recently surfaced. The potential of dilemma analysis in this regard is reflected in the useful insights yielded by the application of the approach to teachers' curriculum work within a restructuring context in Queensland, Australia (O'Donoghue *et al.* 1993). This study showed that restructuring in Queensland provided a context which 'added to the complexity of teachers' work' (p.14). Teachers were 'compelled to redefine their professional lives', which had 'become characterized by a range of dilemmas' (p.15). These findings in relation to teachers' work lives within a context of restructuring might equally well apply to school leaders. Like Cuban (1994) and Maclagan and Snell (1992), Glatter (1994) recognizes the everyday nature of many moral dilemmas faced by managers. Such moral dilemmas may have little clarity or certainty. Quoting Handy (1994, p.83), he continues:

'Most of the dilemmas which we face in this time of confusion are not the straightforward ones of choosing between right and wrong, where compromise would, indeed, be weakness, but the much more complicated dilemmas of right and right.' (Glatter, 1994, p.2)

Taking Handy's argument further, it is suggested that most compromise is not about principles but about interests; in other words, it is as much political as moral. These moral-political choices are endemic to the contemporary school leader's role (Glatter, 1994). They manifest in choices principals find themselves making between the conflicting interests of parents as stakeholders and teachers as professionals, or between parents as consumers and participants, or between the three different perspectives of school effectiveness held by governments, parents and teachers.

In developing the concept of dilemmas further, we need to know more about the nature of dilemmas as perceived by school-site professionals. For example, to what degree are restructuring dilemmas values based? How important are organizational structures and institutional practices as sources of dilemmas in current restructuring? To what extent do dilemmas encountered by school-site professionals in restructuring reflect scarcity of resources? The next two chapters, which focus on principals' and teachers' dilemmas in Western Australia, point the direction which research into these areas might take.

Chapter 11

School principals' dilemmas in restructuring

INTRODUCTION

The following account of principals' dilemmas in a restructuring context is based on data collected from a group of 20 primary and secondary school principals in the government system in WA. These principals were invited to identify dilemmas as they were individually perceived in their context of restructuring. The principals were instructed that a dilemma was a situation which contained elements of the following – contradiction, conflict, inconsistency and paradox – in the ways in which it might be conceived and handled. Thus, in conceptualizing or solving one aspect of a difficult situation, another aspect is left unattended or made more problematic. There is, in economists' terms, a trade-off or opportunity cost.

Categorizing the dilemmas reported by principals revealed two kinds: those which are more general, aptly termed 'states of mind', and those which are more 'specific'. The former appear to equate more with personal and professional concerns. For example, dilemmas which force principals to be introspective and to question their motives and standpoints on issues may be considered personal. They might lead to principals reexamining their self-concept, attitudes and values. Dilemmas which are of a more professional nature, however, relate to principals' ways of seeing their work or conceptual frameworks they use to make sense of and give meaning to events happening in their work lives. Examples include how they view decision making, the job, teaching and learning, ways in which they conceptualize power and control, and the place of individuals and teams. 'Specific' dilemmas, on the other hand, tend to be more related to practical, operational and pragmatic issues and skills concerning structures, processes, resources and curriculum.

Analysis of the 'states of mind' (personal and professional) dilemmas reveals a generic theme focusing on the nature of leadership, including the leader's position, role functions, responsibilities and relationships, all within restructuring. The 'specific' (practical and operational skills) dilemmas of restructuring were sorted into the following sub-categories: the purposes and functions of schooling; structures and processes; human resources; curriculum, teaching and learning; and material resources. It was found that many dilemma situations could be expressed as points of tension between two, or occasionally three, counterpoised states of mind or perspectives, or between two or more specific restructuring issues, or between general states of mind and specific restructuring issues. The remainder of this chapter considers the nature of each of the two types of restructuring dilemmas.

THE NATURE OF RESTRUCTURING DILEMMAS

Leadership, role and position ('states of mind') dilemmas, of a personal and professional nature

A considerable body of evidence testifies that school leaders feel some tension between their roles as educational leaders and corporate managers (Duignan, 1990; Dimmock and Hattie, 1994). Many leaders feel these countervailing pulls of restructuring. On the one hand, the delegation of administrative responsibilities to schools brings financial and personnel functions; on the other, the increased expectations of achieving improved teaching, learning and student outcomes carry responsibilities of a different kind. For many school leaders this dilemma is about whether to focus on professional matters and attend to the technical core activities of the school, or concentrate on a growing administrative workload, a considerable amount of which is, at best, indirectly related to teaching, learning and the curriculum. In the minds of school leaders, the question underlying this dilemma is whether schools are conceived as business organizations, with the attendant values that image conjures, or whether they are a distinctly different type of organization, focused on a fundamentally different set of educational purposes and values. As one principal put it, 'Central office is turning us more and more into administrators while telling us they expect us to be instructional leaders'. This conflicting state of mind derives from asynchronous change taking place in restructuring between burgeoning administrative functions and school leaders' awareness of the importance of educational and instructional matters.

As the administrative and non-educational functions and expectations of their work grow, there is a tendency for many school leaders to neglect the professional and educational aspects. In performing the one set of functions, successful performance of the other is made more difficult. This dilemma reflects two different sets of norms or values, between which the school leader feels obliged to make some sort of reconciliation. In addition, the dichotomous way in which the two sets of values – education and business – are conceived has implications in the institutional domain, with each set generating its appropriate administrative structures, procedures and processes. The two paradigms may also have implications in the resource domain, with their different emphases and priorities for resource allocation.

Another dilemma for school leaders arises from tension between their position as heads of, so-called, self-managing schools, and their strategic position as line managers in the system chain of command from central office, through district office, into school and the school community. An expectation that the school leader will spearhead the drive to create semi-autonomous schools is growing at the same time as the leader is reminded that these schools remain part of a system and are subject to system policy frameworks and guidelines. Indeed, in many systems, decentralization is simultaneously accompanied by centralization, as evidenced by tighter policy frameworks and increased accountability to central offices. The resulting dilemma is aptly captured by the tension between the principal as leading professional on the one hand and as administrator-bureaucrat on the other. This tension has been evident for some 20 years (Hughes, 1976), but has been heightened by recent restructuring. The roles of leading professional and administrator-bureaucrat each has its respective sets of norms, expected behaviours and institutional practices.

A further dilemma for school leaders arises from the tensions between competing elements of leadership, management and administration. Regardless of how these terms are defined, school leaders experience difficulty in deciding the balance between higher order tasks designed to improve staff, student and school performance (leadership), routine maintenance of present operations (management) and lower order duties (administration). Restructuring generates increased expectations for school leadership, while at the same time demanding more work of a maintenance and lower order nature. Many school leaders find difficulty in readjusting their former priorities, values and institutional practices to accommodate the new set of expectations.

Restructuring has led to a transformation in the nature as well as the style of leadership thought appropriate for school leaders. There has been a dramatic shift in expectations that leaders will move from heroic, autocratic styles of leadership to collaborative, participative styles. The expectation that many areas of school life will be characterised by more collegial and collaborative relations among staff and more open, democratic, participative decision making among school community members has challenged school leaders to rethink their leadership styles. Yet principals are well aware that they are still expected to provide guidance and direction, to take initiatives and to take responsibility for what happens in their schools. One principal summarized this dilemma in the following way:

> 'I'm conscious of moving towards a democratic-participative leadership style, which supposedly gives ownership and empowerment to others; all can contribute and more ideas can be forthcoming. However, this may be at the expense of clear direction and the conservative element on staff may be empowered to do very little. On the other hand, the heroic-autocratic style means that I lead towards my vision, it is top down, it stifles initiative and there is little ownership. Now, however, staff, including myself, feel happier with the more participative style, but who sets the direction? And who takes responsibility?'

Asynchronous change between emerging democratic values and norms and former hierarchical normative and institutional practices favours shared, participative leadership and involves different institutional procedures, practices and structures. Many school leaders are caught in the tension of the transition period as they try to decide between respective leadership styles and the appropriate balance between them.

Restructuring has been largely responsible for the introduction of more complex organizational structures. Whereas school leaders have traditionally seen themselves positioned at the head of the school, they are now expected to place themselves at the centre of a complex web of interconnected networks. The school as an organizational entity *per se* has given way to the concept of the school community; a plethora of interest groups and stakeholder groups comprising professional teachers, parents, local community members and students. School leaders are expected to bond these groups, taking into account their points of view while at the same time providing advice and guidance on school policy where appropriate. The political machinations of this new position for school leaders are considerably emphasized. Principals continue to accept responsibility for the management of their schools. However, the shift to a leader role orchestrating a pluralistic network of influence groups, both inside and outside school, has been growing strongly. Many school leaders struggle to adapt to the different sets of values, institutional structures and processes demanded of this more overtly political and pluralist school environment.

A manifestation of the more pluralistic political environment within which school leaders function is the dilemma caused by the tension between reactive leadership to school community concerns on the one hand and proactive leadership of the school community on the other. Underpinning the belief that school leaders reflect community concerns is a set of norms which presents the restructured school as mirroring the local society, based on its ethnic, demographic and cultural features, as well as its social and occupational structure. The school becomes an integral part of the local community's social fabric. Working in contradistinction, however, is the expectation that a school is part of a larger education system, with obligations to prepare students to take their place in national and global economies. Commenting on this dilemma, one principal reflected:

'With more school-based management these days, I am increasingly conscious of the need for our school to reflect the diverse cultural interests of our large immigrant population. On the other hand, I am also aware of forces to standardize curricula across the country, exemplified in the push for a national curriculum.'

Moreover, schools are organizations staffed by professionals with loyalty to their profession as well as to the local community. In this capacity school leaders adopt norms which extend beyond the immediacy of the local environment. School leaders are thus placed at the point of tension between these sets of forces.

A related point of tension concerns the role of school leader as the gatekeeper and preserver of tradition on the one hand and initiator of change on the other. In the pluralist environment of restructured schools it is quite possible that different groups within the school community press for contradictory policies. The school leader plays a key role in preserving established and valued traditions, many of which may have given the school its reputation and ethos in the past. However, new competing sets of norms and institutional structures in the restructuring environment demand that reforms be undertaken. Asynchronous change between the forces driving reform and those sustaining tradition place the school leader at the interface of a real dilemma.

Those schools leading the way in restructuring are invariably undertaking innovative programmes to reform teaching and learning, curriculum and organizational structures. Principals of such schools recognize a dilemma centred on the asynchrony between the rate of change in their schools and that in the rest of the system. They fear that their schools will be seen as too far out of step with other schools, a situation which may provoke central office intervention to curtail their restructuring activities. Evidence from studies of these reforming schools (Rosenholtz, 1989) suggests that when whole school communities align behind programmes of reform the momentum and synergy for change is considerable. Fundamental shifts in norms related to student learning, and the school community's acceptance of responsibility for managing this process, are characteristics of the restructuring school. School leaders are expected to orchestrate this change process at school level. While promoting school improvement in their own institution, they need to take cognizance of the fact that the school is still part of a system. There may be tension between the school's own agenda for, and rate of, change and what the system is prepared to allow.

It is at this juncture that the school leader may experience a tension between being an employee of the system, leader of the local school community, a member of the teachers' union and a member of a professional association. As leader of the local school community the principal has a set of allegiances, interests and accountabilities which may conflict with those held in respect to the central office bureaucracy. As principal employed by an education system there will almost certainly be a line management responsibility to central office.

In some contentious industrial situations this position as agent of the central office may conflict with the leader's interests as member of a teachers' union or professional association. The dilemma arises in trying to serve the interests of two or more groups with opposing sectional interests, each with its own set of norms and policies. This dilemma is expressed in the following way by one principal:

> 'I can see the time not too far ahead when my school community will be wanting to do X, and the central office will be telling me to do Y. I will be serving at least two masters.'

He concludes that while he knows that management and politics is all about reconciling conflicting demands, 'it is easier said than done, especially if and when the school council has the power to hire and fire me'.

Restructuring policies present challenges to school leaders in redesigning the internal work organization of the school, including both classroom activities and decision making in the school as a whole. At the same time, new relationships need to be forged between the school and its external environment. Close links with parents, business and government agencies are considered necessary in promoting an appropriate image of the school. Public relations and marketing are relatively new roles expected of school leaders. These skills are considered necessary in gaining public support, in winning students and in generating additional income for the school. With reduced real levels of public expenditure on education, and growing demands for the provision of better quality school services, government schools are increasingly expected to rely on income from non-government sources.

The dilemmas here are twofold. First, restructuring is taking place on a number of fronts simultaneously. Decisions and choices are necessary regarding how to achieve multiple goals inside and outside the school. Second, the emphasis placed on selling a school image and winning resources (through, for example, private sponsorships) presents a dramatically different school environment to be managed from that which many school leaders have known in the past. A different set of norms, expectations and management practices, many of which have more in common with the commercial world, are called into play.

A common theme reported by many of the school leaders in the present study is the conflict inherent in restructuring policies between, on the one hand, the exhortation to neighbouring schools to share facilities and resources in order to secure economies and, on the other, the promotion of competition for students between such schools. In Australian government high schools it is not unusual for more than one-half of the students to cross school boundaries. Some do so for special programmes, while others are tempted by the prospect of attending a better school (as they perceive it) outside their catchment area. Parental choice is a strong policy theme in many school systems undergoing restructuring, especially in the United States and in England and Wales. Policy makers believe that school quality is improved by promoting parents' ability to select the best schools as though in a free market. From the viewpoint of the school leader, however, fierce competition with other government, as well as private, schools presents a new set of environmental norms within which to lead and administer. This dilemma reflects inherent contradictions between policies fostering cooperation between neighbouring schools and policies creating intense rivalry and competition for students. Survival of one or other school may be at stake.

States of mind of school leaders in restructuring environments are underpinned by points of tension between concerns for effectiveness, efficiency and equity. The school leadership environment in restructuring is characterized by the presence of all three. However, one or two of the three might be dominant at a particular time and place. Effectiveness might emphasize improved student learning outcomes; efficiency might reflect a concern to achieve more with fewer resource inputs or obtain better value from existing resources; equity might be expressed through a concern for equality of opportunity and success for all students. One principal reflected:

'My understanding of restructuring is that the central office is now asking us to improve the learning of all students, but is not prepared to give us any more resources to achieve this. Neither does it offer us much in the way of advice about process and how we should go about it. They say, "we set the outcomes, you handle the process". I understand that as a self-managing school it is our responsibility to determine how we achieve outcomes, but the lack of support from the centre suggests they don't want to know about the difficulties of achieving what they want.'

In the minds of school leaders these are complex dilemmas with which to grapple, predicated on fundamental values and principles. They find expression through attitudes held, through interpersonal relations, through institutional structures and processes, and through resource allocation. In achieving high levels of school effectiveness a school might compromise efficiency. In achieving efficiency a school might forgo equity. The situation appears to school leaders as one of multiple trade-offs and opportunity costs.

School leaders interviewed for the present study report a dilemma captured by the tension between accountability and school improvement. In WA, for example, a major feature of restructuring is the school development plan. Government policy has emphasized its use as an accountability mechanism, whereby schools report to the Education Department on their performance as judged against the goals and priorities set out in the school plan. This accountability thrust is frequently emphasized at the expense of using the plan to secure school improvement. The same school leaders view the development planning process and the plan as involving considerable work, aimed primarily at accountability rather than school effectiveness and school improvement. This apparent dichotomy creates a dilemma in the state of mind of school leaders who see a tension in restructuring between maximizing school effectiveness and improvement, on the one hand, and accounting to central office on the other. The press for accountability is perceived to have grown more strongly than for school improvement. The resulting asynchrony between norms and institutional practices associated with accountability and those associated with school improvement creates a dilemma in the state of mind of many school leaders.

An important role is played by the school leader as a supporter, improver and developer in the restructuring school. Teachers, students and parents require continuous motivation and support to maintain commitment to meet challenging goals of reform. The school leader is cast in the role of colleague, confidante, inspirer, vision sharer, resourcer and professional developer. Another role dimension of increasing importance in the restructuring school, however, is the leader as evaluator and sanctioner. Many principals claim they feel a tension between these two states of mind. One reflected:

> 'I really am finding it difficult to fulfil the joint obligations of colleague and friend, wanting to help staff whenever I can, and the increasing expectation on me to appraise their performance. This is especially so when we all work so closely together every day. If you have critical words with a teacher about their performance one day, you know that you've still got to look each other in the eye the next.'

In the minds of school leaders, each of these roles – developer and evaluator – appears to generate distinctly different sets of norms, expected behaviours, interpersonal relationships and institutional practices.

A further state of mind dilemma for school leaders concerns the responsibilities gained at school level as a result of restructuring, while the concomitant power, authority and resources to support the effective operationalization of these responsibilities is not forthcoming. Asynchronous change between additional responsibilities given on the one hand, and the failure to delegate appropriate powers and authority on the other, creates a dilemma for school leaders. A related concern is the mismatch between the type of responsibility school leaders would like delegated from central office and the actual responsibilities delegated. Many principals feel the responsibilities delegated are either the less important functions or the more politically sensitive ones. In the former case restructuring is perceived to be largely cosmetic, while in the latter situation restructuring is perceived as a means by which governments can escape criticism for certain functions by deflecting it on to schools. These dilemmas are grounded in the institutional domain of administrative responsibilities, powers and authority.

The foregoing dilemmas pervade the general states of mind of school leaders within a restructuring context. They contribute to an explanation of how school leaders conceptualize and draw their cognitive maps in respect to the conflicting norms, institutional practices and resources underpinning restructuring policies. Moreover, these general 'states of mind' dilemmas appear to shape the way in which school leaders view more specific issues arising from restructuring.

Dilemmas based on specific issues (of a practical, operational nature)

Analysis of the dilemmas reported by the principals who participated in the present study revealed that many dilemmas related to specific issues, which generated the following five sub-categories: purposes and functions of schooling; structures and processes; human resource management; curriculum, teaching and learning; material and financial resources.

Purposes and functions of schooling
This type of dilemma is illustrated by the point of tension between the emphasis placed on the school to provide primarily an academic-cognitive service to its student body and the real needs that children have for social, affective and caring services. Two different but related sets of values underpin this dilemma. As one principal reported:

> 'Many students are unable to learn because of their medical problems. Hence, schools attempt to fix these problems to aid the learning process. But the more schools try to solve social problems, the more these problems are dumped on to the school (and schools are held responsible for them). In many cases schools are no better at solving these problems than the rest of society. Many principals refuse to take on these social tasks because they have inadequate resources and little chance of success. Others say "this is the world and to attempt to educate in isolation flies in the face of reality".'

Another essentially normative dilemma concerns the tension between providing a 'moderate' quality schooling for all students, a 'good' education for most, or specialized education for the gifted few. Equity considerations in contemporary restructuring policies tend to emphasize quality education for all. School leaders, however, mindful of the limited resources at the school's disposal and aware of their school's accumulated expertise and reputation gained over time, perceive a conflict between these goals. They feel capable of accomplishing one of these, but not more.

Structures and processes
Responses from principals in this study who are currently engaged in major restructuring at the school site indicate major dilemmas concerning the 'dismantling of former structures' and their replacement by new versions.

Committee structures, student and teacher groupings, curriculum structures and timetables all constitute potential structures for reform in the institutional domain. This specific type of dilemma, however, is more often experienced during the transition period of asynchronous change in structures. As one principal commented, 'you can't knock down the old until the new is up and running'. A school which is embarked on restructuring often operates, therefore, with a combination of confused multilayered structures, some remnants from the past and some embryos of the future. A similar point of tension occurs between the more rigid structures of the past and more flexible structures proposed for the future. Many dilemmas are foreshadowed as more flexible structures, such as school hours, teachers' contact and non-contact hours, and changed schedules and duties, begin to influence teachers' work organization. Employers, in proposing more flexible workplace reforms in schools, are having to consider the implications for teachers' work and conditions. School leaders, positioned between employers and unions, each with their own sets of norms and institutional practices, are at the centre of this dilemma over work redesign.

School development planning and more empowered school councils constitute two central features of restructuring in many systems, and their introduction has caused dilemmas for school leaders. In the case of empowered school councils, many principals are concerned about the implications for the redistribution of power and influence over decision making that this heralds. They declare that the professional base of teachers is threatened while the knowledge base of the parent and community body is problematic with respect to the functions they are expected to fulfil. A dilemma is created whereby asynchrony exists between the investment of school councils with power (an institutional change) and the relative lack of readiness and preparedness of many community and parent groups to assume empowerment for council roles (a normative change). Likewise, a number of the principals surveyed for the present study recognize a specific dilemma centred on the introduction and evolution of school development planning (an institutional change) and resistance to development planning by some teachers and teachers' unions who remain unconvinced of the purposes and benefits of such institutional change.

A related dilemma for school leaders concerns the apparent lack of linkage between policies and practices at different levels in schools. Increasingly, restructuring is seen by policy makers as providing opportunities for improving the quality of teaching and learning. Yet there is evidence that school development planning at the whole school level may not be having the desired impact on instructional activity, classroom organization and the learning of individual students (Logan *et al.*, 1994). The problem for the school leader is how to facilitate institutional change taking place at the whole school level to generate consistent change at the classroom level. In this respect schools appear to be characterized by asynchronous change between whole school and classroom variables within the institutional and normative domains.

Human resource management
Principals surveyed refer to dilemmas concerning the introduction of performance management and appraisal of teachers. They cite union opposition to teacher appraisal, indicating that union norms and beliefs are out of step with this aspect of restructuring policy. These school leaders also comment on the dilemmas confronting them as developers of their staff, on the one hand, and judges, appraisers and sanctioners on the other. This specific dilemma is a manifestation of the more general 'state of mind' dilemma caused by the tension between the leader's role as developer and evaluator. School leaders worry about long-lasting, negative relationships with staff they have reprimanded, and claim feelings of impotence in their inability to fire staff who are consistently underperforming. If a satisfactory appraisal system is not in place, school leaders feel even more impotent in securing improvement in the quality of teaching and learning. These dilemmas can be conceptualized in terms of differential rates of change between norms affecting the introduction of new practices and the development and implementation of institutional structures and processes.

Many principals emphasize the number of dilemmas within the human resource field generated by restructuring. These dilemmas point to the school as an organization with increasing responsibilities in the human resource field, but without the institutional procedures, practices and resources to execute them effectively. In some instances union opposition prevents or delays the introduction of such procedures. School leaders feel the point of tension between wanting to motivate staff and raise morale while realizing their limited ability to reward staff achievements. While the values and norms of school leaders may favour staff motivation, they experience dilemmas in the absence of institutional procedures and resources to support their delivery.

As restructuring proceeds the pressure on personnel at school level, and the resultant stress levels experienced, are likely to increase. Many principals are anxious to invest considerable care and consideration for their staff in appreciation of their reform efforts. However, this is sometimes to the neglect of their own welfare. One principal declared: 'I'm putting a good deal of effort into caring for my staff, but who's caring for me?' A dilemma arises for principals in that the more concern they show for their staff, the more in need of care they themselves become.

Curriculum, teaching and learning
Curriculum reform is an integral part of restructuring in most education systems. Reform issues, particularly in secondary schools, tend to centre on two opposed sets of norms. In many countries the secondary school curriculum has traditionally been controlled by universities and secondary examination bodies, and has consequently catered to the needs of the more academically able, many of whom aim for university. However, as school retention rates in

the 1990s increase, there is a need to cater for a more diversified student population in the upper secondary school. School leaders stand at the interface between traditional curriculum norms and broad-based, diversified curriculum provision catering for all needs. Both sets of norms carry implications for institutional structures, processes and resources.

Accompanying the move to provide diversified curricula are reforms changing the nature of curriculum frameworks. New student outcomes-based curricula are replacing traditional curricula. Student outcomes may provide specificity of knowledge, skills and attitudes, aimed at providing clarity for teachers and students to plan programmes and refine assessment according to individual students' levels of achievement. The transition period of moving to the new outcomes approach, while elements of the old curriculum remain in operation, presents school leaders with dilemmas. Principals realize that new norms and institutional arrangements have to be accepted by teachers.

A fundamental part of school restructuring centres on improving the quality of teaching and learning. However, it is this area, particularly the reform of classroom practice, which has proved to be the most difficult challenge confronting school leaders. The press is to shift from teacher-centred, traditional methods of teaching, with over-reliance on a narrow range of mainly didactic strategies, to a student-centred, teaching-for-learning emphasis, embracing a wider range of teaching strategies. The teacher becomes a facilitator of learning rather than a transmitter of knowledge. Students cease to be passive acquirers of inert knowledge and become active learners. Underpinning these reforms are fundamental changes in norms, institutional arrangements and resources. For example, knowledge is differently conceived; teachers' and students' roles are changed, as is the nature of their inter-relationships; and classroom culture is transformed. Dilemmas arise for school leaders in leading and managing this transformation across whole staffs, with some teachers implementing new practices and others rejecting the new in favour of their traditional methods.

Resources

Discussion of dilemmas in this chapter has noted resource problems as a recurring theme in the life of the school leader. Scarcity of resources is not confined to periods of restructuring. One principal comments: 'there will always be a shortage of time and energy, and in most situations we could always do with more staff and money'. Nonetheless, periods of major reform tend to be resource hungry. Asynchrony between the rates of change of norms and institutional practices, and resource levels to implement and sustain them, are seen by many school leaders as the source of multiple dilemmas. A premium is placed on optimizing the allocation of time, human resources and financial resources between competing uses and, once allocated, ensuring their continued effective, efficient and equitable use.

This account has presented school leader dilemmas as the interaction between changes taking place in their complex environment, embracing school, local, national and global societies on the one hand, and the unique strategic position of the school leader as interfacing this complex environment on the other. The discussion has attempted to capture asynchronous changes in the leadership environment involving norms and values, institutional structures and practices, and resources, and to present these as dilemmas.

CONCLUSION

Restructuring is about transforming the social, educational, political and economic environment of schools. School leaders, positioned strategically at the interface of many conflicting tensions and forces of asynchronous change, are increasingly challenged by complex problems, or dilemmas. Curiously, our understanding of how school leaders perceive dilemmas generated by restructuring efforts in their schools and how they attempt to manage these situations is relatively unexplored. If restructuring is to have beneficial effects in the delivery of a better quality schooling for all students then it is important that school leaders manage these dilemmas as effectively as possible.

If the reality of the workplace for school leaders is largely captured by the notion of dilemmas, a question arises as to how research might contribute to an understanding of the nature of dilemmas, how principals and others perceive and react to complex, problematic situations, and how dilemmas might be useful in the training and preparation of school leaders. This chapter has suggested that research can assist in the analysis of dilemmas as perceived by school leaders working in restructuring contexts and has attempted to clarify how school leaders view problematic work situations in terms of dilemmas. Future research might deepen our knowledge as to how school leaders perceive and manage dilemmas confronting them in the workplace. It should then be possible to use this knowledge base to improve the preparation of school leaders as key managers of change in securing school improvement.

Chapter 12

Teachers' dilemmas in relation to their curriculum work

INTRODUCTION

The nature of the educational developments in Western Australia outlined so far are such that teachers are being compelled to redefine their professional lives. Accordingly, it is not surprising that many teachers are experiencing dilemmas in relation to various aspects of their work. This chapter attempts, in relation to one educational district, to portray those dilemmas which have emerged in teachers' conceptualization of their curriculum work as a consequence of this process.

THE CASE STUDY

Six primary schools were selected within an educational district in the Perth Metropolitan area. These included a primary school in a predominantly middle-class area, a school in a predominantly working-class area, a primary school in an educational priority area, a primary school with a multicultural student population, a 'special school' and a school support centre. Care was taken to ensure that the schools selected were not sites that had attracted continual or intermittent investigation by researchers. A total of 54 teachers was involved.

Method of investigation

Semi-structured, in-depth interviews (Taylor and Bogdan, 1984) were conducted. The teachers were interviewed in groups of between three and six and were provided with the opportunity to engage in discussion (Minichiello *et al.*, 1991). One interview was conducted with each group and lasted, on average, 45 minutes. Before commencing the interviews, the purpose of the research was explained to the teachers and the importance which the researchers placed on maintaining confidentiality was stressed, as was the right of the teachers to remove themselves from the interview process at any time. The researchers had prepared the following *aide mémoire* (Burgess, 1984) to direct the interviews.

First set of questions

The report *Better Schools in Western Australia* advocates self-managing schools within the guidelines of a state education system. What is your understanding of that statement? How should it work in schools?

How do you think curriculum decisions should be made in schools?

Who should make curriculum decisions?

What do you think your role should be in curriculum decision making?

About what curriculum issues should schools make decisions?

What structures need to be in place for this to work?

Second set of questions

How are curriculum decisions made in this school? What are the current practices in this respect?

What structures are in place to make curriculum decisions?

Who is involved in making curriculum decisions?

Are different curriculum decisions made differently? How? Why? What is your role?

About what aspects of curriculum do you make decisions?

Third set of questions

What, from your perspective, are the problems with current policies for making curriculum decisions in the school?

Is there any aspect of curriculum decision making in the school which pleases you? If so, what are the factors which facilitate this?

Neither the wording nor the ordering of the questions were fixed. In conducting the interviews general principles as outlined by Measor (1985) were followed. Probes were used in order to encourage the teachers to describe experiences in detail and to constantly press for clarification of their words, and cross-check questions were asked to elicit an honest account of how the teachers saw themselves and their experiences. The conversations were tape recorded with the teachers' consent, and transcribed. They were 'checked back' with the teachers and modified until they became acceptable accounts of their positions.

Analysis

An examination of the data indicated that, as a result of restructuring, teachers have dilemmas in their conceptualization of their work. These were classified according to Berlak and Berlak's (1981) three main types: control dilemmas, social dilemmas and curriculum dilemmas. The curriculum dilemmas which emerged were then analysed using Winter's (1982) method of dilemma analysis, which is guided by the sociological conception of 'contradiction'. Winter (1982) uses this term to encompass a series of all-embracing postulates:

> 'that social organizations at all levels (from the classroom to the state) are constellations of (actual or potential) conflicts of interest; that personality structures are split and convoluted; that the individual's conceptualization is systematically ambivalent or dislocated; that motives are mixed, purposes are contradictory and relationships are ambiguous; and that the formulation of practical action is unendingly beset by dilemmas.' (p.168)

In this view, a statement of an opinion in an interview is taken to be a marginal option, which conceals a larger awareness of the potential appeal and validity of different and even opposed points of view.

During the analysis it became apparent that the variety of dilemmas in the teachers' conceptualization of their curriculum work could be categorized according to a number of groups within the total teacher population of the schools. The groups were as follows:

A – The Acceptors
B – The Protesters
C – The Enthusiasts
D – The Cynics.

With respect to each group, the transcribed data were analysed in accordance with Winter's (1982) classification of dilemmas as 'ambiguities', 'judgements' and 'problems' to produce perspective documents. Ambiguities are tensions which are tolerated. They constitute background awareness of inevitable complexities of a situation. Judgements are dilemmas relating to the perceptions of those actions which are seen, not as wrong, but as complex and interesting, and which require a requisite skilfulness to be resolved. Problems are those dilemmas arising out of a course of action such that they can undermine its validity and rationality.

Perspective documents were formulated for each group according to procedures outlined by Winter (1982). The technique for this involved:

1. formulating the dilemmas at roughly the same level of abstraction at which they were originally presented in the interview scripts;

2. choosing as a starting point the most elaborate formulation of any given dilemma from among the various episodes in the interview scripts;
3. formulating the dilemma so that it is counterbalanced by an equally held view.

The perspective documents were an attempt to portray in a brief, readily communicable form a summary of the complexities of the social phenomena. The following is an example of one such document from a concurrent study aimed at portraying the dilemmas of the administrators in a school.

EXAMPLE OF A PERSPECTIVE DOCUMENT

The administrators

This group included the principal and the three deputy principals.

Ambiguities

Concerning collaboration with teaching staff in curriculum decision making
On the one hand, they speak about the importance of the decision-making process in all areas, including curriculum, as being a 'whole team' effort.

On the other hand, they constantly refer to themselves as a group separate from the teachers.

Judgements

Concerning the relationship between the school development plan and curriculum decision making
On the one hand, they say that the curriculum components of the school development plan are very important to them as a guide for curriculum decision making.

On the other hand, the principal says that curriculum decisions made by committees in the light of their interpretation of the school development plan would be overruled by him if he saw them as being inappropriate.

Problems

Concerning selection of content in curriculum decision making
On the one hand they speak, albeit in an unqualified manner, of having greater freedom with respect to curriculum decision making than they had prior to the advent of restructuring.

On the other hand, it became apparent in a conversation about LOTE (Languages other than English) that they are not clear as to what degree of independence they have from the Education Department with respect to the choice of language to be taught in the school.

Findings

Ambiguities in the teachers' conceptualization of their curriculum work
'Ambiguities', it will be recalled, constitute a background awareness of inevitable complexities of a changing situation, but the tensions generated are tolerated. The perspective documents indicated a range of 'ambiguities' in the different groups' conceptualization of their curriculum work. Group A, for example, expressed the view that the centralized educational system, with its clear chain of command, prescribed curriculum and support services had served them well: 'We had a very good system. You knew where everything fitted into the scheme of things. You had a sense of direction and good back up'. They also stated that 'the schools and education needed an overhaul'.

Group B was concerned about school-based decision making and associated developments being imposed rather than developed through a joint professional venture. As one member of the group put it: 'Nobody asks what our ideas are for professional development. We are told what will be done'. However, they were ambiguous in this respect since they regularly closed their statements of concern with the comment: 'We just want to be left to teach our classes'.

For Group C the major ambiguity centred on the proliferation of staff meetings as a result of the policy of school-based decision making. On the one hand they argued that 'things are getting worse and worse with all those meetings'; while on the other hand the following comment is not unrepresentative of an equally held view: 'I appreciate the time to sit down and talk to other teachers which you do not normally get a chance to do in a professional manner'.

One 'ambiguity' identified in relation to Group D centred on the amount of extra work which is expected with school-based decision making. On the one hand they argued that 'teachers are worn out with all the extra admin work and meetings and all that is being plonked into the curriculum without anything being taken out'. On the other hand, there was a regular voicing of 'a great need for more in-service'. These curriculum dilemmas have all emerged out of the complexities generated in teachers' lives by restructuring. However, the tensions which they have generated are tolerable. In general, the situation corresponds with Lampert's (1985) image of the teacher 'as dilemma manager accepting conflict as a continuing condition with which persons can learn to cope' (p.192).

Judgements in the teachers' conceptualization of their curriculum work
'Judgements', according to Winter (1982), are dilemmas relating to the perceptions of those actions which are seen not as wrong but as complex and interesting, and which require a requisite skilfulness to be resolved. The perspective documents indicated a range of 'judgements' in the different groups' conceptualization of their curriculum work. Group A highlighted the

need, as they saw it, for all of the members of staff to acquire better curriculum decision-making skills. However, a 'judgement' was evident in the voicing of concern. On the one hand this group felt that the latest developments in the school with respect to curriculum decision making are worth while. As one member put it: 'the situation is better now as we have an input in curriculum decision making'. On the other hand they spoke of the need for all members of the school community to acquire curriculum decision-making skills. This clearly is a dilemma which can be resolved and is also likely to be resolved as the Education Department makes more in-service opportunities available for greater numbers of teachers to acquire the requisite skills.

The major 'judgement' evident in Group B centred on the need by teachers to have the 'caring' aspect of their work valued by the school administration, the Education Department and the wider community. The members argued that nobody values their role as 'carers' of pupils, even though they themselves see it as being at the centre of the education enterprise. There should be little surprise that they are upset about what they see as the 'taken-for-granted' attitude towards their role in this respect since, as Lortie (1975) has demonstrated, one of the great attractions of teaching is the notion of 'giving service'. This emanates from a motivation to demonstrate one's care for fellow humans and in a way in which people may feel they are making important contributions to their communities or their nation. In Australia, for example, Abbott-Chapman *et al.* (1992) have found that the 'human relations' aspects of teaching are paramount in intending student teachers' thinking, yet little emphasis is placed on the importance which teachers attach to their caring role by those policy makers currently restructuring education in Australia. Nevertheless the teachers in the present study state that this situation has 'in some ways drawn teachers closer', with older teachers in particular giving advice and telling them to take it easy because 'things come and go and so it's just best to go along with them at the time'. In other words, teachers have embarked on a process of dilemma management with regard to this 'problem' by adopting an attitude of fatalism as a psychological coping mechanism.

Group C exhibited what Silcock (1990, p.3) terms an ideological dilemma, namely, a dilemma concerning uncertainty about the justifications teachers can offer for what they do. On the one hand they welcomed the recent trend of working towards outcome statements, arguing as one teacher did that 'they give a distinct focus to your work'. On the other hand the same group argued that 'outcome statements are something to worry about. There is a danger that personal development will be forgotten. What about the intangibles? What about the social and emotional side of education?' Here we are reminded of Wagner's (1984) definition of a dilemma as a cognitive knot. What seems to be taking place is a struggle with the idea that outcome statements are useful so long as they do not, as it was put, 'become the engine that drives the curriculum and teachers will have to teach towards them solely since they might become the measure of teacher performance'.

Lampert's (1985) explanatory frame for teachers' dilemmas as pertaining to the gap between ideology and reality was evident in Group D's voicing of its concern. This group stated that the literature emanating both from the Education Department and from the schools' administration teams stresses continually that what is taking place is a process 'which should not and does not need to be rushed'. The members also stated that 'in practice we have to rush around all of the time. Administrators are rushing us so much for things that we cannot possibly give our best to the children'. This, however, would appear to be a dilemma which is capable of being managed. The challenge for school administration teams is, in Wagner's (1984) terms, to search for a balance between reality and what ought to become reality.

Problems in the teachers' conceptualization of their curriculum work

'Problems', it will be recalled, are those dilemmas arising out of a course of action which are of such a nature that they can undermine its validity and rationality. The perspective documents indicated a range of 'problems' in the different groups' conceptualization of their curriculum work. The major 'problem' evident in Group A centred on the involvement of parents in curriculum decision making. On the one hand the group pointed out that parents often come into the school with queries like 'Why are they not doing the new handwriting?' and 'Why are they allowed to have a calculator in Year 3?' and argued that parents should understand these things. On the other hand the members of the group regularly stated that parents should have no involvement in curriculum decisions in the school. It seems that they are torn between professional principles and fear that parental involvement in curriculum decision making will threaten their authority. The overall impression from the tone of the interviews was that such dilemmas are sufficiently emotionally disturbing as to threaten the restructuring process in the curriculum domain.

The matter of teacher planning was a concern for the members of Group B and the focus of a 'problem' which became evident. They drew attention to 'all this school-based curriculum development' and the fact that 'previously it was all laid down by the Education Department and we liked it because we knew that what we were doing was what all other teachers in the state were doing'. But they also said that there is really no school-based curriculum development because the subjects on the curriculum are prescribed by the Education Department and they must teach them. These teachers, it seems, are left in a state of intense inner conversation on this matter such that, overall, they are prompted to protest loudly against the curriculum restructuring process.

The 'problem' for the members of Group C relates to the issue of the promotion of staff empowerment through the process of curriculum decision making. On the one hand the members of the group said that the present process of devolution and curriculum decision making has resulted in feelings of unease about their professional competence. As one member put it:

> 'The engagement in all those school-based decision-making committees is all a big cover-up to make it look like we are all having a say. The administrators can overrule our decisions and they do. We are told that we are being freed to do what the school has decided or someone actually decided in the school and then all of a sudden we are told we'd all decided, like with the language outcome statements, that it was something we were going to look at and now we don't have a choice.'

On the other hand, as a result of their feeling of unease, they said that they have been forced to rethink their professional standing with respect to curriculum decision making. An emerging outcome, as they saw it, is a reaffirmation of their professional competence. This was accompanied by great tension and feelings that this situation could change given the possibility of the introduction of intrusive surveillance schemes into the classroom.

The 'problem' for Group D centred on the members' increased number of absences from the classroom to attend meetings associated with school-based decision making. They stated that these meetings took too much time from the classroom and from preparation; however, they argued that while 'there is definitely much more of the teacher coming out of the classroom, the children are not disadvantaged'. As one teacher saw it, 'the pupils adjust. It's good for them to experience different teachers'. Such a view may be the easiest one for the teachers to adopt, but it may also be pedagogically inappropriate for the students. It would be ironic if restructuring which is taking place with the stated aim of improving student learning is leading to the adoption of strategies which promote the opposite effect.

CONCLUSION

The broad context of this chapter is the widespread restructuring in educational systems throughout much of the developed world. With regard to Australia, the main contention is that while teachers throughout all of the country's states are having to participate in restructuring at the administrative level, their future role in curriculum decision making is unclear because of continuing uncertainties at the state level. The debate which is taking place on the possibility of introducing a national curriculum is one from which they have largely been excluded, and the centralizing thrust of that debate runs counter to the decentralization which has been taking place at the administrative level. Accordingly, they are being compelled to redefine their professional lives and are, in Winter's (1982) terms, experiencing 'problems' along with 'ambiguities' and 'judgements' with regard to this. If this represents the situation throughout the state and elsewhere, then there is cause for alarm among those committed to the involvement of the classroom teacher as a major partner in curriculum decision making, given the potential of 'problems' to undermine the process.

PART FIVE

Conclusion

Conclusion

Chapter 13

Key stakeholders and contemporary educational restructuring: emerging issues

Case studies such as those reported in this book can, in the language of Stenhouse (1975), aid in the development of the capacity to understand relationships and make judgements by constituting frameworks for others within which they can think. To use case studies in this way is to address Lieberman's (1995) point that 'because direct teaching currently dominates much of what the public and many districts consider to be staff development, it is important that teachers, administrators, and policy makers become aware of new and broader conceptions of professional development' (p.593). In this regard, the contention of Darling-Hammond and McLaughlin (1995) is also noteworthy:

> 'Professional development in this era of reform extends beyond mere support for teachers' acquisition of new skills or knowledge... it also means providing occasions for teachers to reflect critically on their practice and to fashion new knowledge and beliefs about content, pedagogy and learners.' (p.597)

Case studies of the sort reported in this book may constitute one source to assist us in breaking away from a notion of in-service education as being concerned only with instrumental ends achievable through 'the recipes of tried and true practices legitimated by unexamined experiences or uncritically accepted research findings' and towards one of 'developing reflective practitioners who are able to understand, challenge and transform' (Sachs and Logan, 1990, p.479).

There is also a strong argument that central-level bureaucrats who are trying to promote change could benefit from reflecting on cases like those reported in this book since, as Fullan (1982) has so strongly argued, to effect improvement (that is, to introduce change that promises more success and less failure) the world of the people most closely involved in implementation must be understood. However, while initially we engaged in this research project with a professional development function in mind, a variety of issues of wider significance began to emerge as the cases were developed. In particular, it became apparent that educational restructuring is taking place in many countries. In some respects the degree of commonality and similarity between each of these restructuring initiatives is both surprising and perturbing. Certainly there are differences between approaches, but they tend to be differences of emphasis rather than substance.

It is difficult to argue that the differences are more related to cultural adaptation, as one might hope, than to administrative expedience or to a particular individual or group that has been able to exert undue influence in shaping the localized version of restructuring. Notwithstanding such differences, it became apparent during the conduct of the case studies that it is possible in most situations to identify common features of educational restructuring around the world. In the light of this observation and the empirical research presented so far, this chapter considers some implications of restructuring for principals, teachers and parents, and concludes with a discussion of a number of policy issues.

THE IMPLICATIONS OF RESTRUCTURING FOR PRINCIPALS, TEACHERS AND PARENTS

Whatever the exact motives may be, there are several major positive outcomes cited as arising from decentralization and devolution. Brown (1990), after conducting a series of interviews with principals and administrators, concluded that a change to school-based management implies flexibility in decision making, changes in role accountability and the potential enhancement of school productivity. He argues that flexibility in decision making allows initiatives to be taken and long-term planning to be encouraged, while the ability to respond immediately to educational problems is best achieved if control of the resources needed to make a response is closest to where the problem is manifest. Because principals and teachers have to implement decisions and live with the consequences, so, the argument runs, it is preferable to have localised decision making because principals and teachers are best able to diagnose students' needs in view of their direct contact with students and access to local information (Beare, 1983; White, 1989). In a similar vein, Knight (1984) concluded that greater discretion over curriculum development at the school site enabled teachers to select instructional materials and methods, and to develop curricula that were most appropriate to the needs of their students. In this way school-based management promises to provide the opportunity to improve the quality of teaching and student learning.

It is customary to assume that devolution entails central office staff having less direct authority over schools, and principals having more control over school resources. In addition, it is argued that increased staff participation in decision making should lead to greater enthusiasm, interest, commitment and effectiveness. In this regard, White (1989) has argued that devolution may improve self-esteem, morale and efficiency of all school personnel. Devolution may also enhance the professionalism of teachers as it empowers them with the authority, responsibility and accountability associated with a professional rank (Caldwell and Spinks, 1988; Hunter, 1989). Principals also believe that schools would be more productive the more school-based management is adopted (Goodlad, 1984; Brown, 1990).

A key argument of those defending restructuring is that parental participation can encourage staff to be more analytical in school matters, and that this results in improved communication between the school staff and the local school community (White, 1989). A decentralized and devolved system is believed to be more responsive and adaptive to the needs of the community. It is also believed that, as school personnel experience more responsibility for curriculum decision making, improvements in teaching and learning will result. Studies by Brown (1990) and Kowalski (1980) found that many teachers acknowledged the value of the broader perspective offered by members of the wider educational community in their contribution to school affairs.

The implications of restructuring for principals and teachers

Notwithstanding the many benefits which, it is argued, can arise from decentralization and devolution, there is much confusion, anxiety and dissatisfaction associated with the transition period involved in bringing it about. The process of changing to school-based management may create confusion in roles and responsibilities (White, 1989). Many principals in devolving systems assume, for the first time, dual accountabilities, both to central office administrators and to the community. As the shift from a hitherto centralized system to school-based management is an evolutionary process, the roles and expectations of principals, teachers and parents are necessarily in a state of continuous flux. Principals, teachers, parents and students may have difficulty adapting to new roles and new lines of communication and consequently may experience considerable role ambiguity. The process of adaptation demands new skills which many participants do not possess. In many educational systems, including WA, more than a century of exclusion from educational policy making in otherwise tightly centralized systems has left a legacy of community and parental inexperience which often seem to result in feelings of inadequacy and reluctance to become involved now that opportunity presents itself (Smart, 1988).

Accordingly, the restructuring process has marked implications for the principal who is expected, perhaps for the first time, to draw on a multitude of roles and skills (particularly in the personnel field) rather than relying on bureaucratic direction, as in the past (Handy, 1985; Duignan, 1990). Technical skills, such as school-based budgeting techniques, short-term and long-term goal setting and policy planning, time management and the art of delegation must be mastered if the ever-increasing demands of a more devolved education system are to be successfully met. In addition, school-based management may lead to a power struggle between principals, teachers, parents and students (White, 1989). Although the principals' decision-making arena has expanded, they are now required to work with new participants who may hold very different values. This calls for heightened political and negotiating skills on their part in order to achieve consensus between diverse groups, leading forcefully from the front on some occasions and steering quietly from behind on others.

There is also a fear that an emphasis on productivity and efficiency may turn the principal and teacher into technicians (Brown, 1990). Some teachers anticipate that there will be a shift in the principals' role from the supervision of instruction to supervision of the fiscal operation of the school. A loss of collegiality and professionalism may result as principals become more like business managers. Accordingly, despite the rationale for, and much acclaimed benefits of, decentralization, it is not difficult to envisage the problems in moving from an entrenched centralized system. Community and parental inexperience and feelings of inadequacy in relation to participation in school affairs, and changes in the tasks and roles of principals and teachers, would suggest that the achievement of self-governing schools is likely to be a long, challenging and evolutionary process. The simultaneous demands for excellence and quality, for economic restraint and accountability, and for an adaptive and responsive system able to meet the needs of a rapidly changing technological society also contribute to the complexity of the change process.

Finally, there have been relatively few research studies of the reactions of teachers and principals to the current trends towards devolution of control to individual schools in government systems. Little has been written about the experiences and reactions of those who have adopted and implemented school-based management responsibilities. It is likely that greater knowledge of the reactions of teachers and principals, who are expected to implement policy at the school level, will provide insights into the difficulties of transforming entrenched attitudes and practices.

Overall, most studies of principals' and teachers' reactions to restructuring reveal an acceptance of the general philosophy and set of ideas underpinning it. There is some evidence to suggest that many would not wish to return to prerestructuring times. At the same time, many express dissatisfaction with the political agenda, the pace of change and the lack of resources provided to support their efforts. It also has to be admitted that the research base in support of restructuring in the form of school-based management aimed at improving the quality of teaching and learning is extremely sketchy. This is also the situation with regard to parental involvement in schooling in restructured educational systems (Dimmock *et al.*, 1996).

The implications of restructuring for parents

The implications of restructuring for parental involvement derive from three corner-stones of government policy and are to be found in a variety of countries. First, there is a widening and diversifying of the forms of parental and community involvement, particularly in school decision making. Second, tighter public spending policies are redistributing responsibilities for the resourcing of schools with consequent ramifications for parents and other non-government sources. Third, emphasis is placed on improving learning outcomes for all students, a policy which involves increased expectations of both parents and schools. A brief outline of each of these three policy themes, and the various issues that they generate with respect to the nature and effect of parental involvement, is now presented.

A major manifestation of a widening of parental involvement is greater school decision-making roles, through legislated representation on school councils, involvement in school development planning and membership of a variety of school committees. These initiatives provide parents with a greater voice in school policy, planning, governance and administration (Hammond, 1986). However, many issues are raised regarding how much or how little power and influence are exercised by parent representatives in the various decision-making groups. A fundamental issue commonly recognized is the extent to which elected parents on school councils can and do represent the diversity of interests, values and views of the parent body as a whole (Brandt, 1989; Tipton, 1989; Burkhardt and March, 1991; Murphy, 1991a). Another relates to doubts about whether this policy initiative is a genuine attempt to embrace parent and community involvement in democratizing school decision making, or whether the reason for shifting responsibilities to the school level is an attempt by governments to avoid criticism of themselves.

There is also an increasing involvement of parents in evaluating and reviewing whole school performance (Cuttance, 1993). Parents in England and Wales, and in some Australian states, are represented on school review and inspection teams. Issues to do with the implications of the parental contribution to quality assurance through school review and evaluation, and how it can be enhanced, are now being raised. Closely associated with this is parental involvement in school accountability. Part of the restructuring movement aims to increase the accountability of schools to parent bodies and school communities. This accountability to parents takes the form of reporting both the performance of individual students and the school as a whole. However, it also raises questions regarding how much accountability is being, and should be, rendered to parents, the form it should take, and the extent to which the performance measures are valid.

Other initiatives are aimed at further widening the role of parents by providing them with the opportunity to choose the school and programme in which their child will be enrolled. This is designed to empower the parent as 'client' or 'consumer' of the school system. Many schools respond to these marketplace conditions by placing greater emphasis on public relations and school image in an effort to attract students. In so doing, the roles of principals, teachers and parents, as well as the relationships between them, are transformed. Many issues and questions centre on both the expedience and the feasibility of parental choice of school as a policy and on the problems and effects experienced in its implementation (Moore, 1992).

The second corner-stone of restructuring policies emanates from the concern shown by many governments to cut public spending and to secure greater efficiency and value for money in education. This pursuit of economic, rationalist policies in education has led to criticism from parents and teachers that governments are placing more responsibilities on schools while failing to provide adequate resources (Dale, 1993). By the same token, there is an expectation by governments that schools will enlist greater parental and community support in the form of time and money. Two issues are of major concern in this respect. First, there is an issue of equity in the expectation that local communities and parents will contribute directly to the human, physical and financial resources of the school. This raises the prospect that schools in more prosperous areas will be further advantaged compared with those in less affluent areas. Second, some parents may consider that the payment of taxes entitles their children to an otherwise cost-free, publicly provided education. The expectation that they will now contribute further is seen by some parents as placing an unfair burden on their already limited resources.

The third dimension of restructuring relates to school effectiveness and school improvement. This policy thrust places emphasis not only on improving student learning outcomes but on doing so for all students, thus posing a dual challenge. Furthermore, the role that parents can play in meeting this dual challenge is seen as vital. A considerable body of literature confirms that parents are a key factor in improving their children's learning (Becker and Epstein, 1982; Henderson, 1988; Ziegler, 1987) and advocates multiple ways in which parents can enhance student learning (Greenwood and Hickman, 1991; Vandegrift and Greene, 1992). As Epstein (1987) argues:

'the evidence is clear that parental encouragement, activities, and interests at home and participation in schools and classrooms affect children's achievements, attitudes and aspirations, even after student ability and family socio-economic status are taken into account. Students gain in personal and academic development if their families emphasize schooling, let children know they do, and do so continually over the school years.' (p.120)

The research base on this general area, along with that on the impact of restructuring on the other major stakeholders, is, however, far from complete.

EMERGING POLICY ISSUES

In many restructuring initiatives the relationship between the central authority and the school is reconfigured. The central authority accepts responsibility for identifying and promulgating system aims and targets, within which schools are expected to draw up their own school development plans. Increasingly, central authorities are adopting student outcome approaches to restructuring curricula, so that aims and targets at both school and centre can be couched in terms of student achievement. As desirable as such approaches may appear, at least from a theoretical level, they are in practice fraught with problems, the first of which is that central authorities are rarely themselves clear about their system aims and objectives. The very nature of devolution and decentralization makes it difficult for the central agency to formulate meaningful systemic aims and goals for scores of disparate and diverse schools without recourse to general platitudes. Establishing more specific criteria, such as those enshrined in student outcomes, only begs questions such as how these will help each school in setting its aims in relation to the system's aims. And how will the centre subsequently evaluate the performances of individual schools, and their performances relative to other schools'? The problem of central authority aims and goals is that on the one hand they tend to be so general and platitudinous as to be functionally meaningless. On the other hand, the more central authorities attempt to graft specificity on individual school goals by specifying student outcome targets, the more they will meet resistance from school groups arguing the exceptionality of their unique school environments.

A lack of clarity, certainty and meaningfulness pervading aims and goals is not the only weak spot in regard to policy on restructuring emanating from central authorities. Typically and deliberately as part of their restructuring strategies central agencies are not prescribing the processes and practices by which they intend schools to undertake the implementation of restructuring. While the frameworks to restructuring are prescribed in top-down fashion, the detail of these frameworks and their operationalization remain largely undefined. As a consequence, schools feel a sense of release, a feeling of being 'cut free', and a great ambivalence about aims, directions, and the ways of going about restructuring. The argument used by central authorities to condone this approach, namely, 'school personnel are the professionals, we let them get on with the job of deciding how they meet the system's aims' is, in fact, the argument used by the professionals as evidence that the centre is unclear about what it wants or expects. The reality is that teachers themselves are unclear about their own pedagogies, structures and processes and could do with good quality support, particularly if it were offered by respected 'outsiders' in ways acceptable to them. Too many system-level policy makers seem to be making policy 'on the run', governed more by fashion and fad than by well thought-out strategies. They have little idea when embarking on the next wave of restructuring initiatives what the requirements are for their success, what problems are likely to ensue in the process, and what are the likely or realistic outcomes and effects.

Characteristics of the policy context to restructuring, underpinned as they are by the uncertain and ill-defined technology of instruction and schooling, are very important in gaining an understanding of the restructuring process to date. Lack of clarity over policy aims and directions, uncertainty and suspicion about the motives driving restructuring policy, absence of support to schools in areas of process and practice, and failure to provide them with sufficient resources, are all explanations for the findings reported in this book. Schools and their communities may experience a stronger sense of democracy, a more pluralistic and political environment within which to function, a widening of choices and options within which to make decisions, or they may feel that these things are more imaginary than real.

Nonetheless, restructuring inevitably brings about changes in the pattern and nature of relationships within and among school communities. A heightened sense of politicization is usually one consequence, particularly in restructuring environments which have incorporated teachers and parents, in addition to principals, in redefining roles. This more political environment has been fuelled by the incursion of market forces into school management and by the redefinition of the meaning of school 'success', from criteria based on inputs and facilities to measures centred on student learning outcomes. Essentially, this book has focused on the working out of a new political order among stakeholders at the local school level.

Depending on whether principals, teachers, parents or any combination of these three groups have been empowered, the political and professional landscape of school management and governance has been reconfigured in a multiplicity of ways. The absence of clear direction and motive from politicians and central agencies initiating the changes only serves to fuel the diversity and range of political arrangements which evolve at the local level. An illustration of this point is provided by the term 'partnership', a concept often used to describe the ideal form which the new relationship between the main stakeholders in the school community might assume. In some cases it provides an accurate description, with principals, teachers and parents agreeing, first, to work harmoniously and collaboratively, second, to adopt the same strategies and, third, to work towards the same goals. In other cases, the term is inappropriate, since teachers or parents are not incorporated as true 'partners'. Genuine trust and collaboration may be rare and there may be little agreement on strategies and goals. More importantly, there may not be the will or the procedural structures in place to allow the differences to be amicably and successfully resolved.

Some observers have commented that restructuring represents a significant change in organizational architecture from hierarchical, bureaucratic structures and decision-making forms to decentralized, cooperative, professional and lay-controlled structures. While this may represent an idealized image of the transformation, it does not necessarily depict reality in a great many cases. For example, the extent to which administrator-dominated bureaucracies in central authorities have experienced a dismantling, 'downsizing' or even erosion of their powers in relation to professional and stakeholder groups at school level is highly questionable. Bureaucrats tend to display a marked resistance to sharing their power and authority with, let alone losing it to, others. Since restructuring is traditionally imposed on schools by central authorities, it is the bureaucrats who play a key role in the process. They are rarely interested in making themselves redundant. Besides, key features of restructuring such as monitoring and accountability even seem to bolster their authority. Meanwhile, evidence continues to accumulate at the school level that the great majority of parents are reluctant to be active participants in formal decision-making structures. Those parents who are willing to participate often express their inability to contribute to discussions on many of the more important technical issues, such as curricula. The professionals tend to dominate discussion and decision making on what turns out to be an uneven playing field. Faced with these realities, it is legitimate to ask how genuine are policy makers and reformists in engineering the shift of power from central bureaucracies to professional and lay members of school communities, and in empowering them in the process.

Murphy (1991a), writing about the complexity of restructuring efforts, recognized different strategies, the adoption of which, he argued, depended 'upon the objectives sought' (p.17). He went on to argue that 'real educational transformation will require the involvement of all the key players, work on all components of the system, and the simultaneous use of four distinct but interrelated restructuring strategies' (p.17). The first, Murphy argues, is teacher empowerment; the second is school-based management; the third is parental choice of school; and the fourth is teaching for understanding. It is indeed rare to find all four elements of restructuring coexisting to underpin policy. School-based management and parental choice are the two most common elements. But, as Murphy suggests, much depends on the objectives sought. And on this issue, we contend, central authorities rarely seem to project ahead to design restructuring policies deliberately to empower teachers or principals or, given the preoccupation with administrative and governance issues, rarely seem to be concerned with redesigning teaching and learning. Far from the clarity, purpose and planned mix of strategy that Murphy advocates, the reality is that restructuring efforts are infrequently driven by any of these, despite the educational rhetoric to the contrary. Rather, the more likely driving forces are financial or political in nature.

In regard to school-based management, the sets of relationships most susceptible to change are those between principals and teachers, and between each of these and parents. Since the principal's role is enhanced from being middle manager and agent of the central authority to senior manager heading a more self-managing organization, while still being subject to system policies and accountabilities, it is the principal who becomes the nexus of restructuring. While more powers and responsibilities are devolved to principals, teachers and parents through school councils and parental choice of school, it is the principal who is at the pivotal point between teachers and parents. However, as the research findings reported in this book indicate, there is often a tension between empowering principals and teachers, as there is between empowering one or both of these groups and parents. In some models of restructuring, decentralization and devolution permeates as far as the principal's office. In Hong Kong, for example, school-based management seems to have empowered principals and enhanced their control and authority relative to teachers and parents. In such instances it can be said that centralization has simply changed its complexion in moving from the central agency to the principal. In some American school systems, however, both teachers and parents appear to have been empowered and the principal's role has been to mediate between, and coordinate the efforts of, the different groups.

Angus (1995), describing restructuring in Australian state school systems in the mid- and late-1980s, admits that while in the USA school restructuring efforts were informed by notions of the 'good' school and with the 'effective schools' movement, Australian efforts were driven by motivation to reform the public sector, particularly the desire to reduce the size and power of burgeoning administrator-bureaucracies, and by a desire to curtail public expenditure and obtain better value for money from educational expenditure. In Western Australia, for instance, it has been suggested that the creation of school councils, and the representation of parents on them, had more to do with the desire on the part of politicians to curb the power of central bureaucrats by creating a countervailing force at school level than with the desire to see genuine parent participation in governing their own schools. Political and economic factors appear to have played a strong part, too, in driving school reform in England and Wales. Interpretation of the real motives and drives underpinning restructuring initiatives is made difficult, however, by the dressing up of policy documents using educational terminology and educational aims. Such policy documents may use educational language and aspire towards educational improvement, but it is rare to find detailed explications in them of how the goals are to be attained, and what the consequences will be for all stakeholder groups involved.

The realization that efforts to restructure education have been complicated by economic and political motives, and by educational aims which lack specificity in referencing better quality schooling, helps explain events and situations which have unfurled at school level and in school communities. It explains why, in many restructuring systems, central authorities seem to have simultaneously decentralized and centralized; why school councils seem to have been given more powers, and why these are sometimes more apparent than real; why some principals, teachers and parents feel more empowered while others feel disempowered. This ambivalence and lack of goal specificity, together with the powerful economic and political factors driving restructuring, have resulted in many restructuring initiatives targeting management processes and governance structures rather than teaching and learning.

In adopting school-based management as one of the central tenets of restructuring policy, central authorities rarely present a clear vision of the reconfigured roles, relationships and influence patterns that might result. Questions of the relative empowerment of principals, teachers and parents are rarely, if ever, explicated. These are important considerations for central authorities, since the empowerment of different groups will necessarily change how the restructured education system looks.

At stake is the question of what is an appropriate balance between central-ization and decentralization. This question needs addressing by each system experiencing restructuring. The appropriate combination of centralized and decentralized elements might expectedly vary between systems depending, *inter alia,* on each system's unique cultural, traditional and political arrangements. Nonetheless, one is reminded at this point of the compelling profundity of Murphy's (1989) paradoxical statement about well-run decentralized organiz-ations: 'successful decentralization depends on strong centralization in certain aspects of the organization' (p.809).

Another way of describing the policy process with regard to restructuring is to acknowledge the almost total absence of any theoretical or philosophical base underpinning it. Rationales for restructuring are rarely articulated, espec-ially in educational terms. Instead, the preponderance of economic, financial and political elements in the restructuring process tends to lead to the school community invariably becoming a more politicized arena, where tensions and insecurities are played out between the major players – principals, teachers and parents – and where education, as a result, may suffer.

The research reported in this book highlights some important consequences of restructuring policy as presented above. The first concerns stakeholders and their newly configured roles with respect to involvement, responsibility and power. Research findings confirm that all groups – principals, teachers and parents – feel more involved in policy and decision making than was the case prior to restructuring. They also admit to having more responsibility. But all are reluctant to say that their particular group has more power as a result of restructuring. Interestingly, each group tends to think the other groups have relatively more power than before. Hence, teachers see principals' and parents' power as having increased relative to their own, while principals believe teachers' and parents' power has increased relative to theirs. From the policy viewpoint, this raises the issue as to what exactly the central authority wants to create in the way of stakeholder contribution. Is it redesigning a system merely to create stakeholder participation and involvement? Or is it going further and transferring responsibilities? If so, to which groups? And is it transferring genuine power to those groups to enable them to fulfil those responsibilities?

A second consequence of the restructuring policy environment is the characterisation of the school policy arena as fraught with interpretation, reaction, innuendo and subjective meanings given to events. Given the regular ambiguity of policy goals, motives and operational detail, school stakeholders proliferate and create their own interpretations and meanings of policy-makers' intentions. The outcome often results in a school climate which is uncertain and rife with rumour, and which displays a lack of trust and respect for the central authority. More importantly, it may also lead to suspicion and even reluctance on the part of school stakeholders to work with each other.

A third consequence of the nature of restructuring policy is the perceived dilemmas, ambiguities and even contradictions experienced by principals and teachers. These make the carrying out of their roles and duties more difficult and stressful. They also lead principals and teachers to search for, and adopt, all sorts of coping strategies, some of which may not necessarily be beneficial to the school community.

In sum, the argument presented is that central policy makers should be more mindful of the effects, both foreseen and unforeseen, that their restructuring policies set in train, particularly among principals, teachers and parents. As Murphy (1991a) has stated:

> 'There are palpable conflicts among various dimensions of the restructuring movement that have received inadequate attention to date. For example, professionalism empowers school employees; choice (and voice) empowers the school's clients; and SBM (school-based management) empowers site-level administrators and, often, teachers. Each strategy is based upon a fundamentally different belief about who should control public education. To empower one group is not necessarily to develop an organization that is more responsive to the others.' (p.84)

Both the nature and form which the restructuring process and its associated policies have assumed to date have generated a set of political and pluralistic forces among stakeholders at the school level. The ways in which this pluralism is operating and the interaction within and among stakeholder groups at school and central levels is too important to be left unattended by policy makers; the quality of schools and of schooling is at stake.

Highlighting the fact that in many education systems restructuring policies have emerged which advocate inclusion of principals, teachers and parents in decision making and in the governance and management of schools does not constitute a rebuttal to this concern. Certainly, on the surface, this policy of democratization has appeal. In addition, it might seem to be a straightforward matter as to how to operationalize it. However, the thrust of this book has highlighted that these two matters are not at all as uncontentious as might seem at first glance. In this regard, three major propositions have been distilled from the case studies and a number of principles for practice have been formulated in relation to each. These are now presented by way of final conclusion.

THE THREE MAJOR PROPOSITIONS AND PRINCIPLES FOR PRACTICE

To date, policy makers may not have given sufficient thought as to why principals, teachers and parents should be engaged in school restructuring

Therefore:

1. Policy makers need to make clear that a prime motivation underpinning restructuring policy should be the democratisation of education.
2. Policy makers need to make clear that another prime motivation underpinning restructuring should be the desire to introduce accountability structures.
3. Policy makers need to make clear that a third major motivation underpinning restructuring policy should be its potential for contributing to the improvement of the quality of the curriculum, teaching and learning.
4. Policy makers need to make clear whether the policy intention is to empower all stakeholder groups or only some.
5. Policy makers need to understand that while their intention might be to empower all stakeholder groups, the process could result in one or more groups being relatively more empowered than the others.
6. Policy makers need to understand that, if they consider a pluralistic balance of powers between the stakeholders makes for a healthy vibrant schoool community, they need to maintain vigilance over a long period in order to achieve it.

Policy presentation and communication have generated ambiguities, dilemmas and uncertainties among stakeholders

Therefore:

1. Policy makers need to involve stakeholder groups in the early formulation stages of policy making in order to understand more fully their respective views, opinions, interests and experiences.
2. Policy makers need to spell out clearly how stakeholder involvement and its attendant features (eg increased accountability and financial devolution) connect with each other and thus lead to the achievement of the overall aim of restructuring, namely, quality schooling.
3. Policy makers need to articulate clearly the roles, rules and relationships between the central administrators and the key stakeholders at the school level.
4. Policy makers need to ensure that while the central authority can decide the administrative, curricular and pedagogical parameters of restructuring, the stakeholders should be allowed to adapt the proposals to their particular circumstances.
5. Policy makers need to ensure that financial and human resources, as well as professional development support, are provided to allow stakeholders to partake fully in restructuring initiatives.
6. Policy makers need to ensure that the language of restructuring is compatible with the professional language of teachers.
7. Policy makers need to appreciate that, regardless of their best efforts, dilemmas will inevitably exist for key stakeholders in the field and so they must be ever alert to the need to deal with them.

Policy environments are rarely created to promote meaningful stakeholder involvement

Therefore:

1. Policy makers need to ensure that structures are configured such that principals, parents and teachers can feel that their involvement and collaboration in restructuring initiatives are seriously considered.
2. Policy makers need to ensure that parental involvement in restructuring is not piecemeal in being restricted to particular communities, but is encompassing of all stakeholder groups, irrespective of their socio-economic standing.
3. Policy makers need to ensure that parents are provided with the necessary professional development such that they can make a meaningful contribution to restructuring initiatives, informed by the requisite knowledge.

4. Policy makers need to ensure that parents are involved in policies relating to curriculum, teaching and learning as well as to management and administration.
5. Policy makers need to realize that in providing principals, teachers and parents with greater opportunities for involvement, they are inevitably increasing the politicization of schooling, and that as a consequence the process needs to be managed carefully to avoid political considerations taking precedence over educational ones.

Finally, in keeping with a main argument running throughout this book, these propositions and the related principles for practice should not be taken as being applicable in each and every context. Rather, they constitute intelligent guides for action. In the words of Stenhouse (1975), they are not to be regarded as an unqualified recommendation but rather as 'a provisional specification claiming no more than to be worth putting to the test of practice' (p.142).

References

Abbott Chapman, J, Hull, R, Maclean, R, McCann, H and Wyld, C (1991) *Students' Images of Teaching: Factors Affecting Recruitment*, Canberra: Australian Government Printing Service.

Armbruster, F (1977) *Our Children's Crippled Future: How American Education has Failed*, New York: The Carnegie Foundation.

Anderson, L W (1990) *Time and School Learning*, Beckenham: Croom Helm.

Andrews, G (1978) *The Case for School-based Decision Sharing: A Discussion Paper*, Sydney: New South Wales School-based Decision Sharing Project.

Angus, L B (1992) 'Quality schooling: Conservative education policy and educational change in Australia', *Journal of Education Policy*, 7, 4: 379–97.

Angus, M (1995) 'Devolution of school governance in an Australian state school system: Third time lucky?' in D S G Carter and M H O'Neill (eds) *Case Studies in Educational Change: An International Perspective*, London: The Falmer Press.

Argyris, C and Schön, D A (1978) *Organizational Learning*, Reading, MA: Addison-Wesley.

Assistant Masters and Mistresses Association (AMMA) (1991) *Assessment Under the National Curriculum: Joint Union Advice on Workload*, London: College Hall Press.

Atkin, J, Bastiani, J and Goode, I (1988) *Listening to Parents*, London: Croom Helm.

Australian Education Council (1991) *Young People's Participation in Post-compulsory Education and Training*, Canberra: Australian Government Publishing Service.

Ball, S J (1993) 'Education policy, power relations and teachers' work', *British Journal of Educational Studies*, 41: 106–21.

Bamblett, C L (1992) 'Decentralisation and devolution in the state education system of Western Australia', unpublished MEd thesis, University of Western Australia.

Barcan, A (1993) *Sociological Theory and Educational Reality*, New South Wales: New South Wales University Press.

Bartlett, L (1992) 'National curriculum in Australia: An instrument of corporate federalism', *British Journal of Educational Studies*, 40, 3: 218–38.

Beare, H (1983) 'The structural reform movement in Australian education during the 1980s and its effect on schools', *Journal of Educational Administration*, 21, 2: 149–68.

Beare, H (1987) 'Changing structures in education', in W A Simpkins (ed.) *Principal and Change: The Australian Experience*, Armidale: The University of New England Teaching Monograph Series.

Beare, H (1993) 'Different ways of viewing school site councils: Whole paradigm is in use here?', in H Beare and W Boyd (eds) *Restructuring Schools: An International Perspective on the Movement to Transform the Control and Performance of Schools*, London: The Falmer Press.

Beattie, N (1985) *Professional Parents: Parent Participation in Four West European Countries*, London: The Falmer Press.

Beazley, K E (1984) *Education in Western Australia. Report of the Committee of Inquiry into Education in Western Australia*, Perth: Western Australian Government Print.

Becker, R and Epstein, J (1982) 'Parent involvement: A survey of teacher practices', *The Elementary School Journal*, 83: 102–14.

Bell, L (1991) 'Educational management: An agenda for the 1990s', *Educational Management and Administration* 19, 3: 136–40.

Berger, E (1991) 'Parental involvement: Yesterday and today', *Elementary School Journal*, 91, 3: 209–19.

Berlak, H and Berlak, A (1981) *Dilemmas of Schooling Teaching and Special Change*, London: Methuen.

Blackledge, D and Hunt, B (1991) *Sociological Interpretations of Education*, London: Routledge.

Blakers, C (1982) *If Wishes were Horses. Discussion Paper Prepared for ACT Schools Authority: The Challenge of Change*, Canberra: Australian Capital Territory Schools Authority.

Blauer, R and Carmichael, L (1991) 'Award restructuring in teaching', *Unicorn*, 17, 1, 24–9.

Boyce, E (1983) *High School: A Report on Secondary Education in America*, New York: The Carnegie Foundation for the Advancement of Teaching.

Boyd, W (1988) 'How to reform schools without half trying: Secrets of the Reagan administration', *Educational Administration Quarterly* 24: 303–04.

Boyd, W (1992) 'The power of paradigms: reconceptualizing educational policy and management', *Educational Administration Quarterly*, 28, 4: 504–28.

Brandt, R (1989) 'On parents and schools: A conversation with Joyce Epstein', *Educational Leadership*, 47, 1: 24–7.

Brown, D J (1990) *Decentralization and School-based Management*, London: The Falmer Press.

Bryk, A, Lee, V and Smith, J (1990) 'High school organization and its effects on teachers and students', in W Clune and J Witte (eds) *Choice and Control in American Education, Vol 1: Theory of Choice and Control in Education*, New York: The Falmer Press.

Burgess, R G (1984) *In the Field: An Introduction to Field Research*, London: Allen & Unwin.

Burgess, R G (1985) 'The unstructured interview as a conversation', in R G Burgess (ed.) *Field Research: A Sourcebook and Field Manual*, London: Allen & Unwin.

Burkhardt, G and March, M (1991) 'Educational restructuring in the ACT government school system, in H Beare, G Harman, G and G Berkley (eds) *Restructuring School Management: Administrative Reorganisation of Public School Governance in Australia*, ACT: Australian College of Education.

Bush, T, and West-Burnham, J (eds) (1994) *The Principles of Educational Management*, Harlow: Longman.

Butts, R F (1955) *Assumptions Underlying Australian Education*, Australian Council for Educational Research: Hawthorn.

Caldwell, B J (1990) 'School-based decision making and management: International developments', in J Chapman (ed.) *School-based Decision making and Management*, Basingstoke: The Falmer Press.

Caldwell, B J (1993) 'The changing role of the school principal: A review of developments in Australia and New Zealand', in C Dimmock (ed.) *School-based Management and School Effectiveness*, London: Routledge.

Caldwell, B J and Spinks, J M (1988) *The Self-managing School*, London: The Falmer Press.

Campbell, R J and Neill, S (1990) *130 Days*, London: AMMA.

Capper, C A (1994) *Educational Administration in a Pluralistic Society*, Albany, NY: SUNY Press.

Carmichael, L (Chair) (1992) *The Australian Vocational Training Certificate System*, Canberra: Employment and Skills Formation Council.

Carnegie Forum on Education and the Economy (1986) *A Nation Prepared: Teachers for the 21st Century*, New York: Carnegie Forum.

Chadbourne, R and Clarke, R (1994) *Devolution: The Next Phase, Western Australian Secondary Principals Association: A Response*. Perth: Secondary Principals Association.

Chadbourne, R and Ingvarson, L (1991) *Advanced Skills Teacher One. Lost Opportunity or Professional Breakthrough?* Victoria: Seminar Series No 9. Incorporated Association of Registered Teachers of Victoria.

Chapman, J (1986) *The Victorian Primary School Principal: The Way Forward*, Victoria: Victorian Primary Principals' Association.

Chapman, J (1987) 'Decentralization, devolution and the administration of schools', *Education Research and Perspectives*, 14, 2: 62–75.

Cheng, Y C (1992) 'A preliminary study of School Management Initiative: Responses to induction and implementation of management reforms', *Educational Research Journal*, 7, 21–32.

Chubb, J E (1988) 'Why the current wave of school reform will fail', *The Public Interest*, 90: 28–49.

Cistone, P (1989) 'School-based management/shared decision making: Perestroika in educational governance', *Education and Urban Society*, 21, 2: 363–65.

Cohen, D K (1988) *Teaching Practice: Plus Ça Change*, East Lancing: Michigan State University, The National Center for Research on Teacher Education.

Collins, C (1995) 'Curriculum stocktake: A context', in C Collins (ed.) *Curriculum Stocktake: Evaluating School Curriculum Change*, Canberra: Australian College of Education.

Conley, D T and Goldman, P (1995) 'Reactions from the field to state restructuring legislation', *Educational Administration Quarterly*, 31, 4,: 512–38.

Connell, W F (1980) *A History of Education in the Twentieth-century World*, Canberra and New York: Curriculum Development Centre and Teachers College Press.

Connors, L (1980) 'The Curriculum Development Centre', *Education News*, 17, 13: 16–24.

Connors, L and McMorrow, J (1990) 'Governing Australia's public schools: Community participation, bureaucracy and devolution', in J Chapman and J Dunstan (eds) *Democracy and Bureaucracy: Tensions in Public Schooling*, London: The Falmer Press.

Cuban, L (1989) 'The "at risk" principal and the problem of urban school reform', *Phi Delta Kappan*, 70, 10: 780–4, 799–801.

Cuban, L (1994) 'Reforming the practice of educational administration through managing dilemmas', Paper presented at the 8th International Intervisitation Program in Educational Administration, 'Persistent Dilemmas in Administrative Preparation and Practice', Toronto, Canada and Buffalo, USA, 15–27 May.

Cumming, J (1992) 'National curriculum: Raising the level of debate', *Unicorn*, 18, 3, 4–8.

Curriculum Development Council (1995) *Target Oriented Curriculum Programme of Study for English Language*, Hong Kong: Government Printer.

Cuttance, P (1993) 'School development and review in an Australian state education system', in C Dimmock (ed.) *School-based Management and School Effectiveness*, London: Routledge.

Dale, R (1993) 'New Zealand: Constituting school-centred leadership', in S Crump (ed.) *School-centred Leadership*, South Melbourne: Thomas Nelson Australia.

Darling-Hammond, L and McLaughlin, M (1995) 'Policies that support professional development in an era of reform', *Phi Delta Kappan*, 76, 8: 597–9.

David, J (1989) *Restructuring in Progress: Lessons from Pioneering Districts*, Washington DC: National Governors' Association.

Dawkins, J (1988) *Strengthening Australia's Schools: A Consideration of the Focus and Content of Schooling*, Canberra: Australian Government Printing Service.

Department of Education and Science (1967) *Report of the Central Advisory Council for Education (England), vol 1: The Report*, London: HMSO.

Derouet, J L (1991) 'Lower secondary education in France: From uniformity to institutional autonomy', *European Journal of Education*, 26, 2: 119–32.

Dimmock, C (1990) 'Managing for quality and accountability in Western Australian education', *Educational Review*, 42, 2: 197–206.

Dimmock, C (1993) 'School-based management and linkage with the curriculum', in C Dimmock (ed.) *School-based Management and School Effectiveness*, London: Routledge.

Dimmock, C (ed.) (1993) *School-based Management and School Effectiveness*, London: Routledge.

Dimmock, C (1995) 'Reconceptualising restructuring for school effectiveness and school improvement', *International Journal of Educational Reform*, 4, 3: 285–300.

Dimmock, C, and Hattie, J (1994) 'Principals' and teachers' reactions to school restructuring', *Australian Journal of Education*, 38, 1: 36–55.

Dimmock, C and Hattie, J (1996) 'School principals' self-efficacy and its measurement in a context of school restructuring', *School Effectiveness and School Improvement*.

Dimmock, C, O'Donoghue, T A and Robb, A S (1996) 'Parental involvement in schooling: An emerging research agenda', *Compare*, 26, 1: 5–17.

Duignan, P A (1990) 'School-based decision making and management: Retrospect and prospect', in J Chapman (ed.) *School-based Decision making and Management*, London: The Falmer Press.

Durbridge, R (1991) 'Restructuring in schools', *Unicorn*, 17, 2, 85–90.

Education and Manpower Branch and Education Department (EMB & ED) (1991) *The School Management Initiative: Setting the Framework for Quality in Hong Kong Schools*, Hong Kong: Government Printer.

Education Commission Report No 7 (QSE-ECR7) (1996) *Quality School Education*, Hong Kong: The Government Printer.

Education Department (1987) *Better Schools in Western Australia: A Programme for Improvement*, Western Australia: Ministry of Education.

Education Department (1989) *School Development Plans: Policy and Guidelines*, Western Australia: Education Department.

Education Department (1990) *School Decision-making Groups*, Western Australia, Education Department.

Education Department (1991) *School Financial Planning and Accountability*, Western Australia: Education Department.

Education Department (1994a) *Report of the Second Survey Conducted to Evaluate the First Phase of the School Management Initiative Scheme*, Hong Kong: Education Department, mimeograph.

Education Department (1994b) *Report of the Advisory Committee on Implementation of Target Oriented Curriculum*, Hong Kong: Education Department, mimeograph.

Education Department (Advisory Committee on the School Management Initiative) (1992) *Staff Appraisal in Schools*, Hong Kong: Government Printer.

Education Department (Advisory Committee on the School Management Initiative) (1993) *The Appraisal of School Head*, Hong Kong: Government Printer.

Edwards, A and Whitty, G (1992) 'Parental choice and educational reform in Britain and the United States', *British Journal of Educational Studies*, 40, 2:101–17.

Eisner, E W (1983) 'The art and craft of teaching', *Educational Leadership*, January: 5–13.

Eisner, E W (1984) 'Can educational research inform educational practice?' *Phi Delta Kappan*, 65, 7: 447–52.

Eisner, E W (1985) *The Educational Imagination*, New York: Macmillan.

Elmore, R (1988) *Early Experiences in Restructuring Schools: Voices from the Field*, Washington DC: National Governors' Association.

Elmore, R (1990) *Restructuring Schools: The Next Generation of Educational Reform*, San Francisco: Jossey-Bass.

Elsey, B and Thomas, K (1976) *The School in the Community*, Nottingham: University of Nottingham.

Epstein, J L (1987) 'Parent involvement: What research says to administrators', *Education and Urban Society*, 19, 2: 119–36.

Feiman-Nemser, S and Floden, R E (1986) 'The cultures of teaching', in M C Wittrock (ed.) *Handbook of Research on Teaching*, New York: Macmillan.

Fullan, M (1982) *The Meaning of Educational Change*, New York: Teachers' College Press.

Gamage, D T (1993) 'A review of community participation in school governance: an emerging culture in Australian education', *British Journal of Educational Studies*, 41, 2: 134–49.

Gigot, P A (1991) 'School reform now turns to revolution', *Wall Street Journal*, 8 April.

Giroux, H and McLaren, P (1992) 'America 2000 and the politics of erasure: Democracy and cultural difference under siege', *International Journal of Educational Reform*, 1, 2: 99–110.

Glatter, R (1994) 'Managing dilemmas in education: The tightrope walk of strategic choice in more autonomous institutions', Paper presented at the

8th International Intervisitation Program in Educational Administration, 'Persistent Dilemmas in Administrative Preparation and Practice', Toronto, Canada and Buffalo, USA, 15–27 May.

Goddard, D (1992) 'Ideology and the Management of Change in Education: Developments in Western Australian State Education 1983–1989', unpublished PhD thesis, The University of Western Australia.

Goetz, M D and Le Compte, J P (1982) 'Problems of reliability and validity in ethnographic research', *Review of Educational Research*, 52, 1: 31–60.

Goodman, J (1995) 'Change without difference: School restructuring in historical perspective', *Harvard Educational Review*, 65, 1: 1–29.

Goodlad, J I (1984) *A Place Called School*, New York: McGraw-Hill.

Greenwood, G E and Hickman, C W (1991) 'Research and practice in parent involvement: implications for teacher education', *The Elementary School Journal*, 91, 3: 279–88.

Guthrie, W (1986) 'School-based management: the next needed education reform', *Phi Delta Kappan*, 68, 4: 305–9.

Hallinger, P and McCary, C E (1990) 'Developing the strategic thinking of instructional leaders', *The Elementary School Journal*, 91, 2: 89–108.

Hallinger, P and Murphy, J (1985) 'Assessing the instructional management behaviour of principals', *The Elementary School Journal*, 86, 2: 217–47.

Hallinger, P and Murphy, J (1991) 'Developing leaders for tomorrow's schools', *Phi Delta Kappan*, 72, 7: 514–20.

Hallinger, P, Murphy, J and Hausman, C (1992) 'Restructuring schools: Principals' perceptions of fundamental educational reform', *Educational Administration Quarterly*, 28, 3: 330–49.

Hallinger, P, Murphy, J and Hausman, C (1993) 'Conceptualising school restructuring: principals' and teachers' perceptions', in C Dimmock (ed.) *School-based Management and School Effectiveness*, London: Routledge.

Hammond, J (1986) 'Reassessing the roles of teachers, parents and governors: Symposium paper 3', *Educational Management and Administration*, 14: 133–8.

Handy, C B (1985) *Understanding Organizations*, 3rd edn, Harmondsworth: Penguin.

Handy, C (1994) *The Empty Raincoat: Making Sense of the Future*, London: Hutchinson.

Hanson, M (1991) 'Educational restructuring in the USA: Movements of the 1980s', *Journal of Educational Administration*, 29, 4: 338.

Hargreaves, A (1993) 'Teacher development in the postmodern age: Dead certainties, safe simulation and the boundless self', *Journal of Education for Teaching*, special issue entitled 'International Analyses of Teacher Education', 95–112.

Hargreaves, D (1993) 'Whatever happened to symbolic interactionism?' in M Hammersley (ed.) *Controversies in Classroom Research*, Buckingham: Open University Press.

Hargreaves, D and Hopkins, D (1991) *The Empowered School: The Management and Practice of School Development Planning*, London: Cassell.

Hargreaves, D and Hopkins, D (1994) *Development Planning for School Improvement*, London: Cassell.

Henderson, A T (1988) 'Parents are a school's best friend', *Phi Delta Kappan*, 70, 2: 148–53.

Hess, G A, Jr (1991) 'Chicago and Britain: Experiments in empowering parents', Paper presented at the Annual Conference of the American Educational Research Association, Chicago, 4–7 April.

Hill, P and Bonan, J (1991) *Decentralization and Accountability in Public Education*, Santa Monica, CA: Rand.

Holly, P (1990) 'Catching the wave of the future: Moving beyond school effectiveness by redesigning schools', *School Organisation* 10, 2–3: 195–212.

Holmes Group (1986) *Tomorrow's Teachers: A Report of the Holmes Group*, East Lansing: The Holmes Group.

Hopkins, D (1993) *A Teacher's Guide to Classroom Research*, Buckingham: Open University Press.

Hughes, M G (1976) 'The professional-as-administrator: The case of the secondary school head', in R S Peters (ed.) *The Role of the Head*, London: Routledge & Kegan Paul.

Hunter, E (1989) 'The role of teachers in educational reform', *National Association of Secondary School Principals Bulletin*, January: 61–3.

Iannaccone, L, and Lutz, F (eds) (1978) *Public Participation in School Decision Making*, Lexington: Lexington Press.

Ignas, E and Corsini, R J (1981) *Comparative Educational Systems*, Illinois: F E Peacock Publishers.

Ingvarson, L (1994) 'Setting standards for teaching: An agenda for the next decade', in F Crowther, B Caldwell, J Chapman, G Lakomski and D Ogilvie (eds) *The Work Place in Education: Australian Perspectives. Yearbook 1994 of the Australian Council of Educational Administration*, Sydney: Edes and Arnold.

Interim Committee for the Australian Schools Commission (P H Karmel, Chair) (1973) *Schools in Australia: Report*, Canberra: Australian Government Printing Service.

Jackson, R W B (1961) *Emergent Need in Australian Education*, Toronto: University of Toronto.

Jackson, P (1968) *Life in Classrooms*, New York: Holt, Rinehart and Winston.

Karmel, P (1973) *Schools in Australia: Report of the Interim Committee for the Australian Schools Commission*, Canberra: Australian Government Printing Service.

Kelly, A V (1990) *The National Curriculum: A Critical Review*, London: Paul Chapman Publishing.

Kendall, I L (1938) *Types of Administration*, Hawthorn: Australian Council for Educational Research.

Kennedy, K (1992) 'National curriculum: An Australian perspective', *Unicorn*, 16, 3: 32–7.

Kennedy, M M (1979) 'Generalizing from single case studies', *Evaluation Quarterly*, 3, 4: 661–79.

Kimbrough, R and Burkett, C (1990) *The Principalship: Concepts and Practices*, Englewood Cliffs, NJ: Prentice-Hall.

Kirk, G (1988) 'The professionalisation of teaching and its frustration', *Scottish Education Review*, 20, 1: 14–21.

Knight, B (1993) 'Delegated financial management and school effectiveness', in C Dimmock (ed.) *School-based Management and School Effectiveness*, London: Routledge.

Knight, P (1984) 'The practice of school-based curriculum development', *Journal of Curriculum Studies* 1, 37–48.

Kowalski, T J (1980) 'Attitudes of school principals toward decentralized budgeting', *Journal of Education Finance*, 6: 68–76.

Lampert, M (1985) 'How do teachers manage to teach? Perspective on problems in practice', *Harvard Educational Review*, 55: 178–94.

Lancy, D (1993) *Quality Research in Education: An Introduction to the Major Traditions*, New York: Longman.

Lauglo, J (1990) 'Factors behind decentralisation in education systems: A comparative perspective with special reference to Norway', *Compare*, 20, 1:21–39.

Lawton, S B (1992) 'Why restructure? An international survey of the roots of reform', *Journal of Education Policy*, 7, 2: 139–54.

Lee, Chi-Kin J and Dimmock, C (in press) 'Curriculum management in secondary schools during political transition: A Hong Kong perspective', Manuscript submitted for publication.

Leithwood, K A (1992) 'The move toward transformational leadership', *Educational Leadership*, 49, 5: 8–12.

Leithwood, K A, Begley, P T and Bradley Cousins, J (1994) *Developing Expert Leadership for Future Schools*, London: The Falmer Press.

Leithwood, K A and Montgomery, D (1982) 'The role of the elementary principal in program improvement', *Review of Educational Research*, 52, 3: 309–39.

Leithwood, K A and Stager, M (1989) 'Expertise in principals' problem solving', *Educational Administration Quarterly*, 25, 2: 126–61.

Levacic, R (1995) *Local Management of Schools: Analysis and Practice*, Buckingham: Open University Press.

Levin, M (1987) 'Accelerated schools for disadvantaged students', *Educational Leadership*, 44, 6: 19–21.

Lieberman, A (1995) 'Practices that support teacher development', *Phi Delta Kappan*, 76, 8: 593.

Linquist, K and Mauriel, J (1989) 'School-based management', *Education and Urban Society*, 21, 4: 403–16.

Logan, L, Sachs, J and Dempster, N (1994) *Who Said Planning Was Good For Us? School Development Planning in Australian Primary Schools. The Primary School Planning Project*, Brisbane: University of Queensland.

Lortie, D (1975) *School Teacher*, Chicago: University of Chicago Press.

Maclagan, P and Snell, R (1992) 'Some implications for management development of research into managers' moral dilemmas', *British Journal of Management*, 3, 3:157–68.

Macpherson, R J S (1996) *Educative Accountability: Theory, Practice, Policy and Research in Educational Administration*, Oxford: Pergamon (Elsevier).

Malen, B, Ogawa, R and Kranz, J (1990) 'What do we know about school-based management? A case study of the literature – A call for research', in W H Clune and J F Witte (eds) *Choice and Control in American Education, Vol 2, The Practice of Choice, Decentralization and School Restructuring*, Basingstoke: The Falmer Press.

Marsh, C (1980) *Curriculum Process in the Primary School*, Sydney: Ivan Novak.

Marsh, C and Stafford, K (1988) *Curriculum: Practices and Issues*, Sydney: McGraw-Hill.

Marton, F (1988) 'Phenomenography: A research approach to investigating different understandings of reality', in R R Sherman and R B Webb (eds) *Qualitative Research in Education: Focus and Methods*, London: The Falmer Press.

Mayer Committee (1992) *Employment Related Key Competencies: A Proposal for Consultation*, Melbourne: Mayer Committee.

Meadows, R (1990) 'The risks and rewards of shared leadership', *Phi Delta Kappan*, 71, 7: 545–8.

Measor, L (1985), 'Interviewing: A strategy in qualitative research', in Robert G Burgess (ed.) *Strategies of Educational Research: Qualitative Methods*, London: The Falmer Press.

Merriam, S B (1988), *Case Study Research in Education: A Qualitative Approach*, San Francisco: Jossey-Bass.

Michaels, K (1988) 'Caution: Second-wave reform taking place', *Educational Leadership*, 45, 5: 3.

Minichiello, V, Aroni, R, Timewell, E and Alexander, L (1990) *In-depth Interviewing: Researching People*, Melbourne: Longman Cheshire.

Mitchell, D E and Beach, S A (1993) 'School restructuring: The superintendent's view', *Educational Administration Quarterly*, 29, 2: 249–74.

Morgan, V, Fraser, G, Dunn, S and Cairns, E (1993) 'A new order of co-operation and involvement: Relationships between parents and teachers in integrated schools', *Educational Review*, 45, 1: 43–53.

Moore, D R (1992) 'The case for parent and community involvement', in G A Hess (ed.) *Empowering Teachers and Parents: School Restructuring*

Through the Eyes of Anthropologists, New York, Greenwood Publishing Group.

Morris, P (1995) *The Hong Kong School Curriculum: Development, Issues and Policies*, Hong Kong: Hong Kong University Press.

Mortimore, P, Sammons, P, Ecob, R and Stoll, L (1988) *School Matters: The Junior Years*, Salisbury: Open Books.

Muller, J and Watts, D (1993) 'Modelling and muddling: The long route to new organisations', *European Management Journal*, 11, 3: 361–6.

Murphy, D (1984) 'The dilemmas of primary curriculum reform', *Studies in Education* 2, 1: 7–21.

Murphy, J (1989) 'The paradox of decentralizing schools: Lessons from business, government, and the Catholic Church', *Phi Delta Kappan*, 70, 10: 808–12.

Murphy, J (1991) *Restructuring Schools*, London: Cassell.

Murphy, J (1993) 'Restructuring: in search of a movement', in J Murphy and P Hallinger (eds) *Restructuring Schooling: Learning From Ongoing Efforts*, Newbury Park, CA: Corwin Press.

Murphy, J, Evertson, C M and Radnofsky, M L (1991) 'Restructuring schools: Fourteen elementary and secondary teachers' perspectives on reform', *The Elementary School Journal*, 92, 2: 135–48.

Murphy, J, Weil, M, Hallinger, P and Mitman, A (1985) 'School effectiveness: A conceptual framework', *The Educational Forum*, 49, 3: 361–74.

Musgrave, P W (1979) *Society and the Curriculum in Australia*, Sydney: Allen & Unwin.

Myers, S S (1990) 'The management of curriculum time as it relates to student engaged time', *Educational Review* 42, 1: 13–23.

National Commission on Excellence in Education (1983) *A Nation At Risk: The Imperative for Educational Reform*, Washington DC: National Commission on Excellence in Education.

National Education Goals Panel (1993) *National Education Goals Report, Volume One: The National Report*, Washington DC: US Government Printing Office.

National Governors' Association (1986) *Time for Results*, Washington DC: National Governors' Association.

Niland, J (1994) *Enterprise Bargaining for Enterprise Agreement*, New South Wales: University of New South Wales.

O'Donoghue, T A (1994) 'The impact of restructuring on teachers' understandings of their curriculum work', *Journal of Curriculum and Supervision*, 10, 1: 21–42.

O'Donoghue, T A and Aspland, T (1994) 'Teachers' curriculum dilemmas in a climate of restructuring: A Western Australian case study', *Curriculum*, 15, 2: 77–85.

O'Donoghue, T A and Dimmock, C A J (1996) 'School development planning and the classroom teacher: A Western Australian case study', *School Organisation*, 16, 1: 71–87.

O'Donoghue, T A and O'Brien, S (1995) 'Teachers' perceptions of parental involvement in school decision making: A Western Australian case study', *International Journal of Educational Reform*, 4, 4: 404–14.

O'Donoghue, T, Aspland, T and Brooker, R (1993) 'Dilemmas in teachers' conceptualisation of the nature of their curriculum work: A Queensland case study', *Curriculum Perspectives*, 13, 3: 11–22.

Organisation for Economic Co-operation and Development (OECD) (1995) *Education at a Glance: Educational Indicators*, Paris: OECD.

Ouchi, W G (1981). *Theory Z: How American Business Can Meet the Japanese Challenge*, Reading: Addison-Wesley.

Perrow, C (1970) *Organizational Analysis: A Sociological View*, Belmont, CA: Wadsworth.

Peters, T J and Waterman, R H (1982) *In Search of Excellence: Lessons from America's Best-run Companies*, New York: Harper & Row.

Pettit, D (1981) *Opening Up Schools: School and Community in Australia*, Sydney: Penguin.

Picot, B (1988) *Administering for Excellence: Report of the Taskforce to Review Education Administration*, New Zealand: Government Printer.

Piper, K (1992) 'National curriculum: An historical perspective', *Unicorn*, 18, 3: 20–4.

Pratt, D (1980) *Curriculum Design and Development*, San Diego: Harcourt Brace Jovanovich.

Purkey, S C and Smith, M S (1985) 'School reform: The district policy implications of the effective schools literature', *The Elementary School Journal*, 85: 353–89.

Pusey, M (1991) *Economic Rationalism in Canberra: A Nation-building State Changes its Mind*, Cambridge: Cambridge University Press.

Quality of Education Review Committee (1985) *Quality of Education in Australia*, Canberra: Australian Government Publishing Service.

Renihan, F and Renihan, P (1984) 'Effective schools, effective administration and institutional image', *The Canadian Administrator*, 24, 3: 1–6.

Robertson, S and Soucek, V V (1991) 'Changing social realities in Australian schools: A study of teacher perceptions and experiences of current reforms', Paper prepared for the Comparative and International Education Society Conference, University of Pittsburgh, PA, March.

Rosenholtz, S (1989) *Teachers' Workplace: The Social Organization of Schools*, New York: Longman.

Rossow, L F (1990) *The Principalship: Dimensions in Instructional Leadership*, Englewood Cliffs, NJ: Prentice-Hall.

Rowan, B, Dwyer, D and Bossert, S (1982) 'Methodological considerations in the study of effective principals', Paper presented at the annual meeting of the American Educational Research Association, New York, March.

Rust, V and Blakemore, K (1990) 'Educational reform in England and Wales: A corporatist interpretation', *Comparative Education Review* 34, 4: 67–79.

Sachs, J and Logan, L (1990) 'Control or development? A study of inservice education', *Journal of Curriculum Studies*, 22, 5: 473–81.

Schlechty, P C (1990) *Schools for the 21st Century: Leadership Imperatives for Educational Reform*, San Francisco, CA: Jossey-Bass.

Schools Council (1989) *Teacher Quality: An Issues Paper*, Canberra: Australian Government Publishing Service.

Schools Council (1990) *Australia's Teachers: An Agenda for the Next Decade*, Canberra: Australian Government Publishing Service.

Scott, B (1989) *School Renewal: A Strategy to Revitalise Schools within the New South Wales State Education System*, Sydney: The Management Review.

Secretary of State for Education and Employment (1997) *Excellence in Schools*, London: The Stationery Office.

Shapira, R and F Hayman (1991) 'Solving educational dilemmas by parental choice: The case of Israel', *International Journal of Educational Research*, 15, 4: 277–91.

Shaw, J (1995) 'Enterprise bargaining in Australia today', *Current Affairs Bulletin*, 11–19 January.

Shinkfield, A J (1981) 'Australian education', in E Ignas and R J Corsini (eds) *Comparative Education Systems*, Illinois: F E Peacock Publishers, Inc.

Shulman, L S (1985) 'Knowledge and teaching: Foundations of the new reform', *Harvard Educational Review*, 57, 1: 1–22.

Silcock, P (1990) 'Implementing the National Curriculum: some teachers' dilemmas', *Education*, 3–13 October: 3–10.

Simons, H (1982) *Conversation Piece: The Practice of Uttering, Muttering, Collecting, Using and Reporting Talk for Social and Educational Research*, London: Grant McIntyre.

Sizer, T (1984) *Horace's Compromise: The Dilemma of the American High School*, Boston: Houghton Mifflin.

Skilbeck, M (1990) *Curriculum Reform: An Overview of Trends*, Paris: Organization for Economic Cooperation and Development.

Slavin, R E (1988) 'On research and school organisation: A conversation with Bob Slavin', *Educational Leadership*, 46, 2: 22–9.

Smart, D (1988) 'Reversing patterns of control in Australia: can schools be self-governing?' *Education Research and Perspectives*, 15, 2: 16–24.

Smart, D and Alderson, A (1980) *The Politics of Education in Western Australia: An Exploratory Study of State Education Department Policy Making*, Centre for the Study of Higher Education: University of Melbourne.

Smith, G (1993) *Public Schools that Work: Creating Community*, New York: Routledge.

Smith, R and Zantiotis, A (1988) 'Practical teacher education and the avant-garde', *Journal of Curriculum Theorizing*, 8, 2: 77–106.

Smyth, J (1991) 'Is it collegiality, or is it another way of controlling teachers?' *South Australian Educational Leader*, 4: 1–15.

Snauwaert, D (1993) *Democracy, Education and Governance: A Developmental Conception*, Albany: State University of New York Press.

Spradley, J P (1979) *The Ethnographic Interview*, New York: Holt, Rinehart & Winston.

Stacey, M (1991) *Parents and Teachers Together*, Milton Keynes: Open University Press.

Stake, R E (1978) 'The case study method in social inquiry', *Educational Researcher* 7: 5–8.

Stenhouse, L (1975) *An Introduction to Curriculum Research and Development*, London: Heinemann.

Stenhouse, L (1978) 'Case study and case records: Towards a contemporary history of education', *British Educational Research Journal*, 4, 2: 21–39.

Strauss A and Corbin J (1990) *Basics of Qualitative Research: Grounded Theory Procedures and Techniques*, London: Sage.

Sultana, R (1991) 'Social movements and the transformation of teachers' work: Case studies from New Zealand', *Research Papers in Education*, 6, 2:133–52.

Sutherland, M B (1985) 'The place of theory of education in teacher education', *British Journal of Educational Studies*, 33, 1: 226.

Swanson, A D (1995) 'Educational reform in England and the United States: The significance of contextual differences', *International Journal of Educational Reform*, 4, 1: 4–17.

Tanner, D and Tanner, L (1990) *History of the School Curriculum*, New York: Macmillan.

Taylor Committee (1977) *A New Partnership for our Schools*, London: HMSO.

Taylor, S J and Bogdan, R (1984) *Introduction to Qualitative Research Methods –The Search for Meaning*, New York: John Wiley & Sons.

Thomas, H (1993) 'The education reform movement in England and Wales', in H Beare and W L Boyd (eds), *Restructuring Schools: An International Perspective on the Movement to Transform the Control and Performance of schools*, London: The Falmer Press.

Timar, T B (1989) 'The politics of school restructuring', in M E Goertz (ed.) *Politics of Education Society Yearbook*, London: Taylor & Francis.

Tipton, B F A (1989) 'Reflections of a parent governor', *Educational Management and Administration*, 17: 39–42.

Tye, K A (1992) 'Restructuring our schools beyond the rhetoric', *Phi Delta Kappan*, 74, 1: 13.

Uhrmacher, P B (1993) 'Coming to know the world through Waldorf education', *Journal of Curriculum and Supervision*, 9, 1: 87–104.

Vandegrift, J A and Greene, A L (1992) 'Rethinking parent involvement', *Educational Leadership*, 50, 1: 57–9.

Wagner, A C (1984) 'Conflicts in consciousness: Imperative cognitions can lead to knots in thinking', in R Halkes and S K Olson (eds) *Teacher Thinking*, Lisse: Swets and Zeitlinger.

Watt, J (1977) *Co-operation in Pre-school Education*, London: Social Research Council.

Watt, J (1989) 'Devolution of power: The ideological meaning', *Journal of Educational Administration*, 27, 1:19–28.

Weiler, H N (1989) 'Decentralisation in educational governance: An exercise in contradiction?' Paper presented at an international conference on the project 'National Evaluation and the Quality of Education', Oslo, Norway, May.

Western Australia Functional Review Committee (1986) *A Review of the Education Portfolio*, Perth: Government Printer.

Western Australia Parliament (1986) *Managing Change in the Public Sector: A Statement of the Government's Position* (White Paper), Perth: Government Printer.

Western Australian Education Department (1987) *Better Schools in Western Australia: A Programme for Improvement*, Perth: Education Department.

White, P A (1989) 'An overview of school-based management: What does the research say?' *National Association of Secondary School Principals' Bulletin*, 1–8.

Wilenski, P (1986) *Public Power and Public Administration*, Sydney: Hale & Irenmonger.

Wilson, B and Corcoran, T (1988) *Successful Secondary Schools: Visions of Excellence in American Public Education*, Philadelphia: Falmer Press.

Winter, R (1982) 'Dilemma analysis: A contribution to methodology for action research', *Cambridge Journal of Education*, 12, 3: 166–73.

Wise, A (1979) *Legislated Learning: The Bureaucratization of the American Classroom*, Berkeley, CA: University of California Press.

Wolfendale, S (1992) *Empowering Parents and Teachers*, New York: Cassell.

Wong, K C (1995) 'Education accountability in Hong Kong: Lessons from the school management initiative', *International Journal of Educational Research*, 23, 6: 519–29.

Wood, G (1992) *Schools that Work: America's Innovative Public Education Programs*, New York: Dutton.

Yin, R (1984) *Case Study Research Design and Methods*, Newbury Park, CA: Sage.

Index

academic performance 9, 10
academic standards 42, 43
accountability 17, 36, 43, 56–7, 144–6, 166, 167, 170
accreditation 75
administrators 165
Advanced Skills Teacher classification (AST) 74
age-weighted pupil funding 33
aims and goals 171
alcoholism 11
A-level 37
'America 2000' education plan 47
annual meeting 32
annual reports 32
Australia 1, 13, 19, 21, 67–83
  first cycle of reform 68–70
  second cycle of reform 70–73
  third cycle of reform 73–8
Australian Education Council (AEC) 73, 77
Australian Schools Commission 19, 76
Australia's Teachers: An Agenda for the Next Decade 73
average-in-actual-out salary funding principle 33, 38

bank accounts 38
behavioural problems 11–12
Better Schools in Western Australia: A Programme for Improvement 71, 109, 124, 130

'better value-for-money' schooling 16
boards of trustees 8
British Columbia 49
budget, *see* school budget

capitation grant 104
caring role 98
Carnegie Forum on Education and the Economy 9, 45
Carnegie Foundation for the Advancement of Teaching 43
centralization 9, 175
Certificate of Advanced Mastery (CAM) 50
Certificate of Initial Mastery (CIM) 49–50
charter schools 49
Chicago school system 46
classroom activity 11
classroom assistants 38
classroom teachers 13
classroom work, impact of restructuring 103–5
collaborative decision making 89
collegial decision making 100
collegiality 168
commercialism 60
committee structures 100
communication networks 100
community management of schools 1
competitiveness 4
computer-assisted learning 14

Confederation for the Advancement of
State Education 19
corporate management philosophies 21
corporate management policies 21, 72
cost efficiency 38
counselling 14
crime 11
cultural features 142
curriculum changes 1
curriculum control 26
Curriculum Corporation 77
curriculum decision-making 100–102
and school development plan 156
collaboration with teaching staff
in 156
role 128–31
selection of content 156
curriculum design 102, 113
curriculum development 92, 166–7
Curriculum Development Centre
(CDC) 70, 73, 98
curriculum improvement 51
curriculum management 35
curriculum planning, school–based 70
curriculum reform 81, 150
curriculum research 92
curriculum role, impact of
restructuring 96–100
curriculum standards 44
curriculum work
impact of restructuring on
teachers 94–106
teachers' conceptualization 152–61,
157–60
teachers' dilemmas in relation to 152

decentralization 8, 9, 16, 26, 27, 63–6,
75, 87–90, 92, 175
decision-making
contrived nature of process 100–101
forms 173
meetings 103
school-based 109
skills 105
see also school decision-making
delegation 168
delinquency 14
demographic-economic structure 26

demographic issues 142
Department of Education and Science
(DES) 27, 32
Department of Employment, Education
and Training (DEET) 73
devolution 69, 78, 81, 84–5, 87–9,
100, 108
dilemmas 18
concept of 137–8
leadership, role and position (states of
mind) 140–7
practical 147–51
see also principals; teachers
disabled students 101
disadvantaged groups 128
Disadvantaged Schools Program 19
dissatisfaction theory 8
dropping out of school 11
drug abuse 11, 14

economic problems 26
economic rationalist policies 21
Edmonton, Canada 8
Education Act 1929 114
Education Act 1944 25, 27
Education Act 1986 33
Education Amendment Regulations
(No.3) 1991 114
education development plan (EDP) 37
Education in Western Australia 71
Education Reform Act (ERA)
1988 25–7, 32, 33, 35, 36
Education (Schools) Act 1992 27–8,
30
educational expenditure 43
educationally disadvantaged 11
effective schools 39, 44, 174
effectiveness 9, 39, 54, 56, 82, 91, 145,
170
efficiency 38, 145, 168, 170
efficiency-effectiveness relationship 39
elementary schools 44
elitism 60
England and Wales 8, 21, 25–40, 81,
92, 101, 104, 174
background to reform 25–7
significance of school reforms 31–40
English language 13, 70

enterprise bargaining 17
equity issues 14, 17, 19, 39, 104, 145
ethnic issues 142
examination performance 39
Excellence in Schools 37

family and work patterns 13
family breakdown 11, 99
Federal Industrial Relations
  Commission 74, 75
feeder schools 39
finance officer 35
financial management 34
financial responsibility of principal 17
flexibility
  in decision making 90, 166
  in school finance 55, 59–60
  of resource use 39
Follow Through 19
free market economists 26
funding flexibility 55, 59–60
further education colleges 27

GDP 26
gender equity 14, 17
General Certificate of Secondary
  Education (GCSE) 37
goal setting 39, 168
Goals 2000 'Educate America Act' 48
governance structures 17
grant maintained (GM) schools 27, 30,
  32, 35

Headstart Homestart 19
headteachers
  and deputies' pay 34
  delegation of functions 34–5
  gain in stature 34
  responsibility and accountability 34
health and safety at work 17
Her Majesty's Chief Inspector for
  Schools 31
Her Majesty's Inspectors (HMIs) 30,
  35
Holmes Group 45
Hong Kong 52–66
  Education Department 54

planned reforms to teaching and
  learning 62–3
school reform initiatives 61–6
school system 54
human resource management 15, 149

immigrant population 13
Individually Guided Education (IGE)
  project 44
industrial relations 73, 75, 76
Industrial Relations Reform Act
  1993 75
information-based society 10
information retrieval 14
information technology 14
Innovations Program 19
inspection reports 32
instrumentalism 60
intellectual disability 13
Interim Committee for the Australian
  Schools Commission 68–9
international policy-based case
  studies 2, 4

Kentucky 46, 49
key competencies 77
key stages 28
key stakeholders, *see* stakeholders

landmark industrial agreement 121
Language Development Project 70
law, knowledge of 15
leadership
  role and position (states of mind)
    dilemmas 140–47
  style 64–5, 141–2
  see also principals
learner-centred methods 60, 63
learning
  disabilities 11
  processes 12
  see also teaching and learning
legislation 17, 43, 49, 73, 75
local education authorities (LEAs) 1,
  19, 20, 29, 32–5, 37
local management of schools
  (LMS) 27, 29, 33–5, 38, 39, 54

macro-reforms 1
management information system
    (MIS) 111
*Managing Change in the Public
    Sector* 71
Manpower Services Commission 29
Mayer Committee 77
micro reforms 1
Minneapolis 49
minority groups 11, 12, 17
motivation 13, 98, 100
multiculturalism 13, 14

Nation at Risk, A 20
National Commission on Excellence in
    Education 43
National Council on Education
    Standards and Testing 48
National Curriculum 1, 8, 27–9, 33,
    36, 37
National Curriculum Briefs, Statements
    and Profiles 77
National Education Goals Panel 47–8
National Education Standards and
    Improvement Council 48
national examination results 32
National Governors' Association 45
National Project on the Quality of
    Teaching and Learning
    (NPQTL) 74–5
National Wage Case 74
negative attitudes 11
New American Schools Development
    Corporation 48
New South Wales 68
New Zealand 8, 21
Norway 20, 100

OECD countries 12, 13
Office for Standards in Education
    (OFSTED) 28, 30–31, 36, 37
OFSTED, *see* Office for Standards in
    Education (OFSTED)
open enrolment 27, 29–30
opting out, *see* grant-maintained (GM)
    schools
Oregon Report Card 50
organization theory 9

organizational architecture 173
Our Children's Crippled Future 42
outcome statements 97
outcomes 17, 43, 87–8

parent-teacher associations (PTA)
    18–19, 91
parental choice 7, 20, 26, 33, 39, 45,
    49, 170
parental empowerment 32–3
parental information 32
parental involvement 20, 65, 91,
    121–38, 124–6, 167, 169–71
  in control over staffing 121
  in life of the classroom 130
  in school decision-making 4, 7–8, 21,
    128–32
  in school governance 81
  in school restructuring 177–9
  teachers' perceptions of 124–6
parents
  changing role 18–22
  communication with 19
  concerns versus teachers'
    concerns 126–8
  democratic rights of 21
  implications of restructuring 169–71
  information on 32
  social background 128
Parents' Charter 21, 36
parochial schools 49
Participation and Equity Program 19
patterns of power, influence and
    responsibility, changes in 88–9
pedagogical strategies 46
performance 17
performance assessment 59
performance indicators 18, 32, 111
performance monitoring 37
performance standards 49
personnel management 15
perspective documents 155–60
physical disability 13
Picot Report 21
Plowden Report 18
policy aims and directions 172
policy assumptions 109
policy changes 109

policy documents 174
policy environment 10, 176, 178–9
policy expectations 10
policy goals and statements 10
policy issues 171–7
  principals', teachers' and parents' roles
    in 177–9
policy making 165, 167, 176
policy planning 168
policy presentation and
  communication 178
political agenda 113, 169
political arrangements 172
political environment 142
political factors 26
political ideology 26, 31
political issues 99
politico-economic case for school
  restructuring 9
practical dilemmas 147–51
primary schools 35, 38
principals
  administrative and non-educational
    functions 16, 141
  allegiances, interests and
    accountabilities 144
  as business managers 168
  as problem solvers and personnel
    managers 89
  changes in role 4, 14–18, 87
  changes in tasks 86–7
  changing nature of work context 16
  cognitive processes 89
  devolution of responsibilities to 81
  dilemmas
    ambiguities and contradictions
      experienced by 176
    in restructuring 139–51
  financial responsibility of 17
  hiring and firing 8
  implications of restructuring 166–9
  leadership
    management and administration
      tensions 141
    role and position dilemmas 16,
      140–47
    style 64–5, 141–2
  levels of operation 15–16

management role 15, 16
new responsibilities and functions 17
new roles for 55
power and influence 92
practical dilemmas facing 147–51
practices of 82
preparation 58
professional development 18
reactions to restructuring 84–93
role in school restructuring 177–9
role-taking and role-playing patterns
  of behaviour 18
see also School Management in a
  Decentralizing System Questionnaire
  (SMDSQ)
private schools 49
private sector 21, 26, 34
professional competence 102
professional development 105, 108,
  165
  and training 66
professionalism 9, 168
Programme of Study for English
  Language 63
public choice 26
public image 39
public sector 26, 53
public spending 170
pupil enrichment 105

qualifications 75
qualitative case studies 2–4
Quality of Education in Australia 70
Quality of Education Review
  Committee (QERC) 70–71
quality of teaching and learning 39, 81,
  169
Quality School Education (QSE) 52,
  57–60, 63–5
  comment on 61–2
  framework for developing and
    monitoring quality school
    education 58–9
  incentives to encourage 59
quasi-market effects 33, 39
quasi-market environment 34
Queensland 68

racism 14
registration 75
relief teachers 103
resources
  allocation 90
  provision of 170
  scarcity of 150–51
responsibility 17, 34, 81, 88–9, 167
responsiveness 39

scholastic failure 42
school-based initiatives 78
school-based management 1, 4, 7, 14,
  16, 17, 39, 45, 46, 59, 63–6, 81–
  2, 108, 143, 166, 167, 169, 174–6
school budget 1, 8, 17, 33, 35, 37, 168
school-business partnerships 48
school competition 91
school councils 111, 128, 174
  empowerment 81, 148
school decision-making 17, 55–6, 72,
  78, 91, 92, 123
  parental involvement in 4, 7–8, 21,
  128–32
School Decision Making Groups 121
school development planning 4, 17, 37,
  101, 107–20, 146, 148
  analysis 111–12
  and curriculum decision-making 156
  case study 109–18
  stakeholders in 108
  teachers' perception 112–18
School Development Plans – Policy and
  Guidelines 121
School Executive Committee
  (SEC) 58, 64–5
school finance, flexibility in 55
School Financial Planning and
  Accountability 121
school funding 69
school governance 51, 108
  parental participation in 81
school improvement 145–6, 170
school management committees
  (SMCs) 54–6, 64–5
School Management in a Decentralizing
  System Questionnaire
  (SMDSQ) 82, 85–6

School Management Initiative
  (SMI) 52–7, 64–6
  comment on 61–2
  flexibility in school finance 55
  framework for accountability 56–7
  new roles and relationships for the
    Education Department 55
  new roles for SMCs, sponsors,
    supervisors and principals 55
  participation in decision making 55–6
  principles of 53
  progress surveys 57
school performance 18, 169
school productivity 166, 168
school purpose statement 111
School Renewal: A Strategy to Revitalise
  Schools Within the NSW
  Education System 108
school restructuring
  administrative 81
  comprehensiveness and complexity
    of 7, 8
  concept dimensions 7
  context 7–22
  emerging policy issues 171–7
  explanations for 8–9
  functions of 45–6
  justifying need for 10–12
  managerial 81
  political explanations 8
  politico-economic case for 9
  real reasons for 99
  school effectiveness studies in 9
  specific foci 2
school revenues 33
school review 169
school secretary 35
schooling, purposes and functions
  of 147–8
Schools Commission 98
Schools in Australia 19
Second World War 20
secondary schools 38
self-governing schools 84, 168
self-managing schools 141
sex education 14
sexism 14
sexual harassment 17

SMDQ
outcomes and reactions 87–8
results 86–9
social justice issues 11, 17
social problems 11, 12
social roles 13
socio-economic groups 105
socio-economic status 36
special education teachers 97
Special Projects Programme 69
special-purpose funding 69
specialist teachers 13
sponsors, new roles for 55
staff, self-esteem, morale and
efficiency 89
staff appraisal 65–6
and performance management 17
staff management 15
staff professionalism 89
staff selection 91
and development function 90
stakeholders 17, 165–79
ambiguities, dilemmas and
uncertainties among 178
in school development planning 108
Standard Attainment Tasks (SATs) 28
State School Teachers' Union of
Western Australia 109, 124
statistically based case studies 2–4
strategic monitoring 37
Strengthening Australian Schools 76
structural efficiency principle 74
student-centred curricula 17
student negotiation 14
student performance 18, 49
student population, changes in 13
subsidiarity 54
supervisors, new roles for 55
support staff 38
syllabus issues 131

target-oriented curriculum (TOC) 52,
60–61, 63, 66
comment on 61–2
curricula planning, teaching and
learning 60
pilot scheme 61
Tasmania 68

Taylor Report 19, 33
teacher-parent relationship 130–31
Teacher Quality: An Issues Paper 73
teachers
appraisal 17, 91
assessments 17
certification requirements 44
changing role 12–14
conceptualization of curriculum
work 152–61
findings 157–60
concerns versus parents'
concerns 126–8
dilemmas
ambiguities and contradictions
experienced by 176
in relation to curriculum work
152–61
empowerment 8, 9, 81, 100–2
frustration 101
impact of restructuring 166–9
on curriculum work 94–106
in loco parentis role 99
job security 34
negative impact on 124–6
new demands on 103–4
participation 102
performance 33
performance management 17
professional roles 13
professionalism 9
reactions to restructuring 84–93
role changes 4
role in school restructuring 177–9
salaries 33–4, 38, 43, 74
social roles 13
terms and conditions 74
time concerns 104
training 58
views on curriculum decision-making
role 100–102, 128–31
views on parental involvement 124–6
views on restructuring effect on
classroom work 103–5
views on restructuring process and
curriculum role 96–100
views on school development
planning 107–20

see also School Management in a
    Decentralizing System Questionnaire
    (SMDSQ)
teachers' aides 38
teaching and learning 44
    grounds of improving 10–12
    improved practices 60
    planned reforms 62
    quality of 150
    reconceptualization 11
    rigidity towards changing approaches
        to 11
teaching for understanding 8
teaching practice, changes in 14
Technical and Vocational Education
    Initiative (TVEI) 28–9
technical decision-making 47
technological revolution 14
trade union negotiations 74
transferability of entitlements 75

underprivileged groups 12
United Kingdom 1, 20

United States 7–8, 10, 11, 19, 20,
    41–51, 81, 100
    curriculum, teaching and learning
        improvement needs 43
    educational reform 41–51
    first wave of educational reform 42–4
    second wave of educational
        reform 45–7
    third wave of educational reform
        47–51

'value-added' concept 36
vandalism 11
Victorian Certificate in Education
    (VCE) 76

Western Australia 2, 68, 71, 76, 78, 82,
    85, 89, 91, 92, 94, 107–8, 152, 174
Western Australian Government
    Functional Review Committee 71
Western Senior High School
    (SHS) 109
workplace agreements 17

For Product Safety Concerns and Information please contact our EU
representative GPSR@taylorandfrancis.com Taylor & Francis Verlag GmbH,
Kaufingerstraße 24, 80331 München, Germany

Batch number: 08160152

Printed by Printforce, the Netherlands